S.G. Cusick
Waterville '02

DECOMPOSITION

Unnatural Acts
Theorizing the Performative

Sue-Ellen Case
Philip Brett
Susan Leigh Foster

The partitioning of performance into obligatory appearances and strict disallowances is a complex social code that was assumed to be "natural" until recent notions of performativity unmasked its operations. Performance partitions, strictly enforced within traditional conceptions of the arts, foreground the gestures of the dancer but ignore those of the orchestra player, assign significance to the elocution of the actor but not to the utterances of the audience. The critical notion of performativity both reveals these partitions as unnatural and opens the way for the consideration of all cultural intercourse as performance. It also exposes the compulsory nature of some orders of performance. The oppressive requirements of systems that organize gender and sexual practices mark who may wear the dress and who may perform the kiss. Further, the fashion of the dress and the colorizing of the skin that dons it are disciplined by systems of class and "race." These cultural performances are critical sites for study.

The series Unnatural Acts encourages further interrogations of all varieties of performance both in the traditional sense of the term and from the broader perspective provided by performativity.

DECOMPOSITION
Post-Disciplinary Performance

Edited by
Sue-Ellen Case, Philip Brett,
and Susan Leigh Foster

Indiana University Press
Bloomington and Indianapolis

This book is a publication of

Indiana University Press
601 North Morton Street
Bloomington, IN 47404-3797 USA

http://www.indiana.edu/~iupress

Telephone orders   800-842-6796

Fax orders   812-855-7931

Orders by e-mail   iuporder@indiana.edu

The paper used in this publication meets the mini-
mum requirements of American National Standard
for Information Sciences—Permanence of Paper for
Printed Library Materials, ANSI Z39.48-1984.

Manufactured in the United States of America

Library of Congress Cataloging-in-Publication Data

Decomposition : post-disciplinary performance / ed-
ited by Sue-Ellen Case, Philip Brett, and Susan Leigh
Foster.
      p.   cm. — (Unnatural acts)
   Includes bibliographical references and index.
   ISBN 0-253-33723-2 (cloth : alk. paper) — ISBN
0-253-21374-6 (pbk. : alk. paper)
      1. Arts, Modern—20th century. 2. Sex in art.   I.
Case, Sue-Ellen.   II. Brett, Philip.   III. Foster, Su-
san Leigh.   IV. Series.

NX456 .D43 2000
790—dc21
                                          99-056968

1   2   3   4   5   05   04   03   02   01   00

CONTENTS

PART 5. DE-COMPOSING THE UNNATURAL

PART I.
CONFERENCING ABOUT THE UNNATURAL

1. Introducing Unnatural Acts, 1997

Susan Leigh Foster

A more or less familiar conference ambiance—the halting flow of papers, and the recesses between them shaped by the estranged architectural setting in a converted Ramada Inn, its brick facade, white colonial shutters, and wrought-iron railings enduring reminders of mid-century middle-class hospitality. The adjacent freeway emits a dull roar. (UC Riverside proudly claimed distinction when it was built as *the* campus within the University of California that sported a freeway running right through it.) At the end of the day we adjourn to the swimming pool, standard Ramada Inn accouterment, where we will enjoy reception food and drink. Milling, talking, munching, and sipping, we become aware at different moments that "a performance" has begun:

Two women in strangely translucent, baggy bodysuits and brilliantly colored sun visors, two each and positioned to form a slit through which to view the world, have appeared in the pool area. They carry a small rubber boat between them, with boom boxes in their other hands. Setting the boat down poolside, they extract from it two small chairs which will host their taped dialogue. Sitting tall and calm, each presses the tape recorder's On button in turn to produce a question or answer for the other. The voices deliver absurd directions for freeway travel and comment on current events. Seemingly edified by this exchange, they place the boom boxes in the boat and launch it into the pool. A voice not theirs continues on the tape, reciting a collage of quotations concerning bodiliness in cyberspace. Speech having sailed away, the performers resort to gesture, complex sequences of hand-arm-head positionings, etched into the space of the pool's rim as they inch by. The performers enter a crowded area of the reception; their gestures mingle with those of the viewers. Small adjustments of bodies, shiftings of weight, alterations to shape, the withdrawal of a foot or elbow, a smile, a widening of the eyes, the embarrassed raising of a glass—all announce the crowd's awareness of these special bodies in its midst. The performers play off these accommodations to their presence, deftly incorporating the viewers' moves into their own. They mimic, mirror, and expand on these gestures, flowing into spaces vacated, extracting themselves from entanglements they have created. Once past the crowd, they dislodge a long pole from the fence surrounding the pool and row, on land of course, to the other end. Here they exchange one navigation system for another: small mirrors held near their eyes but directed so as to reveal the space behind them as they back their way back toward the crowd. The mirrors locate a table of food, which the performers sample by sending their arms behind them toward the plates. Amidst this repast they locate a spool of yellow tape, the kind used to cordon off construction sites. Tying one end to the fence, they begin to wrap the crowd in tape. As it unfurls we see the bold black lettering BIO-HAZARD: DO NOT ENTER. Their costumes and neutral manner as well as the boat's voice with its ongoing recitation of cyber-facts, all take on new significance as the crowd itself becomes a bio-hazard. The bodysuits transform into the uniforms used in transporting dangerous chemicals or radioactive substances; the performers' calm demeanor now evokes, even as it parodies, the anonymous, officious bureaucracy of the state. Is the pool, with its adrift citizen oracularly discoursing on the impending redistribution of corporeality across real and virtual spaces, polluted? Or is it the fountain of youth? Is this social body contaminated, or might it move in a promising direction? All questions raised, all tasks accomplished, the performers exit, leaving the conference-goers to duck under or clamber over the fragile barrier of tape as the boat-voice drones on.

This unnatural performance is a modest event, not a spectacular work of art. Akin to initiatives sustained since the 1960s, this accumulation of choreographic tactics probes boundaries between the theatrical and the quotidian both by using pedestrian movement in the performance and by locating the performance in the midst of pedestrian life. At the same time, it disperses corporeality, dis-integrating the organic melding of peripheral and central body, the functional unity of body as vehicle for expression, and the efficient hierarchization (always momentarily inverted by solemn and precious dancing) of speech and movement. The hand moving backward toward the food constructs a new view of itself. Not the dumb servant of a willful interiority, the hand senses the space through which it moves, deftly calibrating visual and tactile information. It sometimes snacks (these daily motions can attain theatricality), *and* it moves with intelligence. Through this staging of its own physicality, the hand invites us to bestow upon it a sustained, livelier attention. The hand is touching.

The hand's success depends, in part, on the precarious status of the voice. Separated from the body since the beginning, the voice is stranded mid-pool, absurdly isolated in such a dinky boat in such a dinky pool. There it continues to deliver prophecies and proclamations, technological verities and cyber theories. Normally the organizing indicator of the performer's disposition, this voice merely contributes another stream of information, neither more nor less pressing than other kinds of bodily production. The information it conveys, however, intimates a re-organization of body at least as radical as the structuring of voice and body it enacts.

The performers reflect, at the same time as they implement, this re-organization of bodily articulation. Although radically limiting the field of vision, their double-layered sun visors highlight seeing, their own and the viewers'. Shielded from the sun's rays above and below, how must they look? Then, the mirrors, tools of reflection par excellence, open up the space behind the body, facilitating as they comment upon whole new procedures of bodily locomotion. As the performers perambulate around the pool with these prosthetic devices, we see beneath the translucent costume through/to their bodies. What used to be contained beneath the surface, the inner depths of the psyche, is not there. Instead, the costume shows us as inner truth the body, its slimness, strength, and quickness. The body is dwelling inside the body, nothing more and nothing less.

Because I know these women, I know that this piece, which they have titled *Bio-Sentry,* has been made amidst several bodily dramas—failures of ligaments to heal, fantasies of neural disorders and hip replacements. Ah, the body's vicissitudes. Because I work with them, I have been witness to some of the preparations for this event. One is gay, one is straight, but they are equally amused by the instructions accompanying the bodysuits they purchase: "Cut arms and legs to fit." I have heard them recount the story of discovering these wonderful sci-fi oversuits, actually painters' protection garb, at Home Depot. Standing in the line to pay for their costumes, pointing out the instructions to those standing adjacent, their laughter exposes the absurdity of the ambiguous directions: whose/what arms and legs are to be cut in order to fit? I have also heard about how they approached the university's physical plant personnel to request a roll of BIO-HAZARD tape: the refusals, "but we're faculty members"; the restrictions, "of course, we'll bring it right back"; the unwilling interest, "it's for a dance"; the enthusiastic inquiries about subsequent projects, "thanks so much for your help."

A humble intervention into normalcy, this piece, emblematic of so many others, is entwined with the normal. Its making depended on, resulted from a series of ordinary, daily interactions, each of which brought "art" into "life" and "life" into "art." A whole other vision of what it means for artists to be working in the community, this performance's making articulated with and against the working lives of department store staff, janitors, university administrators, students, and secretaries, illuminating ever so slightly the normalizing protocols, the standardizing regimens of behavior that make up our day. It gained momentum from such interactions, relishing as it went its subtle alterations to the expected.

As early as 1974, Michel de Certeau proclaims the existence of an antidisciplinary network of practices such as these. Seeking alternatives to the model of passive consumerism as well as to the panoptic power of the state, so elegantly exposed by Michel Foucault, de Certeau begins to track the meandering and errant traces left behind by ordinary persons moving through their day. He argues that many of these traces, rather than conform to dominant social specifications for behavior, document the thought-filled gestures of those who, having assessed and rejected the normative, simply move in a different way. Erratic, impervious to statistical investigations, these gestures constitute a vital reservoir of resistance to the overwhelming force exerted by dominant orderings of the social.

In order to make the case for the palpable presence of such an anti-discipline, de Certeau imbues action with thought. Drawing upon Austin's notion of the speech-act, he extends to all bodily articulation, whether spoken or moved, the same capacity to enunciate. The acts of walking or cooking, like speaking, all operate within the fields of a languagelike system; individual bodies vitalize that system through their own implementation of it. Each "speech" act positions itself in space and time, and in relation to the enunciations of others. Deciphering these systems of interlocution, one might detect a vast array of seemingly spontaneous or incidental choices that, upon closer examination, signal the exercise of intelligent and creative responsiveness.

De Certeau further refines the anti-disciplinary potential of these enunciations by drawing a distinction between the strategic and the tactical. How better to illustrate this distinction than by revisiting the two performers in preparation for their unnatural acts? "The whole piece began," reminisces Susan Rose, "when we were walking through Nordstrom's, and I grabbed a visor to try on and then added another one." Strategically, Nordstrom department store is organized to enhance and erode confidence in one's appearance. The soporific strains of the live pianist, the artfully arranged displays, the mirrors, all draw the shopper into fervent contemplation of current and imagined identities. Nordstrom devises strategies, "calculuses of force-relationships,"[1] that both create the space between drab reality and fashionable possibility and offer up procedures for moving across this space. But what happens in the moment when these two women, who already fail immodestly to conform to standard images of the feminine or of butch or femme, suddenly peer at each other out the tunnel of vision the visors construct? They crack up; they turn away from each other; visor-laden, they pretend to fit in, gazing at other merchandise, fingering other accessories; they wander about. What possesses them to resume normal behavior in their abnormal condition? The tactical. How long does it last? A minute at most. Does anybody notice? Perhaps.

For de Certeau tactics consist in momentary disruptions to the coercive power of strategic structures. Tactics have no goal beyond the sometimes playful, always critical exposure of the workings of the normative. However, in order to seize effectively the force of the strategic and suspend momentarily its influence, tacticians must assess the direction and flow of force and devise moves that incapacitate power, at the same time revealing its usual path. Because strategies shift frequently, so must tactics:

a tactic depends on time—it is always on the watch for opportunities that must be seized "on the wing." Whatever it wins, it does not keep. It must constantly manipulate events in order to turn them into "opportunities."[2]

Although they attain different degrees of visibility, tactics could never muster the cohesiveness necessary to instantiate an alternative social order. Rather they are a perpetual source of resistance to the normative.

Still, de Certeau does not construct between the strategic and the tactical an absolute opposition. The tactical does not stand for that which is chaotically unknowable. By endowing bodily action with enunciatory intelligence, de Certeau avoids the classical parsing of mindful and bodyful forms of production that would align the tactical with bodily attributes such as ephemerality, insubstantiality, or unorderedness. Although unpredictable, the tactical evinces structure; although disruptive, it contains its own logic. Thus while tactical destabilizations of the status quo observe no predictable pattern, they sometimes share certain moves. For example, the strategic assertion of the sacred purity of the theatre as the site of performance has been disrupted by numerous tactics that redesign theatrical boundaries. Many of these tactics share both an assessment of the need to violate theatrical space and similar methods for constructing that violation.

At the same time, tactics can best be interpreted in relation to the local situation that produced them. The strategic, never monolithic, insinuates itself into local circumstances, and the tactical draws its strength and referentiality from those same circumstances. This is why the Serbian students using bullhorns to lecture police on Plato, Walt Whitman, and the pernicious consequences to posture of bulletproof vests can only be fully understood when situated within the political and social turmoil of 1996 post-Yugoslavia.[3] (And why their voices, disparate and muted, barely register and only on the Internet as Milosevic invades Kosovo three years later.) Similarly, *Bio-Sentry* attains its full impact when located at the suburban campus of UC Riverside, with its transformed Ramada Inn now the Humanities Center. Here, images of global contagion, statistically informed treatments of sickness and health, and unpredictable violence all circulate through the trappings of a conservative community. The re-definitions of public and private space that are resulting from media and cyber technologies and the global capitalist march of generic shopping malls—all resonant within the performance's gestures—impinge upon university's and city's sense of identity. Who better to delineate the motion of this immense social change than these two bio-sentries?

De Certeau never envisioned how the tactical might amass sufficient momentum to instigate social movement, nor did he imagine how it might function as a bridge across gendered, racial, and class-based forms of oppression. These are still projects waiting to be fleshed out. Instead, the speech-act, following Austin's initial formulation of it, has been adapted most often for use in the analysis of written texts and in studies of consumer culture. We now know how words perform, but what do bodies do? We now know something about how consumers "read" and "rewrite" the commodified options available

7

to them, but how do actions figure in their imaginative accommodations to the acquisition and use of capitalism's products?

Writing in the wake of May '68 and the Algerian independence movement, de Certeau had witnessed both the potential for a coalition politics to precipitate social reform and the normalizing mechanisms that re-instated order shortly thereafter. His theorization of tactics, a response to both insurgent initiatives and repressive retaliations, may have aspired to deepen the Left's appraisal of its own revolutionary agendas even as it acknowledged the pervasiveness of the state's organization of power. Did he think that social reform might be accomplished if only the tactics used could be theorized so as to encompass bodily enunciations? Did he determine, instead, that the tactical could never provide enough substance to support the weight of bodies working for such reform?

Does it matter, in other words, whether we gain reflective opportunities on everyday movements from a performance such as *Bio-Sentry*? Can such an event illumine the current status of body as contested site within medical, technological, sexual, and performance discourses? Could the repeated application of *Bio-Sentry*'s performative tactics eventually result in the demarginalization of the arts from the university and of the body from society? How might the "speech" act, as reformulated by de Certeau to include all varieties of human articulation, inform and be informed by the disciplines of performance? Can the arts as performative practices, as practices of the body, collaborate in the creation of new tactics of social critique? Can the performative serve as a locus for exchange among artistic traditions generating new interdisciplinary perspectives on dance, music, theater, and visual arts production? Can the aesthetic and the political be conjoined in ways that bring new meaning to both? These are some of the questions that stand behind this volume of essays and the conference that initiated it.

For the 1997 Unnatural Acts Conference, four roundtables were organized by Deborah Wong, Amelia Jones, Marta Savigliano, and Jennifer Brody, faculty members at UC Riverside in the Departments of Music, Art History, Dance, and English respectively. The essays in this volume grew out of the discussions they hosted. Jones's rationale for her panel is included here to give a sense of the roundtables' orientation, along with Wong's analysis of a performance by Miya Masaoka, an event sponsored by the conference that aroused considerable response not only from university students and faculty but also from the Riverside community. Since Masaoka's stunning combination of high modernism on the koto and Madagascar cockroaches on her naked body, we have all enjoyed numerous discussions with colleagues across the United States about the response she received here. How specific to Riverside was Masaoka's reception we still cannot assess, yet her performance inspired the kinds of questions that Unnatural Acts continues (exuberantly) to provoke.

At the beginning of this century, white, bourgeois women engaged their nearly naked bodies in the practice of something called "de-composition." This relaxation regimen, designed to undo the pernicious muscular patternings that inevitably resulted from living at the hectic pace required by industrialized society, promised to return the body to an original wholesomeness. De-composition yielded up the natural body. In the essays that follow, however, de-composition, a summary term for the methods of analysis they use, accomplishes something quite different. It offers us unnatural bodies, cockroaches, sun visors, and all. Like the bodies of the two performers revealed beneath the translucent painting suits, these variously unnatural bodies, neither extraordinary nor grotesque, move through their day "cutting arms and legs to fit." De-composition performs a critical inquiry into how and why these bodies make the moves they do.

NOTES

1. Michel de Certeau, *The Practice of Everyday Life, trans.* Steven Rendall (Berkeley and Los Angeles: University of California Press, 1984), p. xix.
2. Ibid.
3. For a fuller description of many of the Belgrade students' tactics, see Lawrence Wechsler, "Letter from Serbia," *The New Yorker,* February 10, 1997, pp. 32–41.

2. Acting Unnatural: Interpreting Body Art

Amelia Jones

Discourses of the visual arts—art history and art criticism—have conventionally defined the work of art as a singular object fixed in its significance, valued for its adherence to predetermined aesthetic or political ideals. Within this logic, acts are not perceived as art, and the unnatural is strategically avoided. Here, in an attempt to reverse these exclusions, I begin by excavating the term "unnatural acts"—at once so alluring and elusive—and end by performing a particular body art work as productively denaturalizing. Somewhere in between, I hope to convince the reader of two propositions regarding the performative body/self (the body enacted as a self, in relation to social and interpersonal contexts).

PROPOSITION ONE: IT IS THE ACT (THE IN-PROCESS) AND NOT THE "FACT" OF UNNATURALNESS THAT GIVES CULTURAL MANIFESTATIONS POWER

The term "unnatural acts" begs the old avant-garde question of transgression. Rebecca Schneider has recently pointed out that "transgression, or the inappropriate, certainly props the appropriate"; correlatively, she notes that it is the right wing that yearns for inappropriateness as proof of its own normativity.[1] This observation raises a number of questions. Is the notion of transgression still a viable one? Should transgression be a singular goal for those wishing to gain some kind of cultural power or political efficacy? What does it mean to formulate transgression as the opposition to the "natural," or norm? Doesn't the word "un-natural" incorporate the natural (both literally and figuratively) even as it obsessively poses itself (or is externally posed) as nature's opposite? Who decides what is "natural," and so, by extension, determines the parameters of the "unnatural"?

While the term "unnatural" clearly indicates something that is weird, strange, abnormal, or queer, it also designates something that is not in or of nature. In the words of the *Random House Dictionary of the English Language*, "unnatural" signifies a thing that is, first, "contrary to the laws or course of nature," second and third, "at variance with the character or nature of a person, animal, or plant," or with "what is normal or to be expected." The unnatural can also be, specifically, that which lacks "human qualities or sympathies," and is "monstrous" or "inhuman." Finally, it can also mean that which is "not genuine or spontaneous," something "artificial or contrived."[2] "Unnatural" thus turns out to be, etymologically speaking, an extremely useful term: it is a multiplicitously conceived group of characteristics—artifice, monstrosity, variation, abnormality, contrivance—that might be tapped to rethink the problem of transgression that is built into art-historical notions of the avant-garde.

All of these characteristics, however, can most convincingly be viewed as *articulations* rather than internal truths. That is, they are not inherent: it is by an act of judgment that a person, animal, or plant is understood to be "unnatural" (monstrous, inhuman, etc.). In this same fashion, a person, animal, or plant could (willfully or not) *enact itself as unnatural,* as contrived, not genuine, queer. None of these qualities are fixed in any way. All take place through acts of judgment and self-performance. Perhaps, then, it is in the *act* ("anything done, being done, or to be done; deed; performance"; "to do something, exert energy or force; be employed or operative"[3]) rather than, strictly speaking, in the qualities of "naturalness" or "unnaturalness" (which, as we have seen, are co-constitutive), that the cultural and political significance of a particular practice, gesture, person, animal, or plant resides.

In the realm of visual culture, this observation can be extrapolated in relation to art criticism and art history, which have a long tradition of developing strategies to fix meaning and value through Kantian interpretive models that are said to be disinterested or objective.[4] Through the *naturalized* fixing of meaning and value as "objectively" determined, the commodification of the work as a supposedly inherently valuable, unique object can be ensured. Through this dynamic, normative values are sustained and assigned to objects associated with "natural" artistic subjects (for example, modernist paintings executed by heterosexual Euro-American white males) and those produced by subjects perceived as "unnatural" are repressed, ignored, or otherwise dismissed as non-art.

Given the closed logic of this system of critical analysis, it is clear that by their very performativity works of art posed as acts have the potential to expose the assignment of meanings and values as in process (rather than fixed) and invested. The work of art that is an act potentially unveils the deep motivations underlying the desire for fixed meanings and values: itself in a highly charged "exertion of energy or force" in motion, it engenders recognition of interpretation as a process that is invested and contextual. The performative keeps artistic meaning in motion and refuses at least the *easy* reification of particular (naturalized) meanings and values. In cases of body art, where the artist overtly solicits spectatorial desire through erotic and/or sadomasochistic acts, the art critic or art historian will generally find it even more difficult to ignore the implication of her own desires in her interpretation of the work. The performative—especially as projected across/through the body of the artist in body art projects—thus has a particular and profound efficacy in throwing into question conventional models of interpretation.

Through the act (the performance), the artist effects something quite different from transgression *tout court*. Judith Butler teases out the effects of performativity precisely in relation to the dual logic of Western thought:

> Performativity describes this relation of being implicated in that which one opposes, this turning of power against itself to produce alternative modalities of power, to establish a kind of political contestation that is not a "pure" opposition, a "transcendence" of contemporary relations of power, but a difficult labor of forging a future from resources inevitably impure. . . . For one is, as it were, in power even as one opposes it, formed by it as one reworks it, and it is this simultaneity that is at once the condition of our partiality, the measure of our political unknowingness, and also the condition of action itself.[5]

Butler, who extends Jacques Derrida's notion of performativity (itself drawn from J. L. Austin[6]) specifically in relation to bodies and thus to subjects of meaning (bodies/selves), affords an obvious link from the conception of performativity to that of the embodied identities that are also at issue in the notion of the "unnatural act." As Butler and many other theorists have recognized, understanding the body/self as performative, as constituted through performative acts, points to the contingency of identity and social positionality not only on the context and effect of the performance itself but on the particularity of the other bodies/selves it engages—*on the artwork's coming to meaning through interpersonal engagement and acts of interpretation*. Ultimately, as Derrida suggests in his work on performativity and intentionality, the "live" performance of the body/self, rather than securing the subject's meaning as inherent (as natural or unnatural?), opens it up as fundamentally unstable, the body itself as a supplement.[7] Peggy Phelan extends this formulation when she notes that "[p]erformance uses the performer's body to pose a question about the inability to secure the relation between subjectivity and the body *per se;* performance uses the body to frame the lack of Being promised by and through the body—that which cannot appear without a supplement."[8]

It is the *act*, then, that has the potential to produce a gap between the identity assumed to be attached to a particular type of body/self (for example, as displayed by the artist in body art) and the way in which that body/self actually comes to mean in the social arena—or between the work of art (as a manifestation of the artist) and its cultural meaning as determined through interpretation. It is thus the act that points to what phenomenologist Maurice

Merleau-Ponty has described as the chiasmic intertwining of productive and receptive bodies/selves in the making of culture.[9]

Any kind of cultural product, whether "live" performance or a still object, can be rendered performative (can be made into an act) through the mobilization of particular codes of subjectivity across the spectrum of temporality (identity as process) and the encouragement of interpretive engagements that are explicitly invested and erotically charged (Freud: from the beginning "we knew none but sexual objects") rather than "disinterested."[10] The performative has this capacity of eliciting charged engagements and so of politicizing our comprehension of bodies/selves (and of culture in general) because it specifically marks body/self as contingent on body/other and exposes the investments behind every attribution of meaning and/or identity.

PROPOSITION TWO: THE MOST DISTURBING ACTS ARE THOSE THAT INSISTENTLY PERFORM BODIES/SELVES IN SUCH A WAY AS TO ACTIVATE SPECTATORIAL ANXIETIES AND/OR DESIRES, WHILE AT THE SAME TIME CALLING INTO QUESTION WHAT IT MIGHT MEAN TO CALL SOMETHING "NATURAL" (OR, FOR THAT MATTER, "UNNATURAL")

Take Joseph Santarromana's piece *It's Alive* (1997), for example. We walk in, shoes squeaking on the highly polished gallery floor, to be confronted by a monstrous head, frozen (a still photograph) but mobile in its effects. The torso is only a gap, the gallery wall itself, but a pair of feet are imaged below on a video screen, standing in real time—almost, but not quite, motionless. First, we are encouraged to ask ourselves where, after all, the "act" resides in this configuration that is many contradictory things: a "portrait," yet not a recognizable rendition of an individual subject; an installation, and yet really almost two-dimensional; a "movie," but almost entirely still. Second, the "act" begins to emerge in our relationship, as spectatorial bodies/selves, to this artwork, which is, first and foremost, a staged encounter (and which marks, if not exaggerates, our status as consumers of artworks—our bodies positioned within the gallery space and reflexively marked within the piece itself). Third, we begin to feel that it is precisely this set of relationships that is both the act and what becomes subversively unnatural even as it calls forth our assumption of our own naturalness as viewers who project a particular coherence onto the work of art/the artist.

Beginning with the head, we cannot complete the suture of identification that we so desire. It is grotesque, smeared, out of register—like a piece of meat hammered by a mallet, its features are rearranged (the face is clearly "at variance with the character or nature of a person, animal, or plant," or with "what is normal or to be expected"). The face, it turns out, is a computer morph of the visage of the artist and the grimace of Frankenstein's beast, as played by Boris Karloff in the 1931 Hollywood movie: it is truly monstrous. Expanding upon a century of composite facial imagery (from Francis Galton to Nancy

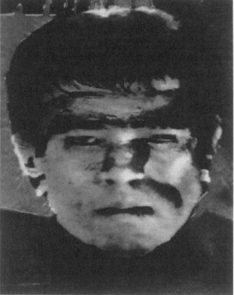

Figure 2.1. Joseph Santarromana, *It's Alive*, 1997. Courtesy of the artist and Post Gallery, Los Angeles.

Figure 2.2. Detail, Joseph Santarromana, *It's Alive*, 1997. Courtesy of the artist and Post Gallery, Los Angeles.

Burson),[11] Santarromana enacts himself *as grotesque.* He is, like Frankenstein's monster himself, made up of gruesome body parts (from "[t]he dissecting room and the slaughter-house"[12]) mashed together into a "self."

Perhaps (in fact, most certainly) I am reading into this image: after all, that is how it comes to mean for me through the act of interpretation. I see it as a kind of performance of what it must feel like to be an artist born in the Philippines, raised in Chicago, living in Los Angeles. I imagine Santarromana acting out the monster he is perhaps very often made to feel. And yet, as I imagine this, I realize it is more likely the monster that *I am made to feel,* and that Santarromana's gift to me—the burden that he allows me—is his encouraging me to fit my body/self into the gap that is the wall/torso of the piece. The first edition of Mary Shelley's *Frankenstein* opens with a quotation from Milton's *Paradise Lost:* "Did I request thee, Maker, from my clay / To mould me man? Did I solicit thee / From darkness to promote me?"[13] To the point: Santarromana "moulds" himself through the act of creation; he "moulds" me (his spectator); I "mould" him (through interpretation).

So there he is, there I am, this absent but monstrous body. No wonder my/his feet are frozen, rooted into the ground, but almost imperceptibly, nervously, active at the same time. The particularly identified body/self is always (almost imperceptibly) in motion, never one with its fantasmagoric projections: with the identities and significances that are thrust upon its visible and invisible codes from both outside and in. The body/self is reversible (inside/outside are a Möbius-strip-like continuum of flesh). The body/self is an "intercorporeal being," fundamentally open to the other.[14] It is the intertwining of self and other (the contingency of each on the other—of the "unnatural" on the "natural") that Santarromana's project brings to mind.

Further, Santarromana's use of multiple media and his deployment of the phenomenological space of the viewing arena points again to the body as a supplement that, far from guaranteeing fixed, singular identity ("presence") exposes the very lack that is, in Jacques Lacan's paradoxical terms, at its core.[15] Santarromana's act is this abyss, that omnipresent gap between me (as perceived by the other) and I (as perceiver); as I engage the piece, it exposes the fact that this primary gap mirrors the secondary gap between self and other. And yet, rather than dwell on Lacan's pessimistic scenario of loss and lack, Santarromana, it seems to me, encourages a more optimistic, or at least less lugubrious, notion of this gap as an intersubjective engagement—more along the lines of that proposed by Merleau-Ponty:

> My body as a visible thing is contained within the full spectacle. But my seeing body subtends this visible body, and all the visibles with it. There is reciprocal insertion and intertwining of one in the other. Or rather, if, as once again we must, we eschew the thinking by planes and perspectives, there are two circles, or two vortexes, or two spheres, concentric when I live naïvely, and as soon as I question myself, the one slightly decentered with respect to the other.[16]

As Merleau-Ponty's formulation suggests, this engagement is one that can politicize subjects by pointing to their entwinement in others.[17] If, on the one hand, I oppress or marginalize Santarromana, he becomes a monster who returns to haunt me (as the unnatural infects the natural that attempts to exclude it). Or rather, more to the point, *I become a monster* (the natural becomes unnatural). If, on the other hand, I view myself as imbricated in his self-enactment through his performative staging of the piece, then I recognize the importance of my behavior in terms of how he *acts* (comes to mean) in relation to me. This is not just a question of acting well so as to avoid being hounded or mistreated in turn. It is a question of understanding my position—as well as his—in the world. When I act, others are affected. When I perceive and attribute meaning, this changes who Santarromana "is" in the world. When Santarromana projects himself toward me (as monster artist), he transforms my identifications.

This is the reversibility of flesh. If by "unnatural" one means to connote a process of disturbance that overturns the very assumptions we have about how subjects come to mean in the world, then this flaunting of the reversibility of flesh is the utmost unnatural act.

NOTES

1. Rebecca Schneider, *The Explicit Body in Performance* (New York and London: Routledge, 1997), p. 4.
2. Or (obsolete) something "lacking a valid or natural claim; illegitimate"—something close to the queer as we now know it; *Random House Dictionary of the English Language,* 2nd ed., unabridged (New York: Random House, 1987), p. 2081
3. Ibid., p. 19.
4. I discuss this problem of art history/criticism at greater length in my essay "Art History/Art Criticism: Performing Meaning," in *Performing the Body/Performing the Text,* ed. Amelia Jones and Andrew Stephenson (London and New York: Routledge, 1999), pp. 39–55, and the issue of "disinterestedness" and its Enlightenment bases in chapter 1, "Postmodernism, Subjectivity, and Body Art: A Trajectory," in *Body Art/Performing the Subject* (Minneapolis: University of Minnesota Press, forthcoming).
5. Judith Butler, *Bodies That Matter: On the Discursive Limits of "Sex"* (New York and London: Routledge, 1993), p. 241. See Sue-Ellen Case's critique of Butler as well as Peggy Phelan (discussed below) in *The Domain-Matrix: Performing Lesbian at the End of Print Culture* (Bloomington: Indiana University Press, 1996), especially pp. 13–17 and 20–23.
6. See Jacques Derrida, "Signature Event Context" (1977), reprinted in *Margins of Philosophy,* trans. Alan Bass (Chicago: University of Chicago Press, 1982), pp. 309–330.
7. Ibid.
8. Peggy Phelan, *Unmarked: The Politics of Performance* (New York and London: Routledge, 1993), p. 151.

9. On the chiasmus see Maurice Merleau-Ponty, "The Intertwining—The Chiasm," in *Visible and the Invisible* (1964), trans. Alphonso Lingis, ed. Claude Lefort (Evanston, Ill.: Northwestern University Press, 1968), pp. 130–55.

10. Not incidentally, Freud makes this comment while discussing the phenomena of transference and countertransference modes of interpreting and relating to other subjects; in "The Dynamics of Transference" (1912), trans. Joan Riviere, in *Therapy and Technique,* ed. Philip Rieff (New York: Collier Books, 1963), p. 112. Phelan corroborates my point about performativity: "While the notion of the potential reciprocal gaze has been considered part of the 'unique' province of live performance, the desire to be seen is also activated by looking at inanimate art," in *Unmarked,* p. 4.

11. On Francis Galton's use of composites to type people racially and in terms of criminality, see Allan Sekula, "The Body and the Archive," in *The Contest of Meaning,* ed. Richard Bolton (Cambridge, Mass., and London: MIT Press, 1989), pp. 363–373; Sekula discusses Burson's work, in a scathing attack, on p. 377.

12. Mary Shelley, *Frankenstein* (1818), published in *Three Gothic Novels,* ed. Peter Fairclough (Harmondsworth, Middlesex, England: Penguin Books, 1968), p. 315.

13. This epigraph is published on the title page of the first edition; reprinted in facsimile in *Three Gothic Novels,* p. 257.

14. Merleau-Ponty, "The Intertwining—The Chiasm," p. 143.

15. Merleau-Ponty writes, "[B]etween the two 'sides' of our body, the body as sensible and the body as sentient (what in the past we called objective body and phenomenal body), rather than a spread, there is the abyss that separates the In Itself from the For Itself," in ibid., pp. 136–37.

16. Ibid., p. 138.

17. Vivian Sobchack uses a phenomenological model of intersubjectivity and interobjectivity to raise this issue of responsibility in "The Passion of the Material: Prolegomena to a Phenomenology of Interobjectivity," forthcoming in her *Carnal Thoughts: Bodies, Texts, Scenes, and Screens* (Berkeley and Los Angeles: University of California Press); I discuss her model at greater length in chapter 5, "Dispersed Subjects and the Demise of the 'Individual': 1990s Bodies in/as Art," of *Body Art/Performing the Subject.*

3. Listening to Local Practices: Performance and Identity Politics in Riverside, California

Deborah Wong

If reception is the most undertheorized area of performance studies, then I am doubly at a loss when trying to explain refusal. How can we theorize audience resistance to a performance, or the audience that refuses to attend? That audience—the one that stays home—executes a different intervention, an intervention of denial that is itself perhaps an affirmation of the performative. Refusing to take in the performative is perhaps the only effective means for eluding transformation. Performance studies has no apparatus for dealing with an audience that closes its eyes and ears; indeed, it is shot through with progressive yet sadly romantic ideals of community. *The Drama Review* regularly carries work focused on community theater and the theater of resistance. How (or even whether) "the community" engages with the performative is another question. Such methodology presupposes a community of the oppressed—a community in such duress that it is willing to engage with the possibility of transforming itself.

But consider an audience that is angry or bored or offended or distracted. This, too, is reception: resistance of this sort is perhaps the strongest expression of agency. Noncompliance is the most difficult gesture of all to parse as it closes up at the moment of interrogation. This essay is, then, an ethnography of reception with a critical edge: in considering unwillingness and repudiation, I will not offer a relativist apology but instead will move toward strategies of engagement and pedagogy.

Miya Masaoka is an Asian American musician and performance artist whose performance at the Unnatural Acts conference, hosted by the University of California, Riverside, on April 11, 1997, created a situation rife with sensationalism and anxiety as well as pedagogical possibility. Various responses to Masaoka's performance suggested that for many UCR students and Riverside residents gender, sexuality, and race intersect in ways that are neither subtle nor abstract. I will consider how performance might have a pedagogical function in a conservative city and will arrive at these strategies through an ethnography of an event and its reception.

As an ethnomusicologist studying performance, I prefer close ethnographies of particular people in particular circumstances because they are a crucial kind of resistance to the generalizing pull of performance studies scholarship focused on crosscultural universals. Interpenetrating relationships of class, race, ethnicity, gender, sexual orientation, etc., are made most visible through close ethnographic work. I also want to take ethnography further into a process that connects scholars to communities and thus creates conditions of accountability and responsibility—conditions refused until recently, but which we can make pedagogical in the broadest sense, as cultural work.

Let me enlarge on each of these points. Taking local lives and local practices seriously is an effective means to reflexively address problematic histories. Anthropologist Lila Abu-Lughod has persuasively argued that "ethnographies of the particular" can subvert the process of "othering" (Abu-Lughod 1991, 149).[1] Carefully noting that she does not suggest reversing older practices by simply "privileging micro over macro processes," she points out how anthropological methods for generalizing about cultures are intrinsically related to scholarly epistemologies of objectivity, speaking what she calls "inevitably a language of power" (150). Instead, Abu-Lughod proposes what she calls "tactical humanism"—that is, a self-conscious attempt to write "against" anthropological generalization by strategically focusing on the local, the particular, the individual. Such a humanistic gesture is tactical, to her mind, because it recognizes humanism's problematic history as a means of celebrating the essentialized individual. Instead, Abu-Lughod calls for the use of humanism as a moral force and as a local language, or one might say, a language consciously made local by mindful writers. As Abu-Lughod says, if Western positionality cannot be escaped, then "our writing can either sustain it or work against its grain" (159). Abu-Lughod's two ethnographies, *Veiled Sentiments* (1986) and *Writing Women's Worlds* (1993), provide vivid models for tactically humanistic ethnography by addressing particular women's worlds and experiences.

The younger discipline of ethnic studies, however, took on issues of difference from its beginning (in the 1960s), largely in reaction to the political sensibilities of certain constructions of history. The incursion of feminist theory in the 1980s and 1990s into ethnic studies is one of its major second-wave changes. Although theorizing race, ethnicity, and class was the focus of the first decade of work in ethnic studies, more recent theoretical influences have led to methodological shifts that theorize race, ethnicity, class, gender, and sexual orientation as interconstitutive. Contemporary ethnic studies thus more broadly addresses the social construction of difference. Introducing gender and sexuality as central to identity work has essentially transformed ethnic studies as a field. Reflecting on this change in Asian American studies, sociologists Michael Omi and Dana Takagi write that

> While Asian American scholars took exception with feminist scholarship and practice which rendered race invisible, failed to grasp the unique circumstances of families of color, and marginalized the role of women of color in scholarly and activist organizations, the overall insights of feminism dramatically reshaped intellectual and political practices within Asian American Studies. (Omi and Takagi 1995, xiii)

Acknowledging the complexity of academic accountability to the communities it touches can be painful. American ethnic studies—as contrasted to area studies and even to so-called American studies—has embraced accountability and made community links central to its purpose. In a 1995 issue of *Amerasia Journal*, the oldest scholarly journal of Asian American studies, editor Russell Leong summarized this problematic in no uncertain terms:

> Academic pimping . . . involves the following: utilizing the communities' "bodies" as informants, studying, collecting and using community culture as material for research, publishing essays, articles, and books based on the above—without giving anything back. As rewards for such intellectual production that is actually based on the labor, experiences and expertise of others (often free), academics get tenure, promotions and royalties from books, article reprints, access to special grant monies for scholars, attendance at symposiums, and so forth. [. . .] Rarely is the work translated for the broader public. Seldom is such work transformed into active political or cultural strategies. (Leong 1995, ix)

Connecting with community has taken two forms. Many ethnic studies scholars in the academy have committed themselves to responding to the needs and directives of communities while also trying to share the largesse of their own position and privilege. In California's public universities, for instance, many of us share a keen awareness that our students *are* members of those communities: if we provide access to certain ideas and experiences, we directly impact the future of those communities by allowing its members a broader range of political possibilities from which to choose. This is not abstract. Many Asian and Asian American undergraduates, for instance, arrive at UCR with little sense of their place in American ethnic politics, let alone a sense of themselves as Asian American *as well as* Chinese American, Vietnamese American, or Korean American. The pedagogical process of asking them to make informed choices about identity based on history, culture, and experience is no simple thing. Certainly our students come to us with experience—they are not blank slates. The important thing is that they leave the university with some sense of how their experiences connect to, or fail to connect, with broader social and political forces. And yet, all this must be inflected with a consciousness of what Patti Lather calls "post-critical pedagogies," i.e., an attempt to activate agency as well as to produce knowledge. As Lather writes,

> [Critical] pedagogies have [too often] failed to probe the degree to which "empowerment" becomes something done "by" liberated pedagogies "to" or

"for" the as-yet-unliberated, the "Other," the object upon which is directed the "emancipatory" actions. It is precisely this question that postmodernism frames: How do our very efforts to liberate perpetuate the relations of dominance? (1992, 122)

Accountability is thus two-tiered. Accountability to the community, certainly, but also a commitment to continuously question the dyadic relationship between community and academy.

So if the ethnography of performance is joined to the progressive political agenda of ethnic studies, much could happen. If we seek to understand the mechanisms of the performative, then this particular disciplinary coalition can lead to a kind of politically performative scholarship.

Why present and discuss an Asian American woman performer? Miya Masaoka is almost the only Asian American woman I will address in detail in my book (Wong, forthcoming) because she is one of very few Asian American woman jazz and avant-garde musicians working in an idiom explicitly constructed as Asian American. I can't help but feel uneasy about her lone female presence even though it's a fact of Asian American musicianly demographics. The historian Gary Okihiro writes that in Asian American studies,

Women's recentering, their inclusion within our "community of memory", has only just begun. [. . .] [R]ecentering women positions gender as a prominent social category in determining relations of power and trajectories of social change—race and class are neither the sole nor principal determinants of Asian American history and culture. (Okihiro 1994, 91)

I am not engaged in a kind of feminist salvage work: I am not writing women or even this woman back into historical reality. Masaoka is busily creating her own Asian American historicity—she doesn't particularly need me to explain what she's up to. Instead, I will address how gender and ethnicity combine powerfully in Masaoka's explorations of the Asian and the Asian American. This performer is keenly aware of the politics of representation: to some extent, she makes this awareness part of her presentation of self.

So I am left with the question of how to present a responsible reading of her to any audience, whether Asian American or not. In fact, I think I failed this exercise in April 1997 when Masaoka came to UCR at my invitation and gave a performance that packed our recital hall for many wrong reasons. I hope to recuperate that extended, compromised moment by doing a better job here —that is, I hope to transform past clumsiness into something pedagogically useful, through re-examination. Elizabeth Ellsworth has criticized the tendency of critical educators to "operate at a high level of abstraction" and the preponderance of journal articles on education that, "although apparently based on actual practices, rarely locate theoretical constructs within them" (Ellsworth 1992, 92). She further wonders whether the use of "code words" like "critical" and "social change" veil the political agenda of critical pedagogy, and I will here question whether my own "posture of invisibility," i.e., my assumption that my agenda in producing this event would be self-evident, was naïve and ultimately ineffective, leaving the event open to conservative reinterpretation (93).

Miya Masaoka is a sansei (third-generation Japanese American) born in 1958; she lives in San Francisco. She is a musician, composer, and performance artist. Her chosen instrument is the Japanese koto, a zither with a long and venerable history. Masaoka has extensive training in traditional Japanese music; she is the director of the San Francisco Gagaku Society, an ensemble that performs the ancient music of the Japanese courts. She has a master's degree in composition from Mills College and is a full-time professional performer. She plays jazz and new music on the koto, and recorded a solo compact disc titled *Compositions/Improvisations* in 1993. This album was released by Asian Improv Records, a nonprofit label dedicated to Asian American new music, and Masaoka is at the center of this circle of musicians in the Bay Area who join music and political activism in very explicit ways.[2] Masaoka has written that, as a Japanese American composer, she has had "no choice but to construct my own musical reality" (Masaoka 1996, 8). She is keenly aware of the cultural politics surrounding her use of the koto, and the possibility of being accused of inappropriately drawing a non-Western instrument into modernist Western traditions of new music. Rather, she justifies the intercultural nature of her activities by saying,

> for me, being of Japanese heritage and born in America, biculturalism and transcultural identity have always been basic to my existence; it is this hybridity that engenders and perhaps necessitates a new cultural expression for me. (8)

I met Masaoka in April 1996 when I helped arrange a three-day residency for her and her Asian Improv colleague Mark Izu in Philadelphia. At that time, I was a member of an Asian American community arts organization called the Asian Arts Initiative, and I spent three days driving Masaoka and Izu around the city, taking them from one lecture-demo to another at different schools and community centers. In short, I got to know Masaoka and her music quickly and intensely, and I liked what I saw and heard. I was intrigued by the diverse influences and ideologies at work in her music: the traditional Japanese, modernist, avant-garde art music, jazz, etc. I also learned that Masaoka was closely involved in several community-based arts projects in San Francisco.

During our free time, Masaoka told me about her performance artwork, especially two works-in-progress. *Bee Project #1* (performed the following month in Oakland) involved three thousand live bees, violin, percussion, and koto; the sound of the bees was amplified and run through MIDI interface: the human performers responded to the resulting sounds. Another piece, titled *Ritual,* featured Masaoka, a number of Madagascar hissing roaches, and a mixed soundtrack of koto and hissing roaches: Masaoka was to lie nude on a table with the roaches crawling over her body while the soundtrack played and a video projector showed close-ups of the insects. We talked about *Ritual* in some detail, as she was in the process of finalizing it; she told me it was to be the first of a series of performance art pieces addressing the Asian American body, and she asked if I could suggest any readings about the body, identity, and performance. I suggested Judith Butler's *Bodies That Matter,* which she consequently read. Fast-forward a year: I had relocated to University of California–Riverside and was involved in the Unnatural Acts conference; the organizers (and editors of this volume)—Sue-Ellen Case, Susan Leigh Foster, and Philip Brett—asked if I could suggest someone for an evening performance and I offered to bring Masaoka to UCR. Arranging it with Masaoka, I asked if she might put together a program of solo koto works plus the performance art piece *Ritual,* and she agreed.

All this was routine enough until the week before the performance, scheduled for April 11, 1997. I made sure that publicity announcements got out, arranged for a poster, and attended to all the details surrounding the recital hall. The performance was advertised as "Miya Masaoka in Performance: Hissing Madagascar Roaches and the Koto Monster," so perhaps it's not surprising that the Riverside County newspaper, *The Press-Enterprise,* called me a week before the event. They ran a preview story three days before the performance, based on a telephone interview with Masaoka (fig. 3.1).

Almost immediately, telephone calls started flooding in to the music department, UCR's University Relations office, the dean, the chancellor—but especially to the music department. Many of the callers simply expressed dis-

Figure 3.1. Concert preview article, *The Press-Enterprise.*

approval, others disgust and outrage. Two days later, a letter appeared on *The Press-Enterprise*'s editorial page from Robert Wild, a UCR professor emeritus of physics (fig. 3.2). Wild argued that professors and administrators should act as moral gate-keepers and hold the "despicable," the "disgusting," and, indeed, the pornographic at bay. (The "brother professor" Wild refers to, Bill Reynolds, was formerly a professor in the music department, once the department chair, now deceased.) "The community" was up in arms over Masaoka and her roaches.

Who *is* "the community" in Riverside, California? In 1992, the population was 238,000, of whom 60.5 percent were white, 26.5 percent were Latino/a, 7 percent were African American, 4.9 percent were Asian American, and 0.9 percent were Native American. Riverside is the county seat and the largest city in Riverside County; it is about sixty miles east of Los Angeles and the river it is named for is the Santa Ana River, which is mostly if not completely dry for much of the year. The city was established after the introduction of citrus trees in the nineteenth century transformed the region—in fact, UCR was once an agricultural college, and a multitude of courses are still offered in soil, insects, and worms. Much of the Latino/a population of the city originally arrived to work as laborers in the citrus groves; the latest waves of laborers are indigenous

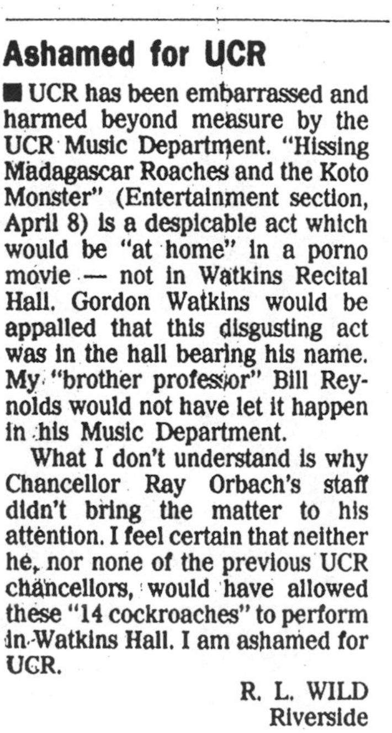

Ashamed for UCR

■ UCR has been embarrassed and harmed beyond measure by the UCR Music Department. "Hissing Madagascar Roaches and the Koto Monster" (Entertainment section, April 8) is a despicable act which would be "at home" in a porno movie — not in Watkins Recital Hall. Gordon Watkins would be appalled that this disgusting act was in the hall bearing his name. My "brother professor" Bill Reynolds would not have let it happen in his Music Department.

What I don't understand is why Chancellor Ray Orbach's staff didn't bring the matter to his attention. I feel certain that neither he, nor none of the previous UCR chancellors, would have allowed these "14 cockroaches" to perform in Watkins Hall. I am ashamed for UCR.

R. L. WILD
Riverside

Figure 3.2. Letter to the editor from Robert Wild, *The Press-Enterprise*.

peoples from Mexico and Central America. Still, the Anglo population is by far the largest. UCR is one of the smallest UC campuses with only nine thousand undergraduates, many of whom come from Riverside County or Orange County, many of whom are the first in their families to attend college. UCR's undergraduate population is dominated by Anglo-Americans, Asians, and Asian Americans. Out of 8,381 students in 1998, the undergraduate population was 42.8 percent Asian /Asian American, 28.6 percent white American, 19.9 percent Hispanic, 2.5 percent "other," 5.5 percent African American, and 0.6 percent Native American ("Self-Study Report" 1998, 95). In short, student demographics do not by any means reflect those of the city.

While I would not describe UCR's undergraduates as particularly radical or even liberal, the faculty and curriculum have repeatedly attracted the attention of the community, and the dismay of the more conservative community has often found a forum in *The Press-Enterprise*. In May and June 1996, for instance, faculty approval of a new minor in lesbian, gay, and bisexual studies caused a major stir in the local newspaper. The Unnatural Acts conference has prompted community outcry several times. In short, "the community" expects something between titillation and the offensive from UCR.

Professor Wild's reference to pornography was echoed in many of the phone calls taken by music department staff members[3] and thus evoked previous controversies. By Friday, the day of the performance, the calls were more focused. One woman caller told the secretary answering the phone that the chair of the music department (Philip Brett) was "no better than a pimp standing out on University Avenue." Another warned that if Masaoka disrobed onstage, he would effect a citizen's arrest on the spot. Others called to threaten disruptions. While most of the phone calls were apparently from community members, UCR students, faculty, and staff were also intrigued, but in other ways. I assigned concert attendance to the undergraduates in my class, "Music and Gender in Cross-Cultural Perspective," and they reported that prurient curiosity was inspiring many of their friends to attend. They assured me that I could expect a full house.

By the evening of the performance, we had arranged for three security officers rather than the usual one, and university legal counsel had advised us that the legal definition of "public lewdness" is that no warning is extended to potential viewers. We therefore posted notices outside the recital hall stating that the performance would involve nudity, thus protecting the school and enabling security officers to remove anyone causing a disruption (fig. 3.3). Watkins Recital Hall seats 208 people, and it was packed by 7:45. I might add that this was unprecedented: the chamber music concerts usually held in this hall generally don't draw hordes of people. The student ushers were so unprepared for the phenomenon of a full house that I had to tell them to close the doors.

Backstage, Masaoka was excited and bemused but not at all worried. She said her performance of *Ritual* in San Francisco hadn't attracted one-tenth of this attention, nor was it regarded by the press as controversial. In short, she was simply pleased at the turnout. I, on the other hand, was tense and perplexed, feeling that the situation had somehow gotten out of hand and won-

THE "HISSING MADAGASCAR COCKROACHES" AND "THE KOTO MONSTER" PERFORMANCE BY MIYA MASAOKA WILL INVOLVE NUDITY. IF YOU THINK YOU WOULD BE OFFENDED BY THIS PERFORMANCE, PLEASE DO NOT ATTEND.

Figure 3.3. Warning notice posted at Masaoka's performance.

dering how I might have better handled it. I had seated sympathetic friends and colleagues in the front row to form a kind of supportive barricade, but it was clear that the second row was lined with conservative community members: they had arrived together—in fact, they were nearly the first people in the recital hall doors, and they looked both grim and . . . prepared, as if they had a plan.

Meanwhile, the excited buzz of undergraduate conversation filled the air. I scanned the audience, at once ashamed of my own attempts to identify troublemakers and compelled to try. I'd say there were three categories of audience members: outraged community conservatives, curious undergraduates, and faculty members and Unnatural Acts attendees ready for a tussle over First Amendment rights and censorship. That middle-aged white man with the crew cut, for instance, sitting right beside the steps up to the stage: was he in position to disrupt the performance? In my role as producer/panopticon, I found myself wondering if every unsmiling, middle-aged white person in the audience represented conservative middle America, and was further distracted by my own readiness to stereotype.

And in the end, nothing happened. Or, rather, Masaoka gave a stunning performance. The first half of the program featured solo koto pieces, some using digital processing and computer interface, one about the Japanese American internment camps based on a poem by Lawson Inada. Masaoka spoke to the audience between numbers as she retuned her instrument, explaining each piece, explaining that the "koto monster" was her koto plus sound technology, a monstrous and often fractious combination. By the second and third pieces, it was clear that many audience members were responding to her virtuosity. During the intermission before *Ritual,* the sense of anticipation was stronger than ever. When everyone was reseated, I went out and (following Masaoka's instructions) explained the technology behind the piece and asked for the audience's silence and concentration, noting that the piece was quite solemn. The curtains opened to reveal a dimly lit stage with Masaoka's nude body, absolutely still, stretched out on a white-shrouded table in its center. The video projection started, filling the back of the stage with such extreme close-ups of her body that precise anatomical locations were unreadable. In the wings, I punched the Start button on the CD player and the amplified sounds of hissing Madagascar roaches moved stereophonically across the hall. Asian American graduate student Yutian Wong, dressed in black, appeared stage right and slowly struck two Tibetan hand cymbals together. Another Asian American student assistant emerged from stage left bearing a box in her hands: she solemnly approached Masaoka and slowly, carefully, began to take Mada-gascar roaches out of the box one by one and place them on Masaoka's body. The roaches sluggishly explored her arms and legs until all thirteen were on her body—and then the assistant began to gather them up, one by one, putting them gently back in the box and finally walking offstage with them. The video ended; the soundtrack ended; the curtains were pulled closed. The piece had lasted fifteen minutes, and nothing had happened. After a long moment of silence, the audience began to applaud. Masaoka pulled on her clothes and went out to bow, announcing that the roaches were for sale if anyone wanted an easygoing pet.

I would like to turn to three textual renditions of *Ritual,* one by Masaoka herself, another by undergraduates in my class who wrote reports about the event,[4] and the third by writers for *The Press-Enterprise.* Despite their *Rasho-mon*-like mosaic, each points to ways that reception can be shaped or resisted, and each suggests pedagogical possibility.

First, it is important to consider that Masaoka offered her own explanation of *Ritual* in her program notes (fig. 3.4). That explanation arose from her creative and political interest in performing the body as well as my earlier suggestion that she read Judith Butler. Masaoka found that Butler's use of performance as a central trope fit perfectly with her ideas. The resulting exegesis of *Ritual* is Masaoka's:

> The *Ritual* is an offering to begin considering the relationships between and the social construction of the body, race, and performance. Recent theoretical work by critical theorist Judith Butler suggests that bodies tend to indicate a world beyond themselves, beyond their own boundaries, a movement of boundary itself. Bodies cannot be said to have a signifiable existence prior to the mark of their gender; the question then emerges, how do we reconceive the body no longer as a passive medium or instrument on which cultural meanings are inscribed? The body can, for example, be thought of as a machine, a work of art, an object of desire/revulsion, a site for hegemony or control, or all of these in fluid and simultaneous flux. The bare skin is the border between our interior self and the exterior world while symbolizing

UNIVERSITY OF CALIFORNIA,
RIVERSIDE
AS PART OF THE
UNNATURAL ACTS CONFERENCE

Figure 3.4. Program notes from Masaoka's performance.

HISSING MADAGASCAR ROACHES AND THE *KOTO* MONSTER: MIYA MASAOKA IN PERFORMANCE

FRIDAY, APRIL 11, 1997
8:OO P.M.
WATKINS RECITAL HALL

cultural representations and triggering cultural memory, illuminating the contradictory nature of female bodies, male bodies, Asian bodies, and even Japanese bodies. This piece addresses issues of power, control, and the social construction of race and eroticism in performance.

In short, Masaoka had rather specific ideas about what her piece "meant," even though its meanings didn't lie at the micro level of, for instance, what the roaches might symbolize. Why she chose the language of critical theory to convey her explanation is another question. At the very least, we can assume it fit her thoughts, since she was already planning the piece and thinking about the body as a cultural construct when she asked me for reading suggestions.

What caught the eye and ear of *The Press-Enterprise,* on the other hand, was the possibility of revulsion. Insects and nudity were all too easy to sensationalize, and Masaoka's phone interview was easily manipulated to point up the vacuousness of contemporary art: she'd originally wanted rats, the roaches didn't "mean" anything, etc. Yet I'm not quite ready to dismiss the newspaper as a rather desperate small-town rag, either. Rather than simply cry irresponsibility (the expected language of liberalism), I have to consider that *The Press-Enterprise* fulfills a pedagogical function (though not the one I wish it did). It filled Watkins Hall, to be sure, and in all fairness I should say that the front-page article the morning after the performance was fair and level-headed (even though penned by one of their sportswriters). Still, "the community" had the last word a few days later, again on the editorial page (fig. 3.5). Despite her venom, I find Alta Armstrong's letter interesting because she keeps coming back to the issues I too am concerned with: teaching and education. Never mind that her use of the possessive "our" is unthoughtful (or that *my* music department has nowhere near a million dollars in either annual budget or endowments). Armstrong's evocation of tax dollars emerges from a peculiarly American idea, a democracy of the imaginary, in which education is ownable through taxes. Indeed, any number of irate callers asked how *their* tax dollars could be supporting *that*. The controllable commodity trope is a pedagogical model that we need to engage with as educators, and we further need to engage with the paradigm of commodity capitalism that lurks behind it.

The undergraduates in my music and gender class went into the event with more information and more directives than other audience members. For one thing, they knew they had to write a short report on it, and I had provided specific questions they had to answer—so in some ways my efforts to shape their reception of the event were quite coercive. Of course, they had read all the pre-performance newspaper materials, and they knew that the roaches had arrived by FedEx that morning, and they knew the event was potentially ex-

Education at its worst

■ How can this be at our UCR? What are they doing at our university? Our tax money paid for this million dollar-plus Music Department. This cannot come under education! It can't even be entertainment. This is not acceptable education....

How can "Unnatural Acts Conference" with "hissing Madagascar roaches" all over her nude body teach our children anything? With close-up video screens so everyone can get a good view.

This is sick, sick, sick....

ALTA ARMSTRONG
Hemet

Figure 3.5. Letter to the editor from Alta Armstrong, *The Press-Enterprise.*

plosive, so I think it's safe to say that they went with a certain excitement and a sense that they had the inside scoop. I was keenly interested to see what they had to say about it in their papers.

Armed with the concept of the male gaze, most of the students addressed audience expectations head-on. A few were honest enough to admit their own expectations were low: as one woman wrote, "For me, [performance art] conjured up images of people dressed in freakish costumes running rampant about the stage and screaming." One student wrote that during intermission the audience got quite "rowdy" because they "couldn't wait to see the 'naked chick.'" Another noted that "the auditorium was completely packed—with fans, horny male onlookers, [and] just plain curious folks." Yet another flatly stated that "one of the primary reasons the hall was so packed . . . was because people knew there was going to be nudity. [. . .] Many men anticipated this performance as they would a live stripper in a bar."

These comments confirm what was evident to anyone in the audience: many of the spectators came to be shocked or titillated or at least to witness controversy—or perhaps even to see *others* reacting outrageously to the performance. All this points to the spectacle of controversy and the spectacle of titillation. In other words, these audience members came to see something happen *around* the performance (e.g., a citizen's arrest of the nude performer) or to see a nude body (as opposed to its performance).

Many of the students openly acknowledged that they ultimately found *Ritual* a bit dull to watch. One man wrote that "the piece [lost] its initial level of excitement for me because it [was so] repetitive. The cockroaches really did not move very much." Others wrote without embarrassment that they weren't sure what it all meant: "I must admit, I felt confused. I had no idea what to think of it," one woman wrote.

Despite their ready admission that interpreting the piece's "meaning" was a challenge, most of the students had a lot to say about its sexual politics. Part of their assignment was for them to consider whether a reversal of the performer's gender would change the piece and its reception. One student suggested that "there is a difference in the way society views the male body and the female body. Women have always been suppressed and held to a standard of virtue, [so that] revealing the body is still considered a degrading and shameful act." One woman wrote that "a woman's naked body is the universal symbol of sex. A man's naked body doesn't have quite the same connotations. A woman has traditionally and historically been seen as a tool for man's pleasure."

All of the students addressed the de-eroticization of Masaoka's body. "She was not viewed as a sex object after the performance," wrote one. "The entire scene created a mood that shifted [us] from lust [to] disgust, and the feeling of being in a morgue," another noted. "What was to be an object of desire—the nude female body—was now a source of repulsion," one woman wrote. And all of them got the bigger point: "[Masaoka] challenged notions of sexuality and gender and tested the comfort level [of] her audience. [. . .] She attempted to disrupt and dispute, but she also showed how these constructed roles are still rigid as evidenced by those who took offense [at] her program."

As pleased as I was by the honesty and thoughtfulness of the student papers, I was struck by the absence of any reference to Masaoka's race or ethnicity. Certainly the students noted Masaoka's connection to the koto through heritage, but no one even speculated about how sexuality and the body are racialized. Certainly, we were only several weeks into the course and hadn't yet addressed in any depth how race, gender, sexual orientation, class, etc., intersect in most forms of performance, nor had I explicitly told them to consider race and ethnicity. Masaoka herself made only passing reference in the program notes to her body as Japanese. But three of the four students from whom I've drawn most of these comments are Asian American (of Thai and Philippine descent). In fact, several of the students made universalizing gestures, suggesting that *Ritual* transcended the body, gender, and race. As one student wrote, "[Masaoka] was trying to show us that race, gender, and color should not matter because they are not significant."

In short, I was nonplussed by the response of both the students *and* the public, because race and ethnicity evidently disappeared into the display of the female body—and I had conceived of the event as Asian American in focus and message. Masaoka's racial politics were absorbed into the politics of the body. And I was caught off guard.

Introducing Masaoka as a campus event was as challenging as introducing non-Western literature into the college curriculum. As an ethnomusicologist, I feel it's my responsibility to produce several performance events every year that will present cultural counterpoints to the usual roster of orchestra and choral concerts; such events complement the curriculum in ways that reflect *praxis,* doing. Whether I help present a xylophonist from Ghana, a Javanese gamelan ensemble of American undergraduates, or Miya Masaoka, some educational gesture *beyond* presentation seems necessary if "understanding" is the goal. Having said that, I immediately wonder why a Brahms symphony is somehow considered more transparently understandable when in fact it begs the same question of how the moment of reception can be made pedagogical. Such moments don't just happen, but on the other hand, I wonder whether —or to what extent—they can be controlled, because my interest in having an audience see beyond its preconceptions isn't disinterested at all; in the case of Miya Masaoka, for instance, I wanted them to see certain things and not others.

Masaoka's exposed racialized gendered body Othered her more profoundly than I could have foreseen. How might I have "taught" her to the audience, to local newspaper critics, to the students in my music and gender class? Considering how she might teach a novel by R. K. Narayan to non-Indian students, Gayatri Spivak worries that the book easily becomes a "repository" for "postcolonial selves, postcolonial*ism*, even postcolonial resistance"—that the novel (or any cultural performance) can be too easily read as "direct expressions of cultural consciousness, with no sense of the neocolonial traffic in identity" (Spivak 1996, 239). Similarly, Masaoka's public reception as Woman Exposed blew away the traffic in identity that she clearly sees as central to her purpose. Ethnic politics vanished into her overwhelmingly female body.

One woman, one event, one community. I've carefully focused on the local and the particular as a means to think about pedagogy and the presentation of the Other. I am of course wondering if the absence of any discussion of race around this event is the result of studied fear—this did happen in California, after all, where even most conservatives know that race and ethnicity are topics to be approached carefully. Were discussions so single-mindedly focused on gender and sexuality because that's what happens when people try to talk about difference—only one parameter can be handled at once? Everything else drops out of the picture. Edna Acosta-Belén notes that issues of gender have traditionally gotten lost in ethnic studies while women's studies has had a hard time dealing with race and class (1993, 177). Chandra Mohanty made this point in her already classic essay, "Under Western Eyes," suggesting that the power of colonial discourses make it difficult even for feminist scholars to get beyond universalizing frameworks. She writes,

> Thus . . . in any given piece of feminist analysis, women are characterized as a singular group on the basis of a shared oppression. What binds women together is a sociological notion of the "sameness" of their oppression. [. . .] Thus, the discursively consensual homogeneity of "women" as a group is mistaken for the historically specific material reality of groups of women. (Mohanty 1995, 262)

Whereas the feminist attempt to get at gendered power relations leads to discursively constituted ideas of shared oppression, the same universalizing frameworks enable a misogynist and sexist reception of an Asian American woman performer as simply pornographic female display.

I should also point out that the most of the public responses came from community members who were not at a performance that had yet to occur.[5] Still, I include them and their response as audience members in the broadest sense. As performance studies has taught us to look beyond the performance "itself" to the totality of the event, I consider this absent, offended critical group as an audience and their rejoinders as reception.

I have been concerned here with praxis in several ways. Patti Lather suggests that "praxis is the self-creative activity through which we make the world" (1991, 11). Praxis can be teaching, or theorizing in concert with others, or any kind of cultural performance. It is a moment when we learn, over and over again, how to turn critical thought into social action. Again, Lather says that "theory adequate to the task of changing the world must be open-ended, nondogmatic, speaking to and grounded in the circumstances of everyday life" (1991, 55).

It occurs to me that I haven't addressed the presence of another audience: the participants and attendees at the Unnatural Acts conference. They were there, too. And we were variously caught up in watching the audience and watching the performance and watching each other while preparing to prevent hostile audience members from disrupting the performance. I haven't theorized the vibrant, enthusiastic, stirred presence of these audience members, nor have I considered the presence of Marta Savigliano on my left and Liz Wood on my right as we watched from the front row. I haven't theorized the readiness of Unnatural Acts participants to fill that row, forming a protective barrier. This praxis of participatory response was both reflexive and performative, and should be acknowledged even as I shy away from valorizing my own cohort.

Finally, I can't know whether "the community" had a *pedagogical* experience. The fact is, after all hubbub preceding the performance, in the end no one disrupted it, and I think we have to ask why not. Of course I (and doubtless many of the Unnatural Acts participants) try hard to believe in and to theorize performance as an activity creating environments that change attitudes and understandings.[6] Or that might change them. At some level, I have to admit I wanted "them" to get "my" interpretation of the performance, but at bottom how can one "know" what happened at the moment of reception? Its ethnographic unknowability irritates and challenges.

To close, I note that Masaoka recounted her Riverside experience to performance artist Guillermo Gómez-Peña, who is considering doing a spot on it in his performative editorial series for National Public Radio's *All Things Considered.* In other words, yet another representation of the event may be forthcoming, again by someone who wasn't there. Furthermore, Masaoka is now planning the second work in her series, Asian Bodies in Performance, so it may well be that performers will have the last word. Her new work is titled *What Is the Sound of Ten Naked Asian Men?* and will in fact feature ten Asian and Asian American men lying on ten different tables; each will have six audio pickups attached to different parts of their bodies. Masaoka's descriptive notes combine cultural theory, politics, and performance detail:[7]

> [The men] will be lying prone, and the amplified sound of their bodies, such as sounds of the stomach, swallowing, natural body shifting on the table, heart-beating sounds, etc., will be amplified and mixed by a sound technician. Later, in the studio, these sounds will be layered and manipulated via computer and digital signal processing. In addition, I will interview each of the ten men participants and the text will be taken from the interviews, recontextualized, fractured and interwoven to the soundscape. Naked men, particularly Asian men, are rarely part of the public and media imagination. By employing Asian naked men into a sound piece, I hope to confront this

current invisibility of Asian, and Asian men in particular, in an upbeat and positive-Asian-male body kind of way.

The goal of the series *Asian Bodies in Performance* is to question the preconceived notions of such social constructions as gender, ethnicity, and sexual orientation. To present the body as a passive canvas, as a passive medium or instrument for which cultural meaning is inscribed is to illustrate this point head-on.

Head-on indeed. As Philip Brett said to me on the afternoon of the performance, "I just don't understand it—*lots* of people have taken their clothes off in Watkins Hall. Tim *Miller* took off his clothes in Watkins Hall." The pornography of insects, of race. The pornography of the performative. I hope this essay opens up broader questions of ethnography, identity, and community, but it also gestures toward the praxis (construction?) of the unnatural in a conservative environment.

NOTES

I would like to thank Jan Monk, Kimberly Jones, and Sandra Shattuck for inviting me to participate in the Southwest Institute for Research on Women's 1997 Summer Institute at the University of Arizona, where I first presented this analysis. In Riverside, Traise Yamamoto, Paul Simon, Piya Chatterjee, Philip Brett, and René T. A. Lysloff provided thoughtful and spirited critique that helped me find the final shape of the essay. My thanks also to Maria Luz Cruz Torres for inviting me to present a version of this essay in the colloquium series of the Department of Anthropology, UCR.

1. I would like to thank Tong Soon Lee for bringing Lila Abu-Lughod's "Writing against Culture" to my attention.

2. Masaoka is mentioned briefly in Susan Asai's article on Japanese American music (1995, 447). Surprisingly, Asai notes that Masaoka's "interest in playing the koto is apolitical and is not intended as an expression of her Japanese heritage. She strives to compose music as a purely artistic endeavor, not meant to make a social or political statement." Masaoka may well explain herself in different ways to different questioners, but in my experience Masaoka explicitly links her musical activities to her Japanese American identity.

3. I would like to thank staff members Andrea Jones and Cindy Roulette for sharing this information with me.

4. I would like to thank the four students in my class who gave me permission to share their papers with you: Kit McCluskey, David Reyes, Michelle Phertiyanan, and Maria Porras.

5. I thank René T. A. Lysloff for this thought and for pointing out that this is *not* the same as John Pemberton's (1987) argument that Javanese don't "listen" to gamelan music.

6. My thanks to Philip Brett for arguing that this *did* happen.

7. Posted on Masaoka's homepage, http://thecity.sfsu.edu/~miya/bodies.html.

BIBLIOGRAPHY

Abu-Lughod, Lila. 1986. *Veiled Sentiments: Honor and Poetry in a Bedouin Society.* Berkeley: University of California Press.

———. 1991. "Writing against Culture." In *Recapturing Anthropology: Working in the Present,* ed. Richard G. Fox. Santa Fe, N.Mex.: School of American Research Press.

———. 1993. *Writing Women's Worlds: Bedouin Stories.* Berkeley: University of California Press.

Acosta-Belén, Edna. 1993. "Defining a Common Ground: The Theoretical Meeting of Women's, Ethnic, and Area Studies." In *Researching Women in Latin America and the Caribbean,* ed. Edna Acosta-Belén and Christine E. Bose. Boulder, Colo.: Westview Press.

Asai, Susan Miyo. 1995. "Transformations of Tradition: Three Generations of Japanese American Music Making." *Musical Quarterly* 79, no. 3: 429–53.

Ellsworth, Elizabeth. 1992. "Why Doesn't This Feel Empowering? Working through the Repressive Myths of Critical Pedagogy." In *Feminisms and Critical Pedagogy,* ed. Carmen Luke and Jennifer Gore. New York and London: Routledge.

Heilbrun, Jacob. 1996. "The News from Everywhere." *Lingua Franca,* May/June 1996, pp. 49–56.

Lather, Patti. 1991. *Getting Smart: Feminist Research and Pedagogy with/in the Postmodern.* New York and London: Routledge.

———. 1992. "Post-Critical Pedagogies: A Feminist Reading." In *Feminisms and Critical Pedagogy,* ed. Carmen Luke and Jennifer Gore. New York and London: Routledge.

Leong, Russell. 1995. "Lived Theory (Notes on the Run)." *Amerasia Journal* 21, nos. 1 and 2: v–x.

Masaoka, Miya. 1996. "*Koto No Tankyu* (Koto Explorations)." *Institute for the Study of American Music Newsletter* 25, no. 2: 8–9.

Mohanty, Chandra Talpade. 1995. "Under Western Eyes: Feminist Scholarship and Colonial Discourses." In *The Post-Colonial Studies Reader,* ed. Bill Ashcroft, Gareth Griffiths, and Helen Tiffin. New York and London: Routledge. (Reprinted from *Boundary 2* 12, no. 3 and 13, no. 1 [Spring/Fall 1984].)

Okihiro, Gary Y. 1994. *Margins and Mainstreams: Asians in American History and Culture.* Seattle and London: University of Washington Press.

Omi, Michael, and Dana Takagi. 1995. "Thinking Theory in Asian American Studies." *Amerasia Journal* 21, nos. 1 and 2: xi–xv.

Pemberton, John. 1987. "Musical Politics in Central Java (or How Not to Listen to a Javanese Gamelan)." *Indonesia* 44: 17–30.

"Self-Study Report: Undergraduate Education in the Context of the Research University." 1998. Submitted in support of an application for reaffirmation of accreditation by the Western Association of School and Colleges. University of California, Riverside, January 5, 1998.

Spivak, Gayatri Chakravorty. 1996. "How to Teach a 'Culturally Different' Book." In *The Spivak Reader,* ed. Donna Landry and Gerald MacLean. New York and London: Routledge.

Volkman, Toby Alice (Program Officer). 1996. "Crossing Borders: Revitalizing Area

Studies." Call for grant proposals issued by the Ford Foundation, December 20, 1996.

Wei, William. 1993. *The Asian American Movement.* Philadelphia: Temple University Press.

Wong, Deborah. Forthcoming. *Speak It Louder: Asian Americans Making Music.*

PART 2.
CONTESTING WHITE SPACES

4. Black Noise / White Mastery

Ronald Radano

It is so difficult with us to tell just where the negro begins and the white man ends.[1]

—G. J. Greene, *Keowee Courier*, 1882

No term in the modern lexicon conveys more vividly African-American music's powers of authenticity and resistance than the figure of "noise." In hip-hop parlance, "noise," specifically "black noise," is that special insight from the inside, the anti-philosophy that emerges front and center through the sound attack of rap.[2] To "bring the noise" means to offer a different logic—a logic of difference—which gives to contemporary America its black musical presence. A little over two hundred years ago, African-American performative culture existed as an absence beyond the grasp of Euro-Western reality. Today, it is arguably the very essence of American musical life, fulfilling what W. E. B. Du Bois proclaimed to be "the most beautiful expression of human experience born this side the seas."[3] The effect of black noise is so powerful, in fact, that it exceeds the bounds of the nation-state. In the transnational repetitions of rap opposition, black noise appears nearly everywhere, creating the illusion that through rap music finally reveals its universal nature. Yet despite this global significance, black noise ultimately conforms to the same American racial logic it seeks to challenge. Rather than radicalizing the stable binaries of race, noise inverts them; it transforms prior signs of European musical mastery—harmony, melody, song—into all that is bitchin', kickin', and black.

The many versions of an oppositional black noise trace across the modern history of American public culture. Together they provide a figurative defense against a tradition of racist assertion as well as a challenge to liberal appeals for a "color-blind" consensus and commonality. "Noise" serves in these instances as a practical response to a legacy of racial insensitivity and incomprehension, just as it sustains through its purported stabilities of form a sense of racio-cultural cohesiveness and belonging. Historically, the claims about black music's essential nature arose as a direct response to the fixed prejudices of white supremacy. In black music, in particular, progressive critics located a powerful weapon to counter the charges of African-American intellectual and creative inferiority—those "Myths of the Negro Past." To ignore the social significance of an oppositional black noise, then, is to deny the real-life effects of race in the United States. And yet to give excessive priority to these same racially deter-mined forms is to perpetuate an interpretation of African-American expres-sive culture that is as constraining as it is enabling. For if "blackness" fulfills a stable difference, it is only difference that blackness can be.

Timeless, essential, and seemingly separate from history itself, the noise of black difference plays by the master's rules to effect oppositions reinforcing not only blackness but the sanctity of whiteness. It is a logic that owns the center of our social life, from the presentations of music in public culture—record stores, radio programming, journalism—to the racial separatism that still dominates liberal musical scholarship. To rely on the interpretation of black music as difference means to acknowledge rather than to overturn a su-premacist racial logic. While this strategy has supported important acts of ad-vocacy at particular times and places, it has never successfully interrogated the root problem of a racially "black music" that perpetuates easy stabilities of the color line.

I want to propose another way of looking at "black music" that might mark the way toward a more subversive critical challenge to white supremacy's logic.[4] What I'll be gesturing to here is a reading of black musical "noise" that, put simply, aims to unseat the hegemony of difference. As theorized here, noise owes its power not to difference as such but rather to the *fear* of what differ-ence brings. From this reading, "to bring the noise"—in the spirit of Public Enemy's familiar phrase—is to reveal the *sameness* that connects black and white at its musical origin.

By proposing an emphasis on racial "sameness" I do not, of course, mean to deny the significance of dialectical logic in modern critical thought. Nor do I seek to reduce blackness to some form of (white) consensus. Rather, I wish to stress points of contact and encounter that subvert the fallacious kind of rea-soning still supporting racialist views of isolated and stable musical cultures, whether black or white.[5] It is the idea of sameness, of black-white contact, recognition, and engagement, that echoes forth from a legacy of modern Afri-can-American music to threaten, as it reinforces, the ideology of racial fixity.[6] What we accept as the "common sense" of black musical autonomy in fact grows out of a prior moment of contact that by the mid-nineteenth century had given way to racialist notions of difference. In order to comprehend this constructed, "second nature" of black music, we need to turn to its point of social origin: not to a pre-colonialist Africa (which nonetheless casts practices resonating into the present day), but to the equally important first musical contacts that begin America's interracial conversation.

When Europe looked with "imperial eyes" to the untapped resource of slave labor, it had yet to recognize the cultural differences that had shaped those newly named "African" lives. Early English and Continental reports of contact provide little documentation of the soundworld of Africans, beyond passing references to performance practices and matter-of-fact observations of an audible terror accompanying enslavement.[7] Expressing a supreme confidence in Europe's self-proclaimed duty to rationalize the naturescape of the known world, early explorers mapped a global territory while looking and listening beyond the non-sites of "blackness." According to Mary Louise Pratt, imperial myopia at first allowed some room for the contrasts between foreign lands and the assumed ideal of Europe. Corresponding musical reports, such as those recorded by Richard Ligon during his travels to Barbados in 1647, support this view, revealing a discernible, if ambiguous, respect for African creativity that seemed inconsistent with emerging racialist views.[8] With the rise of modern institutional racism in the latter half of the eighteenth century, however, European exceptionalism increases to the point of eventually blocking out all that exceeded normative limits. Over time, chroniclers would give less and less notice to cultural expressions that challenged their secure comprehension, as blackness faded into a "blank darkness" of absence and lack. Hegel's frequently cited projection of Africa as a land without history or culture reveals the sentiment of a well-established colonialist perspective at the onset of modern white supremacy. So too does it explain the relative silence of texts appearing across the history of slavery that might have otherwise documented the sonic collisions of so many discoursing "Africans" across the Americas.[9]

In her pioneering studies of African musics in North America (most notably *Sinful Tunes and Spirituals*), Dena Epstein recalls her own bemused response to the paucity of references to black music-making in the colonial literature. After a systematic review of seventeenth- and eighteenth-century sources, she turned up just a handful of accounts detailing African musical practices. Of the references she did locate, most were vague and incomplete, suggesting that European listeners had failed to hear in African performance a truly "musical" significance. Despite the widespread assumption that Africans were "naturally musical"—meaning that they could expertly mimic European music—most white Euro-Americans would increasingly assume that blacks were incapable of actually inventing formally coherent, pleasurable sound.[10] At this point—from 1619 to about 1750—the figure of "noise" becomes central to North American depictions of African absence. Yet unlike our twentieth-century conception, "noise" in the Colonial Era lacked the power of critical opposition that would emerge from the white recognition of black difference. Although noise in this context referred to the threat of an unfamiliar African populace whose numbers would increase dramatically from 1710 on, its significance as a racially transgressive force had yet to dent the armor of Euro-America's imperial imagination. Despite the volumes of sonic excess, black noise remained incomprehensible, virtually inaudible, and nearly always out of music's order.

These missing references to a slave sound world reveal quite literally the white, North American deafness and blindness to African significance. Observers failed to speak or write about a "black music" for the simple reason that they believed it not to exist. To be sure, they heard the screams and cries that accompanied the horrors of the middle passage and the slave auction. So did they witness the "peculiarities" of African performance that prompted occasional comment. Yet the assuredness with which a sober English Christianity determined the moral and intellectual inferiority of African slaves never permitted the recognition of an intercultural, human "sameness" that must have preceded the invention of difference. American slaves—those commodities servicing a new, English economic order—were in cultural terms little more than producers of an anti-harmony, since "music" could develop only within a civilized, Christian world. While it would oversimplify matters to suggest that all whites failed to comprehend the humanity of the slave soundworld, the uniformity of North American discursive practices during much of the Colonial Era suggests that African performance had yet to reach the level of "music" or even of a comprehensible difference within New World epistemological frames. As Frederick Douglass described it, slave sounding remained forever "within the circle," existing as a dimension prior to European recognition and engagement.

Ironically, the shift in this dynamic occurs precisely when the ideology of racial difference begins to harden in the late eighteenth and early nineteenth centuries. By this time, Western racial theory increasingly assumes correlations between color, intelligence, morality, and character that contrast with the more variously constituted prior depictions of Africans. In the United States, as several historians have argued, these racial views would grow particularly virulent as they were articulated within the new circumstances of antebellum society.[11] With the emergence of a discernible African-American culture, the rise of black Christianity, and the threat of the abolitionist challenge, among other factors, blackness achieved a degree of recognizable familiarity or sameness that enabled the ascribing of difference. A preliminary investigation suggests, moreover, that these same circumstances corresponded to the emergence of a publicly acknowledged "black music." With the emergence of a recognizable alternative to American humanity in black, a distinctive black music comes into being. From this first beginning, the idea of black music develops as a crossracial *engagement* conceptualized within similarly changing public discursive frames. What we commonly comprehend to be a stable form of neo-African musical expression is constituted as part of the very flux of rapidly shifting conceptions of racial difference.

The theme of interracial musical engagement has most typically served to support positions of white dominance, depicting a fixed and permanent Euro-American tradition that civilizes the instabilities of morally and formally weaker African-American cultural practices. Formulated this way, instability implies inadequacy: the inferiority of black difference keeps a safe distance from white practices, as African-Americans eagerly adapt and adopt their art to aspire toward the norm of Euro-American achievement. What we might call a narrative of containment thus begins with slavery and linguistic domination. In music, such views informed the white invention/black imitation model characteristic of spiritual scholarship as it was put forward by George Pullen Jackson and others in the 1920s and 1930s. It also informs, albeit in very different political circumstances, the formal preoccupation of jazz music's "new critics" (most notably, Gunther Schuller and the late Martin Williams), as well as the more recent "neoclassical" interpretations that cast a diverse range of musics according to European-informed aesthetics and models of stylistic development.

Less commonly acknowledged are the ways in which white stability has been similarly destabilized as a consequence of interracial encounter. We begin to see considerable evidence of such occurrences at the very same time that the recognition of black music emerges in the late eighteenth century. It is at this time, for example, that the figure of "Sambo," whom Europeans had long enjoyed seeing perform his sport, becomes a familiar comic concept in the white imagination, prefiguring the miming acts of blackface passing. It is at this time, too, that both northern whites and slaves take part in the Pinkster festivals that celebrate a hybrid of Christian and African religious beliefs. And it is at this time, once more, that white Virginians not only begin to make note of the fiddling and dance practices of slaves, but to develop their own versions of black dance and to engage in interracial performances. The phenomenon of the "Negro jig" drew considerable comment in the late eighteenth century, becoming a kind of early fad that prefigures the public cultural dance trends of the early twentieth century. Similar encounters appeared in other venues: in the interracial corn-shucking ceremonies of southern plantations; in the subsequent rise of the white Piedmont style of banjo performance (the instrument itself being of African origin); and in the various elaborations on black dance in white country music—all of which trace a grand process of interracial encounter into the late twentieth century.[12]

Yet what seems to be the key interracial dynamic in the formation of modern black music thus far has received only limited attention from music scholars and historians. It is the moment when large numbers of blacks and whites began to engage in musical acts of religious experience that ultimately lead to the formation of "blackness" as a musical concept. In the musically inspired spiritual conversions of the camp-meeting movement we locate what may well be the originary perceptual space or "contact zone" that fostered religious transformations inscribed with the new discourses of race.[13] Initiated through the activity of performance, these conversions became musical events in themselves, through which actors engaged in multiple levels of spiritual and racial transgression. This pattern of contact and mimesis set the stage for the appearance of a newly acknowledged cultural practice that observers would name "Negro music." Thus, a unique and seemingly stable African-American music emerges out of the racial *instability* of these foundational "white" and "black" contacts.[14]

◈ ◆ ◈

   Social historians have commonly portrayed the early camp meetings as a significant moment of interracial contact, yet rarely do they also acknowledge the extent to which these encounters contributed to equally profound instabilities of racial subjectivity.[15] From about 1780 to 1830, hundreds of thousands of Americans held witness to public rituals of religious conversion. While the actual number of converts was considerably lower, the events as a whole had broad effect, inspiring new and profound intersections of the nation's populace. According to one contemporary estimate, attendance at the camp meetings by the second decade of the nineteenth century had grown to three to four million annually, encompassing about one-third of the American population.[16] These public rituals appeared across the American union, emerging out of the northern models of the Great Awakening. After a flourish of events centered in Kentucky around 1800 (notably the Cane Ridge meeting of 1801), they spread throughout the South and the West, bringing together the poorest of the rural agriculturalists in these territories.

   In the earliest meetings, Methodist and Baptist preachers, espousing strong anti-slavery positions, frequently welcomed African-Americans into the act of worship. This interracial involvement clearly contradicted segregationist sentiments among a laity who had learned to assume the religious and intellectual incapacities of Africans. For a time, however, some poor southerners, having become increasingly skeptical of the authority and wisdom of aristocratic planters, appeared to tolerate if not identify with black slaves. Arising from a common stock of agricultural laborers, these white common folk lived within a religious view that held "divine insight [to be] reserved for the poor and humble rather than the proud and learned."[17] But more commonly, and increasingly into the nineteenth century, white southerners had already begun to voice the fears of interracialism that we tend to associate with modern white supremacy. As such, in the circumstances of the camp meetings, multiple versions of racial difference co-existed alongside a contradictory religious sameness, producing a contested social instability that suggested consistencies with the transgressive powers of the conversion experience.

   Animating and texturing these ritual acts were the public group performances of spiritual sound. Gathered together over the course of several days, African- and European-Americans would witness, often separately, but sometimes together, a grand display of religious performance, from the rhetoric of black and white preachers, to isolated incidents of group or solo singing, to extravagant acts of religious conversion. At various moments, singers would speak out in response to inspiring preacherly fervor, fall in as a congregation to lined-out hymns, or perform in the interactive call/response style commonly associated with West African musics. Historians have described the events as a veritable cacophony of diverse human sound without recognizing how they also complicated racial distinctions. Singing materialized a grand interplay of cultural practices that led back to the religious legacies of Africa and Europe. Whether espousing segregationist positions or grand Christian claims of colorless collectivity, whites and blacks *heard* each other all the same, even if the practice of worship frequently remained racially distinct. After a camp meeting, participants would return to their segregated communities, but carry with them shared behaviors that revealed the hybridities of a new American musical sound. As Epstein observes, the earliest published scores themselves document the end point of a process of oral interaction more than they reveal, as scholars such as Jackson have contended, racially separate traditions of performance.[18]

The conversions were at the center of the camp-meeting rituals and most vividly expressed racial intersection. While these conversions could and often did take place outside of the camp, and then in frequently protracted, undramatic ways, it was the grand performative celebrations that animated Christian evangelism and gave to it a power beyond more genteel, reasoned offerings. Indeed, the revivals took place in part to produce sites of conversion that dramatized the bringing of subjects into the faith. They marked a memorial place of spiritual transformation.[19]

"Conversion" meant to experience direct encounter with the spirit of Jesus, whose presence upon "first contact" transformed and transfigured the very body of the devotee. Reports refer to audible ritualistic behavior traceable to both European and African religions, but most commonly associated in contemporary sources with slaves: chanting, speaking in tongues, trance, ecstatic, "frenzied" shouts. These behaviors suggest that the pinnacle of religious experience was marked by a sounding metaphor of spiritual engagement that took on a racial equivalence in the midst of black-white engagement. The embrace of such equivalence produced a Christian bonding surmounting racial division; the more common fear of this same equivalence limited interaction as it heightened the power of singing as a figure of racial transgression. Viewed this way, conversion carries a double meaning, revealing a religious-racial mix of identity transformation that becomes heightened through the experience of music's supralinguistic powers of "transcendence." In spiritual singing, one hears material evidence of interracialism amplifying the displacement of the conversion exercise.

Now, to argue that music's extra-discursive powers assisted in the experience of the transcendent it may be enough simply to note how commonly in the West this observation had been made over the centuries. Whether or not this is a musical universal, Europeans have frequently thought it to be so and to experience music in this way. Moreover, contemporary and historical evidence of African rituals suggest similar continuities of practice, encouraging speculation that a syncretic alignment of European and African worship was at work. By the 1840s, moreover, Euro-American comprehensions of black music had become noticeably informed by discourses of romanticism, which traced a similar irrational otherness to the musical and racial.[20] It is likely that the public celebrations of black "spirituals" that emerged in the 1860s extended from a prior religious background of "spiritual songs" in the camp-meeting conversions, transforming an early musical articulation of racio-spiritual intersubjectivity into a more stable sublimity associated with post–Civil War imperialist nostalgia. Ethnographic research shows, finally, that music's power to effect transcendence has a real empirical basis, providing what is frequently the key trigger in trance ritual.[21] Steven Feld's observations of what goes on in the musical experience are particularly noteworthy here:

> The significant feature of musical communication is not that it is untranslatable and irreducible to the verbal mode but that its generality and multiplicity of possible messages and interpretations brings out a special kind of "feelingful" activity and engagement on the part of the listener, a form of pleasure that unites the material and mental dimensions of music experienced as fully embodied.[22]

While Feld's assertion may itself be a reflection of the durability of romantic musical concepts, it speaks nonetheless to the way in which we have constructed the musical experience as a state of exception—the aporia revealing racio-spiritual contacts that remain otherwise unconscious in a social environment guided by racial difference. Mid-nineteenth-century designations of slave music as a "spiritual" form expressing the "soul" of a white-dominated American society betray the continuity of this discursive relation, which extends from the camp meetings into the twentieth century.

As performances, then, the camp-meeting conversions became aurally discernible articulations of interracial communion that related to both the embrace and the threat of corresponding ontological transformations. The embodiment of these spiritually and interracially transcendent soundworlds challenged the fixities of identity in ways that appear consistent with postmodern interpretations of decentered subjectivity. Existing literally upon a "common ground" of Christian evangelism, the camp-meeting movement identified a syncretic environment of African and European intersection in which "spiritual song" destabilized as it guided the identities of the converted. This transforming experience of musical conversion, in turn, provided legitimacy and recognition to blacks, as African performance moved from a noise-filled absence to a superior, black difference.

Ultimately, the recognition of a discernible black sound would have a pro-nounced distancing effect, motivating whites to reinforce segregationist prac-tices as the camp meetings grew increasingly divided as the nineteenth century progressed. By the 1840s and 1850s, references to musical versions of racial difference were common. White Americans, in turn, sought to distinguish themselves from blackness, effecting a paradox that led to the distancing from performance practices identified as "black" (e.g., call/response) and the inven-tion of extravagant and ironic displacements of blackness, as in the "love and theft" pageantries of minstrelsy.[23] The enduring trope of blacks' "natural" mu-sical capacities had now taken on a new value, with "nonmusical" whites look-ing to African-American musicians to perform racial difference and religious superiority. Many blacks gladly assumed the role of the nation's performers since "playing for the master" also offered a way to claim a racially and musi-cally determined identity in a hostile white supremacist environment.

Thus, the repeated efforts on the part of whites to transgress racial bounds —in blackface minstrelsy, in the public spirituals after the Civil War—revealed the return of a repressed interracialism that first gave rise to the modern recog-nition of the difference of "black music" during the camp meetings. So, too, have the repeated efforts of many African-Americans to resist the musically prescribed limits of "blackness" (e.g., refusing the limitation of their artistry to concepts of "feeling," "soulfulness," and the "jazz musician") similarly revealed a rather obvious recognition of the artificiality of racial constructs. It may well be that the imagination of black musical difference has played a key role in the modern, helping to stabilize an inherently unstable dichotomy of racial iden-tity. Challenging this stability in ways that transgress race without appropriat-ing blackness into a white whole is perhaps the most positive strategy one can take toward racial emancipation. For it is in the originary noise of interracial recognition that we locate the sonic foundation of being American.

NOTES

1. G. J. Greene, "A New Plan to Govern South Carolina." *Keowee Courier* (Wal-halla, S.C.), May 11, 1882, p. 1.

2. See, for example, Tricia Rose, *Black Noise* (Middletown, Conn.: Wesleyan Uni-versity Press, 1994).

3. W. E. B. Du Bois, *The Souls of Black Folk,* with an introduction by Henry Louis Gates, Jr. (1903; New York: Bantam, 1989), p. 178.

4. I employ "black music" in part because of the familiarity the term now enjoys, but also to stress its formation as part of the American imagination of race. The use of scare quotes here is perhaps enough to suggest that I seek to disrupt rather than to perpetuate an uncomplicated racial significance.

5. It is noteworthy that the assumption of coherence underlying an essential black musical culture derives from nineteenth-century racialism. "Culture" in this context is nothing but a euphemism for "race." Furthermore, my challenges to the historical co-herence of black music should be taken to imply similar challenges to the stabilities of

whiteness. In this regard, it is certainly interesting to observe how the rise of post-structuralist theory in historical musicology has yet to unseat—beyond the work of Gary Tomlinson, Susan McClary, and Kofi Agawu, among others—the coherence and autonomy of "Europe" and "European music."

6. Kobena Mercer's construction of sameness is noteworthy here: "The challenge of sameness entails the recognition that we all share the same planet, even if we live in different worlds. We inhabit a discursive universe with a finite number of symbolic resources which can nevertheless be appropriated and articulated into a potentially infinite number of representations. Identities and differences are constructed out of a common stock of signs, and it is through the combination and substitution of these shared elements that antagonism becomes representable as such. See Mercer, "'1968': Periodizing Politics and Identity," in Lawrence Grossberg, Cary Nelson, and Paula Treichler, eds., *Cultural Studies* (New York: Routledge, 1992), p. 427. For a musicological application of sameness, see Kofi Agawu, "The Invention of African Rhythm," *Journal of the American Musicological Society* 48, no. 3 (Fall 1995): 393.

7. Mary Louise Pratt, *Imperial Eyes, Travel Writing and Transculturation* (New York: Routledge, 1992), p. 48.

8. An excerpt of Ligon's *A True and Exact History of the Island of Barbados* (1673) appears in Roger D. Abrahams and John F. Szwed, eds., *After Africa* (New Haven, Conn.: Yale University Press, 1983), pp. 51–64.

9. Christopher Miller, *Blank Darkness* (Chicago: University of Chicago Press, 1985). Hegel's *Vorlesungen uber die Geschichte der Philosophie* (1813) appears in English translation as *Philosophy of History*. For a view on English perspectives of Africans and slavery, see Betty Wood, *The Origins of American Slavery, Freedom and Bondage in the English Colonies: A Critical View* (New York: Hill and Wang, 1997).

10. In the nineteenth century, Charles Darwin reaffirmed these beliefs: "The musical faculties, which are not wholly deficient in any race, are capable of prompt and high development, as we see with Hottentots and Negroes, who have readily become excellent musicians, although they do not practise in their native countries anything that we should esteem as music. But there is nothing anomalous in this circumstance: some species of birds which never naturally sing, can without much difficulty be taught to perform." *The Descent of Man.* Reprinted in Bojan Bujic, ed., *Music in European Thought, 1851–1912* (Cambridge: Cambridge University Press), p. 317.

11. Henry Louis Gates, Jr., ed., "Introduction," in *"Race" Writing and Difference* (Chicago: University of Chicago Press, 1986); Jan Nederveen Pieterse, *White on Black: Images of Africa and Blacks in Western Popular Culture* (New Haven, Conn.: Yale University Press, 1992); George Fredrickson, *The Black Image in the White Mind: The Debate on Afro-American Character and Destiny, 1817–1914* (1971; Middletown, Conn.: Wesleyan University Press, 1987); David R. Roediger, *The Wages of Whiteness: Race and the Making of the American Working Class* (New York: Verso, 1991); Eric Lott, *Love and Theft: Blackface Minstrelsy and Working Class Culture* (New York: Oxford University Press, 1993).

12. Lott, *Love and Theft*; Joseph Boskin, *Sambo* (New York: Oxford University Press, 1986), p. 37; Eileen Southern, *Music of Black Americans*, 3rd ed. (New York: W. W. Norton, 1996); Epstein, *Sinful Tunes* (Urbana: University of Illinois Press, 1977), pp. 120–124; Roger Abrahams, *Singing the Master* (New York: Pantheon, 1992).

14. I am appreciative of help from my colleagues Jeanne Boydston, Steve Kantrowitz, and particularly Paul Boyer, who introduced me to a bounty of primary and sec-

ondary literature on the camp meetings, of which only a smattering can be represented here.

15. Paul Conkin, *Cane Ridge,* Merle Curti Lectures (Madison: University of Wisconsin Press, 1990); Nathan Hatch, *The Democratization of American Christianity* (New Haven, Conn.: Yale University Press, 1989); Dickson Bruce, *And They All Sang Hallelujah* (Knoxville: University of Tennessee Press, 1974). Conkin observes: "From 1750 on southern presbyterianism was biracial. In fact, blacks almost always composed the largest non-Irish component of southern presbyterian congregations" (39). See also Christine Leigh Heyrman, *Southern Cross, The Beginnings of the Bible Belt* (New York: Alfred A. Knopf, 1997).

16. Hatch, *Democratization of American Christianity,* p. 49.

17. Ibid., p. 35.

18. Dena Epstein, "A White Origin for the Black Spiritual? An Invalid Theory and How It Grew," *American Music* 1, no. 2 (Summer 1983): 53–59. More recently, John F. Garst has challenged Epstein, suggesting that "Jackson's arguments for a general white-to-black transmission are broad and complex" and that "Jackson did not use publication dates as the primary basis for concluding there was white-to-black transmission." While Jackson's efforts may have been more complex than Epstein suggests, Garst's claim seems disingenuous. Jackson's efforts were clearly meant to challenge the primacy of black compositional innovation, and the collections of black spirituals on which he focused were uniformly post-bellum. See Jackson, *White and Negro Spirituals* (1944, New York: Da Capo, 1975), p.141; Garst, "Mutual Reinforcement and the Origins of Spirituals," *American Music* 4, no. 4 (Winter 1986): 390–406.

19. Bruce, *And They All Sang Hallelujah,* p. 61.

20. Ronald Radano, "Denoting Difference: The Writing of the Slave Spirituals," *Critical Inquiry* 22, no. 3 (Spring 1996): 506–44.

21. Renato Rosaldo, "Imperialist Nostalgia." *Representations* 26 (Spring 1989): 107–22; Gilbert Rouget, *Music and Trance* (Chicago: University of Chicago Press, 1985).

22. Charles Keil and Steve Feld, *Music Grooves* (Chicago: University of Chicago Press, 1994), p. 91.

23. Lott, *Love and Theft.*

5. Like a Weed in a Vacant Lot: The Black Artists Group in St. Louis

George Lipsitz

We were voluntary specimens in an experiment to present culture as both an exclusive creation of the people and a source of creation, as an instrument of socio-economic liberation.

—Oliver Lake[1]

Less than a year before he died, I conducted an interview with jazz virtuoso and composer Julius Hemphill in his apartment on Manhattan's Upper West Side. Although I had followed Hemphill's career closely over the years and had listened to nearly all of his recorded music, I had not seen him in person since the late 1960s, when he performed with the Black Artists Group in St. Louis. Mutual friends had warned me that Hemphill's physical condition was deteriorating rapidly, but I was nonetheless unprepared for the sight that awaited me when I entered his bedroom on that hot summer day in 1994. Hemphill lay on his back in bed, wearing only red running shorts on his slender frame. He looked emaciated and exhausted. One of his legs had been amputated up to midthigh, and the stump that remained jerked about spasmodically. Hemphill's deep and rich voice still had the beautiful resonance that I remembered, but he spoke slowly, deliberately, and so softly that I had to place the tape recorder on the pillow right next to his head to pick up his words.

It pained me to see Julius Hemphill like this. I remembered what he had looked like as a young man—when his artistry, imagination, and presence made him appear as if he were a giant who could accomplish anything. Yet as sad as it was to speak with him under such depressing circumstances, Hemphill's message was both instructive and inspirational. He spoke passionately and eloquently about his efforts to envision and to enact an art that came from and spoke to the everyday life experiences of African American people. Affirming his faith in the energy and the imagination of his listeners, Hemphill articulated his intention to contribute to his community by transforming the aggravations and indignities confronting oppressed people into a critical consciousness capable of imagining emancipation. With a winsome smile, he told me, "We were just not trying to say that tooting this horn is going to solve all the problems in the world, particularly living under these wretched conditions over here. That's a bigger issue than any kind of thing we might bring in there in terms of entertainment or whatever. Because first it's got to be entertaining. If there's any deeper meaning or anything attributed to it, it's got to earn that. You can't just say this. It's got to earn that meaning. So we were more than happy to make the place available for some serious dialogue between the city's representatives and the people."[2]

Many artists have spoken in similar ways, but few have experienced as much success as Hemphill enjoyed in creating the kinds of concrete physical and cultural spaces where this vision could be carried out. The Black Artists Group brought together musicians, dancers, poets, actors, and visual artists for mixed-media performances in unlikely spaces ranging from housing project multipurpose rooms to school classrooms, from private lofts to public auditoriums. Hemphill's vision helped shape the World Saxophone Quartet, an ensemble that explored new sounds and sensations through its all-saxophone instrumentation while at the same time making it feasible for other musicians to explore similarly innovative line-ups in groups that include Hornweb, Itchy Fingers, Manfred Schulze Bläserquintett, Kölner Saxophon Mafia, and De Zes Winden.[3] He substituted saxophones for human voices in his opera *Long Tongues,* a piece that deployed film footage, slides, and music by jazz saxophone players, a rhythm section, and members of the Washington Philharmonic Orchestra. With *Long Tongues,* Hemphill created a new kind of operatic space, but he also paid tribute to another kind of cultural and social space by setting the opera in the legendary Washington, D.C., nightclub Crystal Caverns, which was at different times in its history home to performances by swing bands, bebop ensembles, rhythm and blues acts, and jazz artists. Hemphill's libretto traced the history of the club from the early 1940s to its closing after the 1968 riots that were sparked by the assassination of Martin Luther King, Jr.[4]

Hemphill's sensitivity to spaces sparked my desire to interview him in 1994. My recent research has centered on cities and the spaces they create and sustain. Decades of de-industrialization and economic restructuring in the United States have exacerbated racial and class inequalities while promoting profound changes in urban space. Contemporary cities juxtapose pockets of poverty and pockets of privilege that enact in concrete physical form the economic, political, and social divisions that increasingly characterize contemporary urban life. One unacknowledged aspect of these transformations has been the disappearance of social and cultural spaces like the ones that nurtured and sustained Julius Hemphill.

De-industrialization destroyed the high-wage jobs that enabled black workers and their families to visit the nightclubs in Hemphill's hometown of Fort Worth, Texas, where he first heard professional musicians play, as well as in his adopted home, St. Louis, where he perfected his musical technique as a member of rhythm and blues bands. Neoconservative tax cuts for the rich have demolished the financial base for the kinds of public school art and music classes that Hemphill and his fellow musicians took as students and later taught as practicing artists. Direct police repression against the civil rights and black power movements as well as the gradual co-optation and incorporation of that movement's leaders into government positions has blunted the sharp edge of radical activism that gave rise to cultural projects like the Black Artists Group. Conservative attacks on public endowments for the arts and humanities have sharply curtailed the kinds of projects designed to democratize the production and reception of art that enabled Hemphill to secure commissions for his operatic, orchestral, and dance compositions. These assaults on the arts, and on the government institutions and social movements that have sustained them in the past, give more control over culture to the handful of corporations that exercise oligopolistic control over commercial culture as well as to private philanthropists and foundations whose core concerns often compel them to isolate artistic products from the social matrices that give them determinate shape and meaning.

In his original and generative analysis of contemporary culture, Nestor Garcia Canclini argues that commercial marketers and private foundations now serve as the primary patrons and generators of artistic activity, usurping a role formerly filled by social movements and the state. Like so many of the revolutionary transformations of our time, this change has gone largely unanalyzed, even though it has enormous consequences. The imperatives of commercial culture, and of what Canclini calls tax evasion masquerading as philanthropy, are poor substitutes for the kinds of support previously given to artistic endeavors by social movements and the state. The new forms do not erase the oppositional potential of art by any means, but they do function to suppress systematically the kinds of self-expression and self-activity characteristic of the community-based art making that did so much to create new artistic and social spaces in the past by linking artistic practices to social conditions.

For a little more than five years during the late 1960s and early 1970s, the Black Artists Group in St. Louis emerged from within the social networks and cultural institutions of the African American community to carve out a unique cultural and social space. Best known for its prestigious alumni—including musicians Julius Hemphill, Oliver Lake, and Hamiet Bluiett; visual artists Oliver Jackson and Emilio Cruz; poets, playwrights, and writers Quincy Troupe, Ntozake Shange, Robert Malinke Elliott; and actor Vincent Terrell—BAG played a vital role in nurturing and focusing the talents of important figures in contemporary music, painting, poetry, and theater. Along with the Association for the Advancement of Creative Musicians in Chicago, the Watts Writers Workshop in Los Angeles, and many other collectives identifying with the Black Arts Movement of the 1960s and 1970s, BAG functioned as an "alternative academy," to borrow a phrase Robert Farris Thompson uses to describe the many sites where people who have no standing in society as artists learn to make art. While innovative and even revolutionary in its artistic vision, as a social space for making art BAG drew productively on a long tradition of alternative academies in black St. Louis, borrowing forms, functions, ideas, inspiration, tools, and traditions from a WPA-sponsored "people's art center," neighborhood jukeboxes, drum and bugle corps, military bands, grade school music, art, and drama classes, gospel choirs, and the sights and sounds of the central city and its crowded, lively, and exuberant street life.

The black community and its institutions permeate the history of BAG. Coordinated community pressure by African American activists established Sumner High School as the first comprehensive black high school west of the Mississippi in the nineteenth century, and Homer G. Phillips Hospital as the first—and for many years the only—full-service teaching hospital for black people west of the Mississippi during the twentieth century. Oliver Lake grew up on the north side of St. Louis near Homer G. Phillips Hospital, Sumner High School, and Poro College of Cosmetology, established by Annie Malone, one of the nation's first female African American millionaires. These institutions drew members of the black middle class to St. Louis from all across the country while the city's factories, wharves, and freight terminals attracted working-class blacks from the vast hinterlands of the South and West where travel to St. Louis by road, rail, or river was the fastest and easiest way to a new life.

Lake learned to play marches in a drum and bugle corps sponsored by the American Woodman Insurance Company, but he also received an early education in the blues from the jukebox at the Five Sisters Cafe, a family business that his mother co-owned and co-managed on Whittier Street, close to Homer G. Phillips Hospital and Poro College. Lake liked the rhythm and blues he heard on the jukebox at the Five Sisters, and that music remained with him in his later years as a jazz artist. "The blues have always been the basis of my music," he told an interviewer recently. "Even when I play chamber music, the blues are always there."[5]

Hamiet Bluiett chose his instrument and his favorite sounds to play on it because of the part of the St. Louis area in which he was raised. Bluiett lived in Lovejoy, Illinois, near Scott Air Force Base in East St. Louis. He remembers the way his house shook when jets flew over it, and he took up the baritone saxophone because it was the best way to make music that resembled the sonic booms to which he had become accustomed. Drawn into jazz and rhythm and blues by the success of Jimmy Forrest, a neighbor and family friend who scored a major hit record with "Night Train" in the early 1950s, Bluiett took his baritone saxophone into many musical forms that seemed to have little room for the instrument. The bands that Bluiett joined in college and in the Navy were often unprepared for a baritone sax player, so Bluiett learned to play parts written for alto on the baritone. "That's how I developed my high register," he remembers. Bluiett also played chamber music with the Gateway Symphony but found that group even more resistant to his sonic-boom style than were jazz and rhythm and blues ensembles. "I liked the sound [of the Gateway Symphony] when everyone was getting in tune," he recalls, but "not when we started playing."[6] Although he played with extremely skilled classical musicians and jazz musicians, Bluiett's admiration gravitated more toward eccentric innovators like the member of rhythm and blues singer Marvin Gaye's band who "played fretless Fender bass and made chord changes that expanded Bluiett's conception of what music might be.[7]

Julius Hemphill had a similar passion for innovation, claiming many times that "I'd rather be a so-so original than a highly regarded imitator."[8] Growing up in Fort Worth, Texas, Hemphill lived near his second cousin, Ornette Coleman, whom he remembered as "[t]he first person I ever saw holding a saxophone." Yet Hemphill also insisted that he felt a connection to music independent of his famous relative. "I didn't discover music one day," he explained to an interviewer. "I grew up with it all around me. I lived in the block where the night life would carry on. There were three jukeboxes, and you could hear them about twenty-four hours a day."[9] Hemphill came to Missouri to study music theory and harmony at Lincoln University in Jefferson City, but, unhappy with "an all-Black school where you couldn't study Black music," he dropped out of school to play alto saxophone for rhythm and blues aggregations including the Ike and Tina Turner Show.[10]

St. Louisan Lester Bowie met many of the musicians who would later become central to BAG when he played trumpet in many different kinds of musical groups in the early 1960s. "St. Louis was really a great town for a young musician to grow up in," Bowie later recalled. "When I think back on it, it was really unbelievable." Bowie received his early training on his instrument from Enrico Carrion, who played with the St. Louis Symphony, but he also learned by watching local trumpeters David Hines, Clark Terry, and Miles Davis. Bowie left for Chicago in 1965 and soon became a part of the AACM (the Association for the Advancement of Creative Musicians) along with another St. Louis expatriate, Phil Cohran. He maintained close ties to BAG, however, and played with members of the group in Europe in the early 1970s along with the woman who was then his wife, vocalist Fontella Bass, a St. Louisan who secured a national hit record with "Rescue Me" in 1966, and whose mother sang gospel music with the Clara Ward Singers.[11]

In the mid-1960s, Oliver Lake and Julius Hemphill moved into Laclede Town, a low-rise federally funded urban renewal housing project located near St. Louis University. The manager of the complex, Jerry Berger, sought to make Laclede Town a stable integrated community in a city increasingly polarized by residential racial segregation. At that time, artists and activists in civil rights groups made up a natural constituency for integrated housing in St. Louis and Berger attempted to make Laclede Town attractive to them. He granted them preferential treatment in rental applications and established a venue for live performances, the Circle Coffee House, in a centrally located space in the complex.[12] Civil rights activists Percy Green and Ivory Perry took up residence in Laclede Town, using the nearby Berea Presbyterian Church and the complex itself as a base for their community organizing. Oliver Lake lived next door to Perry and Hemphill lived near Percy Green. Berger contracted with Oliver Lake to have his Lake Art Quartet play regularly at the Circle Coffee House, and Hemphill was one of the regular patrons of the establishment.

In an environment suffused with the energy of the civil rights movement and the self-affirmation central to the Black Arts Movement, the Circle Coffee House quickly became a site for politically charged artistic expression as well as a locus for political consciousness-raising. As anthropologist Victor Turner notes, "Pleasure becomes a serious matter in the context of innovative change."[13] Oliver Lake reflected some of that seriousness in a 1970 interview explaining his intentions as an artist working within the contours of BAG. "We try to make our music relevant to everyday life, day-to-day existence," Lake asserted. "Often, we open our concerts with verbal phrases or lines of poetry. We use voices while we're playing, groans, moans, screams, but even these are aimed at relating to the lives of black people."[14] The informal atmosphere and emphasis on experimentation at the Circle Coffee House encouraged an improvisational art that blurred the lines dividing music from poetry and audiences from performers. It enabled people to put on their own readings and concerts in a place outside the control of commercial entrepreneurs and cultural institutions alike.

Yet cultural institutions still played an important role in transforming a neighborhood network of artists, intellectuals, and activists in the Black Artists Group. A theater group at Webster College in suburban Webster Groves put on a performance of Jean Genet's play *The Blacks* and recruited African American actors, musicians, and dancers from the entire St. Louis area. Members of the Circle Coffee House group developed ties with dancers trained at Katherine Dunham's art institute and community center in East St. Louis, with visual artists trained at the WPA-originated People's Art Center in north St. Louis, with musicians from local jazz and rhythm-and-blues ensembles, and with artists engaged in preschool education and academic enrichment through the city school system and the St. Louis programs supervised by the federal government's Office of Economic Opportunity's "war on poverty."

Aided by activists in the anti-poverty program and civil rights groups, the Arts and Education Council of St. Louis received grants of $100,000 each from the Rockefeller Foundation and the Danforth Foundation for "an experimental program of community cultural enrichment" providing classes in dance, theater, and music for two thousand children and young adults in St. Louis and East St. Louis. The Arts and Education Council appointed Julius Hemphill as the director of the St. Louis program, and he set up instructional programs in drama, dance, poetry, and music under the rubric of BAG—the Black Artists Group. Initially established in ground-floor rooms leased to Project Head Start and other anti-poverty programs at the Pruitt-Igoe housing project, BAG eventually used the grant money from the Rockefeller and

Danforth Foundations to set up permanent studios and performance space at the Sheldon Auditorium at 2665 Washington Avenue, about five blocks from Laclede Town.[15]

The headquarters of BAG in the Sheldon Auditorium was a new kind of urban space: a center for the arts intended less for individual uplift than for collective mobilization, a place where artistic and social barriers could be contested. Hemphill described the music made at BAG as "a sounding board for social issues," observing that "unsatisfactory conditions" affect everything in a person's life and therefore have to affect music. "It's not just about tooting your horn when you have these wretched conditions all around you."[16] Visual artists in BAG loaned their talents to community groups, making signs for a rent strike by tenants in public housing and for demonstrators protesting the lack of testing and treatment for lead poisoning among children in inner-city neighborhoods.[17] At the same time, those involved in BAG tried to create an artistic space appropriate to their political and social vision by transcending the limits of genre and form.

Collaborations among musicians, writers, painters, and dancers encouraged individuals to reconceptualize the internal properties of their art by exploring the ways in which sight, sound, movement and timing influence all artistic expression. Hemphill reconceptualized the saxophone as an extension of human vocal processes, as less of a musical instrument than a prosthetic for speaking and singing. He also spoke of music in terms that a sculptor might use, talking about it as a kind of "clay" that enables people to "just start making things."[18] Oliver Lake claimed that working with visual artists in BAG led him to think about "color" when he played the saxophone. Visual artist Oliver Jackson, on the other hand, found that working with musicians taught him about the role of "time" in painting. "A musician knows when he is losing the attention of his audience right away," according to Jackson. "Working with musicians taught me about the whole matter of *time* in a painting, the need to eliminate the dead spots, the parts that don't move. From musicians, I learned how to get into a painting, to find an opening. And the most important thing you learn from the best musicians is: just play the tune. There are some tunes, certain thematic ideas, that call for lots of notes and speed and intricacy. Others simply have to be done with very few, and very simply. The same is true of a painting."[19]

In artistic terms, BAG succeeded in nurturing and promoting the talents of an extraordinary group of individuals who have gone on to secure fame and recognition as artists. These artistic achievements played a role in mass mobilizations and changes in individual consciousness in their community as well. The BAG dance and drum ensemble offered dance classes on Wednesday nights and drum classes on Saturdays for only fifty cents per week to people who had no other access to training in the arts.[20] Contemporary jazz saxophonist Greg Osby heard his first concerts as a youth because of BAG. "I always related to Julius Hemphill and Hamiet Bluiett," he later recalled. "They used to play in these lofts around St. Louis. And while I was too young to get in, I'd sit outside where I could hear them just fine because they'd play real loud, with the windows open."[21]

The broader social movement of black activism that was so central to BAG's genesis also enjoyed significant victories in the late 1960s and early 1970s. Percy Green's protests at construction sites called attention to discriminatory hiring practices in the building trades and contributed to the process that eventually produced federal affirmative action programs for the construction industry. Ivory Perry played a crucial role in the 1969 rent strike by tenants in public housing that led Congress to pass legislation limiting the maximum rent for tenants in government housing projects all across the country, and Perry similarly led a successful campaign to secure testing and treatment for children victimized by lead poisoning.[22] Yet these political and artistic victories also jeopardized the main source of funding for BAG when local elites protested the group's actions to the Danforth and Rockefeller Foundations.

In announcing its support for what was to become BAG, the Rockefeller Foundation defined the problem to be addressed as primarily psychological and personal: the debilitating effects of racism and poverty on black people themselves. "We believe that the arts, thought of in the broadest sense, do offer a direct remedy for some of the underlying ills—voicelessness, isolation, depersonalization—that affect the economically underprivileged members of our urban society," proclaimed George Harrar of the Rockefeller Foundation in announcing the original $200,000 grant in May 1968.[23] The foundation also argued that the arts themselves would profit from identifying, acknowledging, and refining the talents of inner-city residents, announcing in a press release, "The American Negro has already shown, through his creative writing, his music composition, and his performance in music, theater, and dance, that he can make a valuable contribution to American society."[24]

Intending to speak to the psyches of deprived individuals and to augment the arts as they already existed, foundation officials found themselves deeply disappointed in the practices that emerged from BAG. They complained that the group's "lessons and teachings have been mainly for blacks, not whites. Therefore the effect on black-white understanding has been very limited." They judged the group's theater performances as having more "shock value" than "cultural value," and complained that "certain artists have been more interested in social reform than in art."[25] While conceding that "much that is good" came out of the program, the foundations decided that BAG's accomplishments did not conform to the definitions of urban problems and their desired solutions as envisioned by officials at the Danforth and Rockefeller Foundations, and consequently they terminated its funding. Obviously, the foundations had a different understanding of what constituted the "community" than did members of BAG.

BAG lost its funding in the midst of a general attack on the institutions that generated and sustained the civil rights and black power movements in St.

Louis. The war in Vietnam diverted funding away from the war on poverty during the Johnson Administration, then revenue-sharing and federal block grants initiated by President Nixon redirected funds away from direct aid to the poor and toward property tax relief for businesses, equipment for police and fire departments, and subsidies for office buildings and civic amenities. The Federal Bureau of Investigation's COINTELPRO operation secured the cooperation of the "Red squad" of the local police department and a young journalist named Pat Buchanan, then working for the conservative *St. Louis Globe-Democrat,* to vilify, intimidate, and harass a number of activists, including Percy Green and Ivory Perry. At the same time, seniority-based layoffs during the recessions of the early 1970s had a particularly disastrous effect on black workers, many of whom had secured access to skilled jobs only after the passage of civil rights legislation and direct action protests during the 1960s. As the last hired they became the first fired. In addition, federal subsidies and incentives to move manufacturing to new plants in low wage regions of the United States and overseas had an especially negative impact on black workers in older industrial cities like St. Louis.

Although some people connected with BAG secured employment at local educational institutions, most of the artists had to leave the city in order to find professional work as musicians, actors, artists, or writers. They enjoyed extraordinary success, artistically and commercially. Emilio Cruz moved to the Studio Museum of Harlem. Vincent Terrell became a successful actor and educator in Boston and New York. Robert Malinke Elliott gained recognition as a poet on the West Coast. Quincy Troupe joined the Watts Writers Workshop and earned distinction for his efforts as a poet, teacher, and biographer in New York and San Diego. Oliver Jackson attained great success as a painter in the San Francisco Bay Area. Julius Hemphill, Oliver Lake, and Hamiet Bluiett moved to New York, where they connected with David Murray (who was briefly married to St. Louisan, BAG alumna, and award-winning playwright Ntozake Shange) to form the World Saxophone Quartet.

The World Saxophone Quartet created a sensation in the jazz world during the 1980s through the innovative compositions of all of its members but especially Julius Hemphill. The group had no percussion or keyboard accompaniment, and made an art out of breaking the conventional rules of jazz music performance. "We don't have drummers," Murray explained to a reporter. "We have heart beats."[26] Lake saw their art as a challenge to commercial culture, to "the almighty dollar which moves a lot of the stuff in America. You either fit or don't fit in this framework. It affects creativity and awareness because everyone pursues it. It comes before human life."[27] Yet the very things that secured recognition and praise for the World Saxophone Quartet as innovators on the world jazz scene grew organically and easily from local networks in St. Louis when a space existed for them to flourish. Looking back at BAG from the perspective of his successful career with the WSQ, as a solo artist, and with other small ensembles, Lake emphasized, "The fact that we had poetry, dance, music, and so forth all together stayed with me. I've been doing that sort of thing pretty much throughout my career."[28] Similarly, on one of his last visits to St. Louis before his death Julius Hemphill spoke fondly of his memories of a time when "there was a lot of interest in exploring unfamiliar territory, in putting on concerts instead of waiting for someone else to do it, in playing in places other than clubs."[29]

Although celebrated around the world as modernist innovators, the members of the World Saxophone Quartet shunned the label of the avant-garde, thinking of themselves as products of a musical and social environment which refused to recognize limits rather than of one that honored limits all the more by self-consciously "transgressing" them. "I never really thought of myself as like that, avant-garde," Lake explained to a reporter in 1993. "At first it really used to make me mad because it was so limiting, but I've gotten used to it. I like to think of myself as a person who likes a lot of different styles."[30] Hemphill similarly located his music within community traditions rather than outside them, telling a reporter from *Down Beat*, "I think that the American people, particularly black people have a kind of intimacy with the music that we play. There is a cultural dynamic that has to do with the reality of the music being all through the black communities. It results in a kind of awareness and exuberance that people bring from the whole history of listening to the guy next door."[31]

The history of the Black Artists Group offers an important illustration of how the state and social movements during the 1960s combined to fashion a space for dynamic cultural activity. At the same time, this history shows how ill equipped charitable foundations and commercial culture are to unleash the kinds of creativity that emerged from the Black Arts Movement in general and from BAG in particular. The destruction of anti-poverty programs, cutbacks in state spending on the arts, and the defeats suffered by the social movements of the 1960s leave young people in St. Louis and other cities today with fewer options and opportunities for the kinds of self-expression that BAG nurtured and sustained. No monument marks the spot where BAG once was, and no individuals have been able to pick up the torch that BAG members put down where they scattered to the far corners of the globe in the 1970s. "We were like a weed in a vacant lot," Julius Hemphill told me during our 1994 interview.[32]

Yet the conduits of commercial culture and foundation-supported expressions that now occupy the artistic space that once included egalitarian collectives like BAG also call our attention to the histories they have erased through the presence of Oliver Lake, Fontella Bass, Julius Hemphill, Oliver Jackson, Hamiet Bluiett, Vincent Terrell, Robert Malinke Elliott, Ntozake Shange, Quincy Troupe, Lester Bowie, and many others in many different places. Through songs that recall their formative experiences in St. Louis, including Julius Hemphill's "Messin' with the Kid," Hamiet Bluiett's "Night Train," and Oliver Lake's "Love like Sisters," the members of the World Saxophone Quartet have inserted into their art some of the energy, imagination, and inspiration they drew from their community and its social movements in the 1960s.

These performers and artists carried traces of their BAG experiences with them into their subsequent work. In addition, while historical appreciation and nostalgia alike feed a deep sense of loss about the disappearance of groups like BAG from cities like St. Louis, we have to acknowledge that these endeavors were fugitive and ephemeral even then. Julius Hemphill came to St. Louis from Fort Worth. Oliver Lake was born in Marianna, Arkansas. Ntozake Shange lived in New York before she set foot in St. Louis. Katherine Dunham's art center in East St. Louis drew upon the great dancer's experiences in New York, Paris, and Haiti as well as on local traditions and expressions. When Hemphill, Lake, Bluiett, Shange, Troupe, and Terrell moved to New York they followed in the footsteps of previous exiles, including Josephine Baker and Miles Davis, who found St. Louis too harsh an environment for the survival of their art. Far removed from the physical places and cultural spaces that gave determinate shape to their art at one time, they continued to construct discursive spaces to keep alive the memory and the provocation of a different kind of culture. Their art is ephemeral, fugitive, and elusive, but it retains the extraordinary moral power and sense of cultural connection characteristic of the art-based community-making of the 1960s, evocative of the "weed in a vacant lot" that nurtured and shaped their talents.

Some people think weeds are ugly, that they fail to conform to the standards of beauty that earn plants designation as "flowers" rather than weeds. But weeds spring up in the most unexpected places, they push through seemingly impregnable concrete and asphalt. They are hardy and hard to kill. They also do not need to remain in their native soil; they can survive and thrive everywhere. They have many of the features that all of us will need in the days ahead as we try to make our way in a world dominated by commercial marketers and private foundations intent on pressing down as hard as they can on social movements and the cultures they create.

NOTES

1. David Jackson, "Profile: Julius Hemphill, Oliver Lake," *Down Beat*, June 1975, p. 32.

2. Interview with Julius Hemphill, New York City, July 31, 1994.

3. Herb Boyd, "World Saxophone Quartet: New Life after Julius," *Down Beat*, September 1996, p. 26.

4. Mike Joyce, "Julius Hemphill, Making the Sax Sing," *Washington Post*, September 27, 1989, sec. C, pp. 1–2.

5. Harper Barnes, "Jazz Threads through Life of Oliver Lake," *St. Louis Post-Dispatch*, February 14, 1993, p. 3.

6. Richard Woodward, "Four Saxmen, One Great Voice," *New York Times*, April 12, 1987, magazine, p. 47. Harper Barnes, "Visit to St. Louis Stirs Memories of '60s for Julius Hemphill," *St. Louis Post-Dispatch*, April 9, 1989, sec. E, p. 3.

7. Ibid., p. 72.

8. Joyce, "Julius Hemphill," p. 2.

9. Ibid., p. 72.

10. Barnes, "Visit to St. Louis Stirs Memories," p. 11.

11. Darrell McWhorter, "Bowie in Line for Crown of St. Louis Trumpeters," *St. Louis Post-Dispatch,* February 3, 1992, sec. D, p. 1.

12. Jack Schmidt, "Former Tenant Says Laclede Town Discriminated in Effort to Integrate," *St. Louis American,* July 30–August 5, 1992, letter to the editor (copy in author's possession, n.p.).

13. Victor Turner, *Dramas, Fields and Metaphors: Symbolic Action in Human Society* (Ithaca: Cornell University Press, 1974), p.16.

14. Cassandra Johnson, "Esoteric Expression," *Proud* 1, no.6 (June/July 1970): 21.

15. Cathee Allen, "Dance—Black Artist Group," *Proud* 2, no. 6 (June/July 1971): 31. Arts and Education Council of Greater St. Louis, Arts and Education Fund Press Release, May 14, 1968. Rockefeller Archives. Tarrytown, N.Y.

16. Interview with Julius Hemphill, New York City, August 8, 1994.

17. Summary of telephone conversations with Merrimon Cunninggim and Gene Schwik, September 16–18, 1969. Rockefeller Archives, Tarrytown, N.Y.

18. Joyce, "Julius Hemphill," p. 2.

19. Jan Butterfield, "Oliver Jackson Interview," in *Oliver Jackson* (Seattle: Seattle Art Museum, 1982), p. 7. Leah Ollman, "Oliver Jackson's Fluid Realm," *Los Angeles Times,* November 27, 1991, Orange County edition Calendar section, p. 9.

20. Allen, "Dance—Black Artist Group," p. 31.

21. Paul A. Harris, "Living and Playing in the Present: Saxophonist Greg Osby Embraces Contemporary Black Pop Styles," *St. Louis Post-Dispatch,* September 29, 1991, sec. G, p. 3.

22. George Lipsitz, *A Life in the Struggle: Ivory Perry and the Culture of Opposition* (Philadelphia: Temple University Press, 1989, 1995).

23. Arts and Education Council of Greater St. Louis, Arts and Education Fund, May 14, 1968. Rockefeller Archives. Tarrytown, New York.

24. Arts and Education Council of Greater St. Louis, Rockefeller Foundation 1-2 200R, Box 289, Folder 2720. Rockefeller Archives, Tarrytown, N.Y.

25. Danforth Foundation summary of telephone conversations with Merrimon Cunniggim and Gene Schwik, September 16–18, 1969. Rockefeller Archives. Tarrytown, N.Y.

26. David Ruben, "World Sax Quartet Swings to Its Own Beat," *San Francisco Chronicle,* April 9, 1989, Datebook, p. 48.

27. Clifford Jay Safane, "The World Saxophone Quartet," *Down Beat,* October 1979, 29.

28. Barnes, "Jazz Threads through Life of Oliver Lake," p. 9.

29. Barnes, "Visit to St. Louis Stirs Memories," p. 3.

30. Barnes, "Jazz Threads through Life of Oliver Lake," p. 9.

31. Safane, "The World Saxophone Quartet," p. 28.

32. Interview with Julius Hemphill, August 8, 1994.

6. Yayoi Kusama's Body of Art

Kristine C. Kuramitsu

> Power belongs to s/he who succeeds,
> in the rat(extermination)race,
> to consume most before(/while) being consumed.[1]

—Trinh T. Minh-ha

Painter, sculptor, and performance artist Yayoi Kusama has emerged as one of the keystone figures in a newly revised art-historical narrative of modernism. This story highlights artists given little attention in the previous twenty years, such as Carolee Schneemann and Eva Hesse, while continuing to keep the "old masters," such as Marcel Duchamp, Jackson Pollock, Andy Warhol, and Donald Judd, central. Kusama has appeared in a number of important group exhibitions in venues around the globe on equal footing with these long-canonized artists of the postwar era.[2] Her unique usefulness to this reframing project arises from her participation in the mainstream avant-garde art world in New York City and her simultaneous "outsider" status as a Japanese woman with psychological problems; thus, Kusama's body of work and her actual body are the sites of this rethinking of modernism.

Interest in Kusama in recent literature is generally characterized by a deep fascination with her biography and how that biography manifests itself in the objects and environments which she has created over the past forty odd years. In a recent *Artforum* article, author Andrew Solomon begins: "There was no mistaking Kusama. Tiny, old, dressed in a red embroidered silk jacket, loose trousers, and sneakers, her long black hair free-falling down her back, she stood surrounded by attendants like some marvelous glass ornament enveloped by protective cotton . . . she shuffled forwards and looked at me with alarming intensity, as though she were seeing a vision in my polite smile."[3] Although Solomon's article is intended as a biographical profile, the tone of this description quite vividly captures the tenor of writing about the artist and her work. The drama of the narrative culminates in the image of Kusama as a sort of lunatic sage removed from the mundane world. She fascinates with her simultaneous "fragility" and "intensity." Admittedly, Kusama's story is a compelling one that makes for enthralling art history; her persona itself is so overwhelming that it is difficult not to see her work only as its product.

This is not to say that Kusama is an unwilling victim of critics; indeed, Kusama's own words have always packaged her works. She herself places primary importance on her mental/psychic and disembodied biography. She creates herself and is critically understood as a neurotic obsessive, perhaps manic-depressive, compelled to work for days at a time and then collapsing from mental and physical exhaustion. During her entire life, she reports, she has had powerful hallucinations in which everything in her visual field is covered with repeated patterns of polka dots or nets, which spread like a virus. She has been in therapy for most of her life to work out her feelings of fear and hostility toward men, stemming from a difficult childhood in which her father and mother were her direct adversaries. This discourse of mental illness, circulated by the artist and propagated and multiplied by critics around the world, consistently packages her art as psychic autobiography, as therapy for a diseased mind. Positing her insanity as a singular interpretive reference point also guarantees her originality; she cannot be influenced by, let alone be derivative of, other artists because of the entirely interior derivation of her imagery. This approach deftly foregrounds her obsessive mode of creation as well as her defiant and heroic independence, providing a seamless interpretive framework through which we can view all her work.

Kusama's masterful manipulation of her physical body into the physical body of the work enacts the exoticist and sexist dynamics of the culture at large to her advantage. She uses these normally silencing stereotypical images as a point of entry into the New York art world; they become her signature. This provides her with the tentative identity of an "outsider" to the avant-garde, but one who is understandable within its frame. She is not only foreign and female, but "insane," which distances her yet again from the power centers of the avant-garde. Thus, by the very fact of her gender, race, and mental instability, she occupies an extremely problematic locus. I contend that her self-conscious exoticization (sexual, ethnic, and mental) was a virtual parody of the racist and sexist frameworks imposed upon her, a winkingly over-the-top performance of her subject position which might open avenues to aesthetic posterity. Kusama was, in a sense, acknowledging and exploiting tropes that were being written across her body and her work. In her desire for fame and acceptance, she proactively prefigures the criticism and reception of her work, increasingly over time positing a sexualized, racialized body literally among her works. At the same time that she performs these excesses of ethnicity and sexuality, she simultaneously insists upon the purity and truth of her avant-garde aesthetic. As Kusama tries to inhabit both worlds—exotic outsider and purist insider— particularly in her later work, she ultimately becomes ignored by critics. This tension in the field of gender and cultural politics, blatant sexualization and transcendent aesthetics, generate potentially subversive ruptures in the master discourses of the avant-garde. Through the exploration of some of these unexcavated spaces of race and gender in Kusama's oeuvre, I hope to illuminate some of the social and aesthetic strands of meaning that are woven together into the body (of work) created by Yayoi Kusama.

In the criticism of her work during the late 1950s and early 1960s, the tension between explicating Kusama's work in the terms of the prevalent aesthetic language while writing around the spectacular sexual and racial difference of her body is most vividly manifest. Before turning to the critical texts surrounding Kusama's work in the late 1950s and 1960s, I will briefly establish the cultural currency of Japan and Japaneseness in the United States in the decades prior to and after the artist's arrival in 1958 as a background for the discussion of the complex racial and aesthetic discourses that Kusama inhabits and complicates.

The trope of Asia, and in particular Japan, has been crucial to the development of the Western avant-garde. The advent of *Japonisme* in nineteenth-century France, Britain, and the United States became a key factor in the construction of Impressionism as a movement and the constitution of the modern avant-garde in general.[4] Japanese commodities, aesthetics, and bodies became the signifiers of fashionable refinement in the cutting-edge circles of the West. This notion of the East-as-aesthetic persists throughout the twentieth century. As John Tchen clearly iterates: "Asian elites have been perceived to embody the revered Orientalist traits of hyper-aestheticism, refinement, simplicity, and arcane knowledge of ages past. Artists in particular have been cast as mystic masters whose work should deal with eternal beauty, timelessness, naturalism, harmony and antimaterialism."[5] These characterizations endure and inform the perception of Eastern objects, ideas, and people as beautiful, wise, and innocuous.

World War II caused virtually anything associated with Japan to fall out of favor with all the Allied nations. However, in the late 1940s and early 1950s, the fad for things Japanese came back into fashion. On the mass cultural level, Japanese-themed "friendship gardens" were cultivated in communities across the country, and images of screens and Asianesque decorative arts flooded interior decorating magazines.[6] The specific figuration of the exotic Japanese female gained new currency in films such as *Sayonara* (1957), in which Marlon Brando's Korean War pilot falls for a Japanese actress. The alluring Japanese female appeared as well in popular women's magazines. In a 1957 issue of *Vogue,* we are treated to a lesson in how the geisha achieves her "beguiling" look. The article begins: "On his month's tour of Japan, artist Bouché found . . . 'a world of femininity of which we have no idea.'"[7] Japan, now sufficiently tamed into a friendly nation, could resume its place as enticing exotica in the mass cultural imagination.[8] Regarding this moment of Japanese-American cultural relations, Bert Winther states: "Japanese and Asian culture was the object of a widespread desire for *possession;* that is, subsumption to American self identity."[9]

For the artists and writers in elite circles across the United States, this renewed fascination with Japan primarily manifested itself in an attraction to intellectual and philosophical ideas. Zen, as transported to the United States in this postwar era, was a significant influence on the aesthetic practices of the avant-garde. In New York, academics and artists flocked to the lectures of a Japanese scholar named Dr. Daisetz Suzuki, who spoke at Columbia University between 1951 and 1958. Drawn to the romance of attaining universal transcendence through self-forgetting, writers, musicians, and artists read translations and interpretations of Zen teachings, which they assimilated into their working processes.[10] This burst of interest included major exhibitions of Japanese calligraphy and other Zen artworks and, along with Suzuki's lectures, strongly impacted intellectual communities across the United States. Publications by artists, writers, and musicians on the Zen-ness of their productions as well as a number of popular books based upon Zen philosophy proliferated.[11] These philosophies were absorbed into the artistic practices and formal styles of artists across the country, perhaps most famously in the music and writing of John Cage. Hugo Munsterberg, commenting on U.S. artistic interest in Zen in the *College Art Journal,* wrote: "Living as we do in a conformist society where the man in the gray flannel suit has become a symbol of the goal for which the average person is striving, Zen offers a drastic antidote to the prevailing mood. Zen is indifferent to secular values; it is immediate in its experience; it accepts life as it is; it penetrates beneath the surface to the essential self."[12] Such avant-garde artists framed Eastern wisdom, and more specifically, Zen, as an escape from the drudgery of Western realities and a means to transcendent knowledge.

Zen as an alternative (Other) lifestyle merged with avant-garde artists' conceptions of Japanese culture and Japanese people. Japan and the Japanese, then, assumed the role of muse in this dynamic, the Other by which an artist (read: male, white, and, ostensibly, heterosexual) might achieve pure creative genius.[13] In fact, I would argue that it is not even the real country or its people that sustain this dynamic, but the *idea* of Japaneseness. As the quintessential champion of modernism Clement Greenberg characterizes the avant-garde in "Avant-Garde and Kitsch":

> The true and most important function of the avant garde was not to "experiment," but to find a path along which it would be possible to keep culture *moving* in the midst of ideological confusion and violence. Retiring from public altogether, the avant garde poet or artist sought to maintain the high level of his art by both narrowing and raising it to the expression of an absolute in which all relativities and contradictions would be either resolved or beside the point.[14]

Greenberg's scenario of the avant-garde artist ultimately producing a universal expression of truth was meant as a general characterization of the process of aesthetic creativity and its most noble manifestation as art. More often than not in the 1950s and 1960s, the path traversed on this journey was formed by and through Zen. As the specificity of this cultural practice, Zen, and cultural location, Japan, are both obscured, Japaneseness becomes a means, a muse, a methodology.

Asian subjects, though, must be absent from the space of the "transcend-er"; their presence is necessarily symbolic. The presence of the Other as subject disrupts the dynamic of creator and muse.[15] When the Other does not occupy the position of guest lecturer or aesthetic ideal, but is manifest in physical bodies that exist in space and time, the ideological dynamic implodes. Actual bodies disturb the fantasy of desired objects/desiring subjects; the objects become subjects, however tenuously so, with desires and fantasies of their own. This ruptured framework demarcates a space for understanding Yayoi Kusama's position in the New York avant-garde of the 1950s and 1960s.

Just as artists and writers in the United States formulated fantasies about the transcendent possibilities of Zen and Japaneseness in general, Kusama cultivated equally cherished fantasies about the possibilities of the New York avant-garde. Here, it will be useful to look at the development of Kusama's career in Japan, her early image of the New York avant-garde, and her self-production as one of its distant relatives.

Motivated by her success in the Brooklyn Museum's watercolor biennial in 1955, she thereafter concentrated her energies on emigrating to the United States. Although there were a large number of artists who went to the United States from Japan in the early to mid-1960s, Kusama and three other painters, Kenzo Okada, Minoru Kawabata, and Tadoaki Kuwayama, were the first few to do so. Her persistence in pursuit of a visa is now part of the Kusama legend, including her extensive correspondence with Georgia O'Keeffe asking for advice and an introduction to a New York art dealer.[16] In an early letter to O'Keeffe, Kusama writes: "I hope with all my heart that I will be able to show my paintings [to] dealers in New York... I also know that I am very optimistic in this regard that I seek such a chance. I, however, have been aiming for this for some past years that my paintings be criticized at New York."[17]

Kusama was vocal about her desire to leave Japan for the United States. She embraced the notion of the West and its art world as liberated places of artistic independence. There, she could not only be free of her family and a restrictive Japanese society, but also free of what she perceived as a deadly Japanese provincialism, in the art world and otherwise. She, like her other Japanese contemporaries, had just been exposed to the work of the Abstract Expressionists in a series of government- and corporate-sponsored art exhibitions in the early 1950s; this work made a tremendous impression on Japanese artists, as did the avant-garde movements in France. The impact of the shows would have been quite dramatic, since there had not been any exposure to works of art from the Allied nations, or for that matter, the West in general, since the late 1930s. These exhibitions, sponsored by government, newspapers, and various Japanese companies, particularly department stores, featured recent paintings from Europe and the United States. In 1951, there was a large exhibition sponsored by the *Yomiuri* newspaper that featured works by established European modernists, such as Pablo Picasso, Georges Rouault, and Henri Matisse, as well as several works by the Abstract Expressionists, the first ones to be seen in the country, including canvases by Jackson Pollock, Mark Rothko and Clyfford Still.[18] Thus, the fantasies about the New York School were extremely powerful and became a part of Japanese contemporary artists' definition of modern aesthetic expression.

Kusama, it would seem, had already established herself as such an individualistic artist. She had not joined any of the groups to which most artists belonged in the Tokyo art world, rejecting the prevailing styles of *Yoga* ("Western-style" painting) and *Nihonga* (a neo-Japanese painting style aligned with nationalism), and had even distanced herself from the newly emerging modernist groups such as Gutai and the Surrealists (both aligned explicitly with the Parisian art world). Instead, Kusama showed a single-minded desire to be original and independent—to be "avant-garde," American style.

As Kusama's desire to enter the spaces of New York's art circles developed, she clearly began to develop her artistic persona. Her unusual means of entry into the artistic circles of Japan via her mental illness established a framework for her reception from the outset. Thus, she cultivated her image as an outsider to facilitate her entrée into the New York avant-garde. Her imagery, she asserted (and still asserts) in interview after interview, springs from lifelong hallucinations of proliferating polka dots and nets which spread over all that she saw. She was compelled to create these images as a sort of therapy, to work through these hallucinations compulsively. Her insanity, as the sole source for her aesthetic, established her individuality and marked her work as nonderivative. She could conveniently claim no influences save those conjured by her unique mind. Foregrounding her obsessive mode of creation as well as her defiant independence in one of her first letters to Georgia O'Keeffe, she declared that she had shown only in solo exhibitions; she wrote, "I am in Tokyo alone. . . . I like to work hard from morning to night in silence."[19] She embodied the mad loner and genius in her self-presentation. Even at this early stage, she promoted herself as quintessentially individual, separating herself from Japan and aligning herself instead with the notion of Western mastery and unique creativity.

In the publicity written by her first art dealer, Richard Castellane, she described her impetus to go to such an enormous and unwelcoming city as New York, in which she knew no one, especially in light of the fact that she spoke virtually no English: "I wanted to go to the top of the Empire State Building to see the view or even to jump off—anything to become famous . . ."[20] Her desire to engage with such a symbol of American might and modernity shows her determination to conquer the city as well as her dramatic bent toward hyperbole.[21] Kusama asserts that "America has freedom"; Kusama imagines and enacts New York's art world as a space in which she can exercise her "freedom" as an artist.[22]

Here, I do not wish to dismiss Kusama's very real psychological problems; her mental condition is not wholly imagined, nor is it to be taken lightly. I do, however, want to point out Kusama's manipulation of her condition in public presentations. In other words, she actively participated in her promotion and was complicit in the construction of her public persona, working within spaces that she could access and exploit as a foreign woman.[23] Her illness is, in fact, a self-designated foundation upon which she has built a career. This has resulted in Kusama's vacillation between the designations "mad genius" and "hysterical woman," depending on whether or not the assessment is positive.

Critics typically frame Kusama's insistent presentation of her physical body as a manifestation of her exhibitionist tendencies, a by-product of her mental illness and a colorful appendix to her art-making activity. Thus, such "exhibitionism" has recently been either dismissed or ignored altogether in favor of recuperating her as a foundational figure in a realigned canon of artists working in a modernist idiom. I would argue instead that her insistence on the body is in fact crucial to formulating a picture of her work and its previous as well as contemporary interpretations. Discussion of her overtly displayed body, however, is strangely absent from the imputation of sexuality in her art and psychosexual illness in her life history, perhaps because an acknowledgment of her corporeal (sexual and racial) specificity in direct, formal relation to the work would totally displace her from the status of modernist male hero that she has been granted; referencing her body would demean her "genius."[24] However, the ways in which her very particular body is highlighted in and through the work is what I find most intriguing. Instead of separating her racially and sexually marked body from her oeuvre and its criticism, interconnecting the three might produce more nuanced readings of Kusama and her work.

The work with which she juxtaposed herself is telling: in 1962, Kusama stopped creating her acclaimed net paintings and began working on a series of sculptures which she alternately termed "compulsion furniture," "sex obsessions," or "accumulations." These were a series of objects (rowboats, household furniture, kitchenware, clothing, and canvases) overtaken by stuffed cloth protuberances. The initial works were painted white; later, her palette expanded to include solid metallic colors or primary-colored dots or stripes. The works were created as a collective installation, meant to be displayed together in order to heighten the effect of these "growths"; the furniture and objects would create an all-encompassing environment (see fig. 6.1). The pouches vary in shape and size, at times evoking organic growths bubbling to the surface of the furniture, mushrooms or fungus-like masses, diseased (or benign) tumors, fingers, cilia, or phalli. Critics such as Lucy Lippard and Dore Ashton placed the objects in a lineage of surrealist subversions of the material world, as they make absurd the commonplace and banal. One immediately thinks of Meret Oppenheim's *Object* (1936), the fur-covered cup, saucer, and spoon with which Kusama's accumulations were exhibited in a group show in 1966. Likewise, they can be seen in relation to the work of her contemporaries, such as Louise Bourgeois and Eva Hesse. These frameworks, however, are subsumed through an insistence upon and attention to the body and biography of the artist. Kusama said of the pieces: "I was trying to fight against males—it was like my own art therapy. I had two brothers and a father who were always bothering me, and I had to struggle to be myself."[25] These protrusions, which she specifically refers to as phalli, serve then as therapeutic images (the first of which were created after she re-entered psychoanalysis with a Japanese therapist in New Jersey) through which she confronts her issues with the men in her life and her much advertised fear of sex and sexuality. She locates these works for the viewer autobiographically, within a psychic disorder, and the visual representations of the work and performances in the work itself direct the viewer to see these as her compulsive sexualization of the environment.

Photographs and photo collages are the primary ways in which Kusama's body and art are imbricated. These highly staged images often featured Kusama, nude or nearly nude, on top of or in the midst of her work as the evidence of the "psychosexual" nature of the environments. These images circulated in an astonishing array of incarnations in which the line between "artwork" and self-promotion blurred. She used the photographs to create photo collages which were then displayed as artwork on the gallery walls; some of the collages featured her body, others did not. A collage that is perhaps the most widely recognized image relating to Kusama's career depicts her lying on her stomach,

Figure 6.1. Kusama's studio, New York (1962–64). Courtesy Yayoi Kusama.

covered with polka dots and wearing nothing but black spiked high heels, staring straight at the camera atop *Accumulation #2* (1962) (see fig. 6.2). Her heavily lined eyes, long black hair, and frosted white lips coyly meet the viewer's gaze as she strikes the classic pose of the *Playboy* centerfold. One of her critically acclaimed paintings forms the backdrop. Kusama has collaged onto the bottom of the photograph a macaroni-strewn floor—many of her environmental installations feature pasta-covered clothing, furniture, and mannequins. The circa 1966 image includes a reference to several of her major series of objects produced in the United States: the "infinity net" paintings, "sex obsession" sculptures, and "food obsession" environments. Thus, six years of her artistic production are collapsed into this collage, which includes most prominently Kusama herself. She is literally located in the midst of her artwork, and her body is produced as an artwork as well as a sexualized object. At the same time, these dots ironicize and parody the sensuality of her nude body. One could also read such images in relation to contemporaneous images of the nude in Pop Art, such as the canvases of Tom Wessleman or Mel Ramos—except here, Kusama is the artist and creator of her own image. Like many other collages of this nature, this photo of Kusama was reproduced in numerous magazines, both in art journals and the non-art press, as illustrative of her artwork. Eventually, a cartoon version of this pose adorned flyers and advertisements for her performances. This and other similar images later appeared in mainstream newspapers and magazines, and finally, internationally, in men's magazines such as *Men, Bachelor, Mr.*, and *Sir*.[26] The resultant conflation of her sexual and racial body with her work is amplified by the multiplication and proliferation of the reproductions as well as by art critics and criticism.

The static images, though, were only part of her art-world persona. Her racialized and sexualized public body was equally integral to her self-production. She would attend art openings in a self-designed kimono, fabricated in a variety of outlandish colors and fabrics—gold lamé was a favorite—and "tell anyone who would listen her life story."[27] A photograph shows Kusama at the center of a group portrait in Holland, at the opening of the 1965 Nul and Zero group exhibition where she exhibited the *1,000 Boat Show* (see fig. 6.3). In a relatively casual group photograph, flanked by smiling artists such as Hans Haacke, Lucio Fontana, Günther Uecker, Heinz Mack and Jiro Yoshihara, Kusama, the diminutive kimono-clad figure dead center, stares at the camera with a characteristically solemn face.

After being overlooked for the 1966 Venice Biennale, she consulted with a gallery owner in Milan with whom she had exhibited earlier in the year and decided to crash the party, creating a piece called *Narcissus Garden* outside one of the pavilions (see fig. 6.4). It consisted of several hundred palm-sized mirrored balls spread across the grass. Wearing her gold kimono, Kusama wordlessly handed out flyers printed with a statement that Herbert Read submitted on the occasion of a 1964 exhibition of her accumulation sculptures: "Now with perfect consistency, she creates forms that proliferate like mycelium and

Figure 6.2. Kusama on *Accumulation #2* (1962). Macaroni floor, Sex and Food Obsession, Infinity Nets. Photo by Hal Reiff. Courtesy Yayoi Kusama.

Figure 6.3. Artists at Nul group exhibition, Stedelijk Museum, Amsterdam (1965). *Left to right:* Jiro Yoshihara, Hans Haacke, Henk Peeters, Rotraut Klein-Uecker, Jan Schoonhoven, Lucio Fontana, Pol Bury, Gianni Colombo, Mrs. Fontana, E. L. L. de Wilde, Nono Reinhold, Yayoi Kusama, George Rickey, Jesus Raphael Soto, Otto Piene, Nanda Vigo, Alfred Schmela, Heinz Mack, unidentified woman, Günther Uecker. Photo courtesy of Otto Piene and the Los Angeles County Museum of Art.

seal the consciousness in their white integument. It is an autonomous art, the most authentic type of super reality. This image of strange beauty presses on our organs of perception with strange persistence."[28] This quotation was often disseminated by Kusama in catalogues and essays as it basically articulated her own preferred reading of her work in the voice of one of the most respected art critics of the time. The statement emphasizes the very points which Kusama self-promoted: the ability of her work to affect the perceptions of the viewer, her aesthetic authenticity and autonomy, and the beauty of the work.[29] After introducing the Biennale audience to her work through such critical praise, she then tossed the balls in the air, entertaining the bewildered spectators. Finally, after trying to sell the balls to Biennale attendees as artworks for $2 apiece, she was thrown out of the space by the organizers for her circuslike "cheapening" of this high-art event. Her engagement of the late sixties "anti-capital" discourses, vending pieces of her artwork for such trifling sums, sends up the absurdity in commodifying art objects and something as ephemeral as a site-specific performance. Ironically, however, she was actually being quite businesslike and material in the very act of commodifying her performance in such a blatant manner. But the effort was certainly not a loss, for she received coverage in journals and newspapers around the world for her installation. Eventually, a photograph of Kusama in the installation would be featured on the cover of the catalogue for a 1966 group exhibition at Galerie Potsdamer in Berlin and Gallery Orez in The Hague. It seems that this performance and its fallout, then, enacted Kusama's relationship to the avant-garde and the commercial art world in general, a relationship which would become more and more extreme throughout the late 1960s and early 1970s: if you can't join them, at least you can get some public visibility.

Kusama's intense ambition for artistic fame and personal recognition led many to assess her work as sheer narcissism. However, while she engaged discourses of narcissistic reflection using mirrors and other imagery, she also tried to engage the multiplication and infinite refraction and reconstitution of the "outside" (the material and social) world as well. In a 1965 environmental exhibition called *Floor Show—Infinity Mirror Room*, mirrored walls reflect a floor covered with white protrusions polka-dotted with red (see fig. 6.5). Even in the title, she playfully evokes a performance, perhaps a burlesque one, as well as making a direct reference to the term most commonly associated with Eastern philosophy: infinity. The spectacle enveloped the viewers as active participants in the performance itself since a narrow path cleared away at the edge allowed them to walk around the field of growths. The viewers thereby joined Kusama's endless burlesque. One reviewer said that Kusama's *Floor Show* is

> nothing if not obsessive . . . insofar as it has no visible close antecedents in the world of art, Miss Kusama's acting-out of her own compulsions may be said to be a highly original genre . . . spiritually, however, she is one with the ingenious fanatic who constructs an Eiffel Tower of toothpicks, engraves the

Figure 6.4. *Narcissus Garden*, 33rd Venice Biennale (1966). Courtesy Yayoi Kusama.

Lord's Prayer on a pinhead. . . . the basic flaw in her oeuvre is that it has no autonomous life, but depends for its effects, such as they are, on its references to Miss Kusama herself and her very, very personal problems.[30]

The installation and others like it are likened to the grandiose project of a raving mad woman. Kusama is an "outsider artist," although exhibiting and working in the midst of the New York avant-garde; she is not a creative artist, like perhaps Oldenburg, who created his papiermâché environments three years earlier to wide critical acclaim, but an anomaly. Clearly, her work has been encrypted entirely through her mental illness, her pathologized psyche and body manifesting themselves in the work and becoming one with it. Here, her intentional imbrication has backfired, presaging reaction to her later work.

Figure 6.5. *Floor Show* (1965) at the Castellane Gallery. The artist in *Infinity Mirror Room.* Courtesy Yayoi Kusama.

Simultaneously with her inscription of her work with/on her body, she occasionally frustrated the conflation of her ethnic and gender identity with the content of her work. In interviews conducted in the 1960s and today, she often comments on her frustration with the orientalization of her work (although not in so many words). Today, she notes with a tone of exasperation the Western reduction of Japan to geisha girls, Mount Fuji, and gold folding screens. Her work is not at all about these references, she argues. On the contrary, she is at the leading edge of the avant-garde. There is a disruptive and potentially very powerful dynamic at play here. While one could argue that she is being exploited as an exotic object or that she is strategically using her marginal status as a position of power, I would assert that these two moments of marginalization are not mutually exclusive. For Kusama, at least, these moments are simultaneous and nearly impossible to disentangle. Perhaps one can contextualize these images within this complex dynamic, not to imbue them with Kusama's intentions or call them retrograde self-exoticism, but to understand how they function as a site for potentially subversive possibilities. The character that Kusama performs is Japanese female sexuality; this benefits her career, pro-actively claiming a space that would have already been assigned to her. Like O'Keeffe, Louise Nevelson, Eva Hesse, and countless other American women artists in the twentieth century, Kusama in effect staged her entry into modernist discourse by presenting herself as flamboyant and eccentrically feminine. Her subversion, then, could be seen at the level of her simultaneous insistence upon her marked presence, her "articulated difference," and her participation in the avant-garde.

Kusama engages the popularly recognizable sexualized Asian female, the marginal and dangerously titillating culture of the "free love" generation, while simultaneously and contrarily rejecting those frameworks for those of avant-garde aestheticism and performance. She oscillates between the formal aesthetic and the playful throughout her body of work; broadly speaking, she simultaneously engages Western definitions of the East and Eastern definitions of the West. The discourses of the displayed and objectified Asian woman and the actively displaying artist/genius here are confused and conflated in a way that explodes traditional art-historical narratives. She conflates the subject/object dichotomy, refusing to be naked in public while drawing attention to sexuality. Kusama, today enjoying perhaps her widest audience since the 1960s, is surrounded and buoyed by the mystique of her decade in New York. The overall effect of her performance is a literal subject/object slippage: she makes the art, she is the art, her work is her body, her body dictates the work. For audiences today and yesterday, Kusama is often reduced to a gendered and racially specific artist who simultaneously embodies "avant-garde genius" alongside hysterical femininity. However, her truly radical potential is seeing her body of/as work within a complex web of cultural significations.

NOTES

For their invaluable help with this essay, I would like to thank Amelia Jones, Donald McCallum, Richard Meyer, Mario Ontiveros, Donald Preziosi, and Cécile Whiting. I would also like to thank the editors of this volume for their suggestions. Finally, I am grateful to the artist for providing the photographs that accompany this essay.

1. Trinh T. Minh-ha, *Woman, Native Other: Writing Postcoloniality and Feminism* (Bloomington: Indiana University Press, 1989), p. 108.

2. For example, she appeared in the landmark exhibition "L'informe: Mode d'emploi" (Formless: A User's Guide), curated by Rosalind Krauss and Yves Alain-Bois, which created new formal categorizations for postwar Western art.

3. Andrew Solomon, "Dot Dot Dot: The Lifework of Yayoi Kusama," *Artforum* 35, no. 6 (February 1997): 66.

4. After re-establishing trade with Japan in the nineteenth century, Europe and the United States were flooded with Japanese art objects and goods. Particularly of interest to artists were Japanese prints, which introduced radically different pictorial conventions for depicting space as well as a visual vocabulary of foreign objects and bodies. There is an extensive body of scholarship on the phenomenon of *Japonisme*. See Clay Lancaster, *The Japanese Influence in America* (New York: Walton H. Rawls, 1963), for an overview of Japonisme in the United States; for both Japanese and Western perspectives on, see Chisaburo Yamada, ed., *Japonisme in Art: An International Symposium* (Tokyo: Committee for the Year 2001, 1980); and see Sigfried Wichmann, *Japonisme: The Japanese Influence on Western Art in the 19th and 20th Centuries* (New York: Harmony Books, 1981), for a well-illustrated volume on the general impact of Japan in European and American aesthetics from the opening of Japan to the current day.

5. John Kuo Wei Tchen, "Believing Is Seeing: Transforming Orientalism and the Occidental Gaze," in *Asia/America* (New York: The Asia Society Gallery, 1994), p. 19.

6. A forthcoming book by Kendall Brown will critically examine the popularity of Japanese gardens in the United States. See also *House Beautiful* 102 (August 1960), which is an entire issue devoted to Japan. The cover, an idyllic image of a Japanese house and garden, reads: "Discover, the word for the highest level in beauty."

7. Rene Bouché, "Make-Up of a Geisha," *Vogue* 129, no. 10 (June 1957): 98–101.

8. Here, I should mention that this was primarily manifested in a desire for handcrafted "native" Japanese objects, Japanese women, and, generally, "harmonious" and "timeless" Japanese aesthetics. However, mass-manufactured goods made in Japan and marketed to a U.S. audience were considered shoddy substitutes for their domestically manufactured counterparts. It seems that as long as Japan did not emerge as an economic force and maintained its position as aesthetic Other to the West's scientific and industrial pre-eminence, cordial relations could exist between the two.

9. Bert Winther, "Japanese Thematics in Postwar American Art: From Zen to the Assertion of Asian-American Identity," *Scream against the Sky* (New York: Abrams, 1994), p. 59.

10. See Daisetz Teitaro Suzuki, *An Introduction to Zen Buddhism* (London: Random Century Group, 1969), for a general overview of his teachings. Also see Eugen Herigel, *Zen in the Art of Archery* (London: Routledge and Kegan Paul, 1976) as a popular example of the interpretation of Suzuki's teachings. See Alan Watts, "Beat

Zen, Square Zen, and Zen," *Chicago Review* 12 (Summer 1958), for an influential early article about Zen. Also, see Catherine Elmes Kalbacher, "Zen in America" (Ph.D. dissertation, University of Michigan, 1972), for an overview of the Zen phenomenon among the intelligentsia of the United States during this era.

11. For an examination of this phenomenon specific to the post–World War II period in the United States, see Bert Winther's "Japanese Thematics in Postwar American Art." Also, see the catalogue for the exhibition of Zen calligraphy mounted in 1955 at the Museum of Modern Art, New York.

12. Hugo Munsterberg, "Zen and Art," *College Art Journal* 20, no. 4 (Summer 1961): 201. Other notable publications include the Fall 1958 issue of the *Journal,* which focused primarily on the Western interest in Japanese art and the writings of John Cage, particularly in the volumes *Silence* (Hanover, N.H.: University Press of New England, 1961) and *A Year from Monday* (Middletown, Conn.: Wesleyan University Press, 1967).

13. See Andrew Perchuk, "Pollock and Postwar Masculinity" in *Masculine Masquerade* (Cambridge, Mass.: MIT Press, 1995), for a discussion of the construction and circulation of this Abstract Expressionist, male genius trope.

14. Clement Greenberg, "Avant-Garde and Kitsch," in *Art and Culture* (Boston: Beacon Press, 1961), p. 5. Greenberg, in his 1955/58 essay "American-Type Painting," denies the import of "Oriental" art to American painters, but nonetheless, this idea that there is a "path" that must be followed to an essential and absolute expression was echoed in many of the artists mentioned in the paragraph above in reference to their interest in Japan/Zen. For an overview of Greenberg's scholarship, see John O'Brian, ed., *Clement Greenberg: The Collected Essays and Criticism* (Chicago: University of Chicago Press, 1986–93).

15. Interestingly, the repeal of the race-based immigration quota laws in 1965 (affecting actual immigration in 1968), allowing for a flood of Asian bodies into the United States, coincides with a marked drop of interest in Asian philosophies, particularly Zen.

16. Here, I would like to note Kusama's choice of correspondent. She aligns herself with a famous female modernist, who, essentially, was the most successful woman artist in New York in the early twentieth century. This, I think, was no coincidence. Other allegiances and alliances that she would forge in New York helped her career in no uncertain terms; this speaks volumes about her social savvy and acuity.

17. Yayoi Kusama to Georgia O'Keeffe, c. August 1956, the Center for International Contemporary Art Archive, Archer M. Huntington Art Gallery, Austin, Texas.

18. I should acknowledge here that the modern French works had the widest general impact on the artists in Tokyo; the Gutai group of artists, based in Osaka, found inspiration in other Parisian sources such as Art Informel. A few artists, such as Kusama and a handful of others who would have seen the work of American artists in reproduction or at exhibition, found inspiration on the Abstract Expressionists and other American movements.

19. Yayoi Kusama to Georgia O'Keeffe, December 13, 1955, the Center for International Contemporary Arts Archive, Huntington Art Gallery, Austin, Texas.

20. Untitled biographical sketch of Yayoi Kusama, c. 1966, personal papers of Richard Castellane, New York.

21. Kusama was an avid fan of the work of Yves Klein, whose career served as somewhat of a model for her own. He was a successful minimalist painter, first and foremost. His *Leap into the Void,* a photograph of Klein's "suicide leap" staged exclusively

for the camera, and his *Anthropométries de l'époque bleue*, in which the tuxedoed maestro conducts naked, paint-covered women across canvases on the floor to create paintings (the art exists in performance, photographic document, and canvas), are particularly of note in relation to Kusama's career. We can see her emulating this command in her self-presentation, which wholeheartedly participates in the romance of the artist as daring, mad genius.

22. Dana Friis-Hansen, "Yayoi Kusama's Feminism," *Art & Text* 49 (1994): 51.

23. Bert Winther, when analyzing the careers of several Japanese artists in the United States, observed that Kenzo Okada (active in the United States in the 1960s) "succeeded [in the United States] by glossing his style with a Japanese veneer which appealed to the elite American collectors who supported him" (Winther, "Japanese Thematics in Postwar American Art," p. 63). Although Okada and Kusama are certainly very different artists, one might find parallels in the self-conscious cultural savvy with which they guided their careers.

24. Here I must distinguish the career of Kusama as inflected by her body and the career of many other male artists of the postwar era as inflected by their bodies. Images of Jackson Pollock reproduced famously in *Life* (August 8, 1949), as well as those recorded by Hans Namuth for "Pollock Paints a Picture" in *Art News* 51 (May 1951) and for a film on the artist, were crucial to the definition of the modern artist-hero, as well as to the ultimate success of his own career. Images of Kusama, however, engage the entirely different registers of exoticization and sexualization, producing objectifying rather than heroic images.

25. Quoted from an interview with Diana Friis-Hansen, "Yayoi Kusama's Feminism," p. 51.

26. See the Center for International Contemporary Art Archives, Archer M. Huntington Art Gallery, Austin, Texas.

27. Donald Judd interviewed by Alexandra Munroe and Reiko Tomii, December 8, 1988, the Center for International Contemporary Art Archives, Huntington Art Gallery, Austin, Texas.

28. See the Center for International Contemporary Art Archives, Huntington Art Gallery, Austin, Texas.

29. Of course, her insistence upon her aesthetic autonomy and formal purity seem quite contradictory when considering the promotion of her career using sexualized, racialized images of her body. The ironies of this inconsistency produces the tensions which have caused considerable critical vacillation about her career and her place in the history of art.

30. Jay Jacobs, "In the Galleries: Yayoi Kusama," *Arts Magazine* 40 (January 1966): 61.

7. "Oh, You Can't Just Let a Man Walk over You": Staging *Threepenny Opera* in Singapore

Sue-Ellen Case

In 1819, Sir Stamford Raffles established a trading station for the British East India Company in what would become Singapore. Raffles wrested a city from jungle, dividing land by auction among those who would "responsibly" develop it. He cleared areas for "white men" to build their houses, using local Chinese as coolies. A garrison was built to protect the store of opium and hand goods kept there in the warehouses. He outlawed gambling and passed other laws to maintain an orderly society. In 1824, a Dutch officer recorded an impression of Singapore that foresaw its present sense of accomplishment: "I feel that no person with any feeling can help being impressed when setting foot in Singapore, because he can now see as a seat of European trade and industry a place which only five years before was a cavern and hiding place for murderers and pirates" (Nahuijs 1996, 19). In 1824, Singapore was ceded, in perpetuity, to the British East India Company by the Sultan of Johor; it became a crown colony in 1867, as part of the "Straits Settlement" program. When the British surrendered to the Japanese in 1942, Singapore "witnessed the triumph of an Asian power over a seemingly invincible European one" (Fook 1996, 6–7). Following that disappointment, Singapore moved toward independence, which it achieved in 1959. Yet Singapore Airlines still calls its business class "Raffles Class." The Raffles Hotel recently enjoyed a multimillion-dollar facelift. It is beautifully maintained and displayed for tourists and well-heeled locals to enjoy the historic "Singapore Sling" in its Long Bar (where locals were once not allowed). The country proudly displays its colonial heritage as part of its current claim to the same principles Raffles deployed to develop it.

Upon the heels of Raffles and the British colonial government, a single man, Lee Kuan Yew, led Singapore from 1959 until 1990. Singapore held its first presidential election in 1993. It was Yew who created the modern "economic miracle" in this tiny nation with no natural resources. Singapore has no foreign debt. Over 86 percent of the population lives in Housing Development Board flats and 80 percent own the flat they live in. Compared to many neighboring countries, the general population enjoys a relatively spacious and modern accommodation, with swimming pools in many of the developments. The city is modern and clean. It has no malaria and enjoys the most modern health and hospital system in its region.[1] As the language of historical progress and betterment, English remains the lingua franca—the language of business and higher education. It is found on most road signs, shopping areas, and foodstuffs, and is spoken by most cabbies, college graduates, men in middle management, and those working in the state bureaucracy. The historical relation between "strong" leadership and prosperity does not seem to create a critical attitude in the people, toward either their colonial past, their recent leader, or their current controlled environment. As Raffles banned "immoral" practices to guard the safety of successful trade, Yew, and others following him, banned homosexuality, and spitting in public places. They set up a censorship board for film and theater, along with laws against chewing gum. Yet, while ethnic cleansing, dramatic economic decline, and street violence take place in many of the neighboring countries, Singapore remains at peace, enjoying prosperity and order within a nationally sanctioned multicultural society.

In this environment, following this national history, the prospect of directing *Threepenny Opera* by Bertolt Brecht and Kurt Weill, in English, set in London, making full reference to the Queen and other British tropes, took on a completely different set of affects than those which Brecht and Weill would critically propose.[2] Brecht and Weill, like Mack the Knife, could wittily "steal" John Gay's *The Beggar's Opera* for their own political and aesthetic agenda, foregrounding its distance through translation into German and through their innovative musical and theatrical inventions. Berlin, after all, had not served as a colonial site for British trade, so London could offer an apt and distant setting for class politics, with a spectacular tradition of collusion between the upper class and the government. However, it seems that by translating the German text into English, and making full reference to the tropes of the British Empire in a country so plundered by it, the performance might actually reproduce colonial, docile bodies, rather than the critical gestures that Brechtian practice would encourage. In terms of this project, Polly Peachum's song "You Can't Just Let a Man Walk over You" seemed to say it all, for the final verses of the song conclude that you *can* just let a man walk over you, when he is as devilishly effective and attractive as Mack the Knife, or perhaps Sir Stamford Raffles. *Threepenny*'s stinging portrayal of sexual and economic submissiveness seemed to sing Singapore's old, familiar tune. Moreover, as Brecht structures the action, the opera can offer any sort of ending, ineffectually portraying a critique of social relations that, in itself, can change nothing. The critique hangs (or doesn't hang, in Mack's case) just behind the curtain of municipal, state, and business practices, whose requirements for a smooth-running society define personal and social relations.

REHEARSING THE LOCAL

In 1999, Dr. KK Seet invited me to Singapore to direct the graduating class of theater studies majors at the National University of Singapore in their final production. I guessed that Dr. Seet had chosen *Threepenny Opera* because his class was composed of fine singers and I was known for studying the Brechtian tradition. I thought it would provide a rich opportunity to bring a more traditional Marxist critique into line with new ideas about transnational capital and a postcolonial critique. I had been inspired by Ackbar Abbas's fine book *Hong Kong* to imagine that the stage might provide an accurate lens on the conditions of appearance and disappearance in the transition from colonial to global status on the part of a major Asian city. Abbas argues that Hong Kong cinema actually offers one of the most accurate registers of change for considerations of the city, noting that "[t]hese films do not so much thematize Hong Kong culture as they give us a critical experience of Hong Kong's cultural space by problematizing the viewing process" (Abbas 1997). Brecht certainly tried to produce a similar effect for the stage, by somehow distancing the action to encourage critical reflection on the *gestus,* or gesture of the social. However, by the end of the process, I felt that perhaps the only visibility I might have managed to produce was my own, as an American expat. What follows is an attempt to describe, within the full play of contradictions, the process of trying to practice the theory I had read.

The cast had mostly Chinese surnames, with the exception of a few Indians, Malays, Sri Lankans, and others. To me, the cast looked like the multiethnic environment of Singapore, with a majority of Chinese, alongside a mix of other immigrants from the Malay peninsula and the Indian subcontinent. All of the students were fluent in English, with their own versions of a colonial accent. When speaking among themselves, they often used Singlish, a local dialect difficult for the American ear to parse, or they spoke in one of the four major dialects of Chinese found in Singapore: Cantonese, Teochew, Hokkien, or Hakka. I was familiar with the sound of Indian English, but I had never heard the British pronunciation formed with a Chinese accent. To my ear, two elements of the Chinese language resonated through the English. The students spoke with a more staccato rhythm in the sentence, which lightly broke the British articulation of vowels as mellifluent. At the same time, when speaking rapidly, they tended to drop out the consonants, thus intensifying the sense of the sentence as composed of a rhythmic assortments of vowels. The result could be very charming, sounding as if the Chinese prompted the English to emphasize more the motor of the sentence than its ride—an appropriate timbre for the colonial relationship. When I heard this accent onstage, I could not really associate it with the music of the play, which is composed of chromatic slides. I think this sound of the accent encouraged me to want to change the orchestration, as I will describe in the next section on the music.

Even if the stage language sounded like a Chinese version of British English, it still resonated in my ear as a strong, vibrant echo of Singapore's colonial past. After a talk on women and postcoloniality in Malaysia by Chin Woon Ping in the sociology department, I heard a discussion of local uses of colonial English, in which people seemed to agree that the Indians had made English their own language in a way the Chinese could not. The group agreed that perhaps the Indians were perhaps the most successful group in assimilating that language. This prompted me to offer that, in fact, the Americans had successfully made colonial English their own language. As a theater scholar, I am often reminded of our postcolonial relationship to the works of Shakespeare and the "great" history of theater in English. Yet in this discussion in Singapore, I became aware of the fact that, somehow, others might hear American English as naturalized, seemingly cut loose from its colonial heritage. Perhaps the strength of our American accent veils the imported history of the language itself. Speaking daily among Indian and Chinese scholars at the National University, my ear heard the distance of my own accent from the local, more British inflection and vocabulary of the English in Singapore. In rehearsal, this accent, compounded with the setting of the play in London, kept prompting me to want to somehow distance the production from its colonial consonance. Possibly, I was playing out my own American, revolutionary rejection of that colonial past, in the midst of their more casual, or perhaps more cynical, use of its advantages. Accents aside, the greater distance between American English and the Singaporean British was in the subtext. I was proud to say exactly what I thought, within a Singaporean language tradition that finds that habit annoyingly aggressive and short of diplomacy. So, a scholar of the Brechtian tradition, I was cut loose from the German context of Brecht's work, from the American language, and from the local uses of translation.

Searching for some context in which I could stage this language, I sought to discover the tradition of English theater in Singapore. Two contemporary groups, Theatreworks and the Necessary Stage, produce most of their productions in English. They are innovative and vital components of the cultural scene in Singapore. Historically, the tradition seemed to gain momentum in the 1930s, with the import of London hits along with the flourishing of amateur theatricals by expatriates. Singapore has a strong tradition of expatriate cultural importation, still encouraged by the government as "foreign talent" for the university, business, and culture. The English theater tradition was not as strong, historically, as Chinese street theater; Singapore Mandarin drama, which began in the 1920s; forms of Indian dance and drama; the Wayang Kulit; and other local traditions.[3] Yet the English stage continues there, to be reviewed in the English-language newspaper, *The Straits Times.* In fact, the tradition of English-speaking theater, moving from expats to Asians performing in English, is a fascinating marker of the assimilation of colonial practices by the locals. The work of Brecht plays a positive role in this history. In 1962, *The Straits Times* heralded the successful all-Asian production, in English, of *The Good Woman of Setzuan* (Birch 1998, 24). Interestingly, Brecht is associated with the English language. The Necessary Stage uses English to brilliantly critique and confirm Singaporean policies and traditions. Theatreworks produces a variety of fascinating formal inventions, borrowing from performance practices in the States and England. In a discussion with my students of Theatreworks' new pan-Asian production of *Lear*, which was performed in several Asian traditions and languages, the students noted that when they listened to the Chinese on the stage they could hear that the Japanese playwright, who wrote the dialogue for the sections done in the style of Beijing Opera, had worked from Japanese, through English, into Chinese. Thus, even this melting-pot Asia qua Asian production used English as the intermediary language among Asian languages and styles, marking them with its imperial role, even as they performed the "local." English, if not the language of the stage, still remains a player within the multi-language environment of Asia.

Given this history of playing in English, I first considered just doing the play, as it is, in "whiteface" in order to emphasize the colonial heritage. However, this decision would overlook the local assimilation and integration of this past. After all, Brecht was distancing the London setting, anyway, as an apt site for class relations and royal presumptions. The example of his play *The Good Woman of Setzuan* suggested still another set of contradictions. The development of Brecht's own dramaturgy and some of his plays presents a troubling version of orientalism. Brecht records the influence of Beijing Opera on his own understanding of "distance," using his distance from the tradition as a strategy within Western European stage practices. His "good woman" is a Chinese one, the kindly prostitute/mother visited by outmoded Chinese gods and plagued by Chinese poverty. Brecht's notion of China seemed to be as a fertile ground for revolutionary consciousness. In *The Measures Taken*, Communist agitators try to better the lives of coolies and factory workers. In both *Setzuan* and *Measures*, China plays as a parable of poverty to the possibility of betterment. The critic Rey Chow, in her book on modernism, women, and China, notes that "China, like woman, is unknowable, but also archaic" (Chow 1991, 9). In Brecht, China is merely desired, as a ground of revolution, having no wishes of its own.[4]

How, then, to imagine *Threepenny Opera* in Singapore? The students were not critical in ways the text might want them to become. Should I import a politics, as in *The Measures Taken*? Would I use the Brecht text and ancillary Marxist analyses as a source of political knowledge like the role of The Party in *Measures Taken*? Should I play the role of the American "Big Brother" of critical understanding, or the role of imposition and relief designed by the International Monetary Fund? Should I, a feminist, feminize the local by making it a compassionate, contradictory, impoverished character within a parable, like the "good woman"? Regarding "good women"—or in the case of *Threepenny*, "bad women"—how could I my produce my own feminist critique of the play? What could I do with Brecht's romantic portrayal of the prostitutes (translated as a word I had not said for years, "whores") and the brothel?

Should I try to deconstruct or decompose the text, using strategies borrowed from performance art traditions and the feminist critique?

These interrogations of the process led me to discover another set of contradictions. None of the strategies of resistance with which I am familiar are allowed to play a productive role in Singaporean society. Feminism is not sanctioned in Singapore. It is perceived as an aggressive, Western, confrontational politic that does not work within Asian, particularly Chinese, traditions of social problem solving. The government has attempted to address the problems of women within its overall policy, downplaying the issues as particular to women. Women do not organize as an interest group. On numerous occasions, I was informed either that women did not have problems in Singapore or that they would address their problems in an entirely different manner. I can certainly understand how feminism, as I know it, derives from my own cultural heritage. I also did not want to argue with the women who felt that the social structures in which they lived were adequate, nor did I want to use feminism as part of American cultural imperialism. I thought, then, to look to, say, Thailand to work on the problem of prostitution, since it was "nearby" and generally perceived to be the center of the sex trade. Perhaps I should set the play in Thailand, in order to make a less colonial critique of proximate conditions. Along with my embrace of feminism, I also learned that the strategies of performance which I felt were accurate and empowering were not practiced in Singapore. Forum theater, Augusto Boal's Brecht-derived idea for theater as social change, is not allowed. Boal had been identified as a "Marxist ideologue." The audience participation was regarded as playing "dupes" for well-placed Marxist agitators. Performance Art was also banned. In 1994, the Home Affairs Ministry stated that these art forms "pose greater risks to public order, security and decency."[5]

Still convinced I would not let a "man walk over me," I doggedly sought to perceive how I could produce the appropriately critical staging of *Threepenny* without directly crossing the lines of cultural censorship (known there as "o.b. markers" or "out of bound markers"). Yet these interdictions against my own version of politics and theater made me increasingly aware how American culture had been cast into a particular role from which it could not be extricated. "Seduced and abandoned," one of my favorite refrains from popular culture, seemed to aptly describe the ambivalent relationship Singapore has with American influence. While American culture seems ultimately seductive and desirable, it is also carefully contained. Walking through one section of metropolitan Singapore, I observed the signs of the seductive success of American cultural imperialism and transnational capital and its containment. Orchard Road is the district of upscale department stores, malls, and other businesses. On the way, one might pass the American club, where expat wives spend time during the week, joined by their husbands on the weekend. Their children cavort in the pool while they drink in the bar, or dine in the formal dining room, under the seal of the United States, which is frosted into the glass partition. These expats live an affluent but separate life within those walls and that membership. They relax in the comfort of a nostalgic rendering of "home," both erecting their distance from local culture and confined within it. Further down the street, an enormous Borders bookstore sits on one corner, touted as the largest bookstore in that part of the world. The books are in English, of course, and it is crowded with customers. Borders is about two doors down from Planet Hollywood and across the street from Starbucks. In a renovated section of Chinatown, which is now a steel and glass mall, huge TV screens project images from MTV. At the local cinemas, I could see a multitude of the latest Hollywood films, while queen *Elizabeth* still occupied a certain cultural throne.

I tried to collect these various observations into a profile of my own character in Singapore. I was an American director on a Fulbright grant, who self-identified as one who ascribed to alternative political views, in a country where my own homosexuality, feminism, expertise in performance art, and a Marxist version of Brecht were not allowed, and where the authority of American culture was as alluring as Mack the Knife. I soon decided that probably all I could manage to produce was exactly that compound of elements. Rather than any idealistic notion that I could make the production "mean" something, I decided it would simply reflect the set of contradictions in which I found myself.

MUSIC AND GESTURE

Although I had studied *Threepenny Opera* from a critical perspective, I had never worked on it for production. It was fascinating to discover the surface and fragmentary nature of the text. As is commonly known, the characters are stock characters, with little individuality and no subtext. What I had not registered is that they seem most themselves when singing. Moreover, Brecht fragmented the play into scene titles and short episodes, in his familiar style, but I discovered that the songs stand out as fulsome and whole. In his practice of separating the songs out from the action, they actually took center stage. In this sense, the piece is foremost an opera. In spite of Brecht's dramaturgical innovations and Kurt Weill's use of popular cabaret idioms, *Threepenny* plays almost like recitatives and arias. Perhaps it is the dramaturgical success of the songs, along with Weill's talented scoring, that has constituted the songs as the cultural memory of the play. While the play is not widely known, "Mack the Knife" has been recorded across genres and audiences: 101 Strings as *Cocktail Hour Hits of the 50's and 60's*; Arthur Murray as "Most Fabulous Ballroom"; Duke Ellington/Ella Fitzgerald, Oscar Peterson as jazz; the Nashville Superpickers as country; the Psychedelic Furs as a form of rock, and Peggy Lee as torch. "Pirate Jenny" fares less well but has been taken up by leading female vocalists, such as Nina Simone and Judy Collins.[6]

Brecht's notion of opera is complex and critical. However, when playing in proximity to Asian performance traditions, it seems quite Eurocentric. Even Weill's musical setting, which was radical for its time in rejecting the Wagnerian tradition and incorporating popular music idioms, works in direct contra-diction to Asian theater-music traditions. Its biting irony and heart-on-sleeve sentimentality, so redolent of the cabaret world of the Weimar Republic, are at complete odds with both traditional Asian musics and the familiar Asian ar-rangements of Western songs. Weill emphasizes the chromatic structure of the songs, while Asian music is played in the pentatonic scale. Unlike the tra-dition of the Beijing Opera, the scenes are structured like recitative and aria. Unlike, say, Balinese and Indian forms, dance plays no role in the gestural system. Rather than whiteface, then, to foreground the colonial roots of the London setting and the English language, it seemed to me that I could simply foreground the "roots" of this form by staging it *as* an opera, with a sense of lavish costumes, formal gestures, blocking, and settings. Further, referencing the lavish spectacle of European opera staging traditions within a country proud of its "economic miracle" seemed a more appropriate sense of mise-en-scène than trying to replicate a distant "poor."

While the elements of cultural imperialism in the project seemed to re-quire strategies that foregrounded their operations, the power of Singaporean cultural assimilation also needed to be scored. So, together with Adrian Tan, the student who would eventually arrange the music and conduct it, I decided to mix the orchestra with Asian and Western instruments. Why not simply put together the sounds of two traditions as if they meet in this place? Wouldn't the sound of the music better match the accented English? Without trying to accommodate the full mix of Southeast Asian musical traditions, we decided to mix certain Chinese sounds and rhythms with the Western ones. First, we chose the *er-hu*, which is used in most Chinese traditional music and is possi-bly one of the most popular instruments. I had heard it in a concert in Shang-hai, where its similarity to the violin marked its ability to play within the West-ern chromatic register. Yet, the tuning of the instrument to the pentatonic scale forced the *er-hu* player to estimate positions between two notes to get a flatted or sharped note as required by the music. Tan added the *zhong-hu*, a stringed instrument with a deeper sound and lower octaves. This played the more somber songs. The Western keyboard sound was played on the piano, while the *yang-qin* was used as the Chinese equivalent. The sound of the *yang-qin*, however, is unique and emphasized the Asian texture of the sound. For the aggressive military sound of the "Cannon Song" Tan added the trumpet and trombone. The large assortment of Chinese percussion instruments were what colored the music most of all, most prominently the *yue-luo*, which is a gong that is able to alter in pitch after it is struck.[7]

In addition to the orchestra, I decided to use a convention from the Beijing Opera which emphasizes the conclusion of a gesture, or, more correctly, some-thing like Brecht's notion of the *gestus*. I thought this inclusion might wittily cite Brecht's own discovery of his method from having seen the Beijing Opera and also might provide a more local strategy of distanciation. We used a com-bo instrument made up of the *ban gu* (the drum with the clicking sound), the *yueluo*, and a Chinese temple block (*mu yu*). The sequence of sounds is composed of a staccato beat that increases its tempo until a crescendo is struck on the gong. I used it primarily to highlight moments of hierarchical oppression. We would match the words to the beat, making the stage picture of corruption or alienation, pausing on the gong and falling out of character. Then we would pick up the next beat of the dialogue. I also used this instrument to underscore Brecht's sexism in scenes in the brothel and elsewhere. Sexist jokes about Mack's sexual prowess were thus accented, while the women broke out of the scene.

Most of the songs were played in a spotlight before the curtain, emphasizing their distance from the dramatic action, their fulsome form, and their cabaret roots. Unfortunately, the circumstances of the stage forced us to put the orchestra in the wings, miking it as well as the singers. The mikes produce an intimacy of sound that is foreign to Brecht, yet the sound of technological intervention seemed more contemporary, more like the global sound of MTV. The young cast seemed familiar with miked singing, possibly from popular uses of karaoke and MTV. It was difficult to break their habit of imitating the slides of sound, the break of the voice, and other tropes of heartbreak and passion they had learned from these global forms.

THE UNNAMABLE ASIAN CITY

Threepenny Opera engenders a hearty but fruitless anger, since it offers a forceful portrait of unjust conditions with no alternatives. Designed to reveal the corrupt base of the entire economic, judicial, and state system, Brecht's great dramaturgical achievement resides in combining a critical critique of corruption with a portrait of corruption as alluring. Mack the Knife is deadly attractive, with several "wives" and favorite "whores" who do his bidding until they realize that his interest in them is worth money. Their betrayal of him is portrayed as ubiquitous. Because of the Singaporean self-image I have outlined above, as well as its national and cultural "markers," it seemed impossible to set the opera in Singapore. After all, it is neither corrupt nor decadent. Before "reunification" in 1997, Hong Kong might have provided a perfect example of the London of the East. Bangkok, while geographically proximate, was culturally quite different, and China, as we know, is "Red." Since I wanted to drop London out of the stage picture, I needed some equally distant, but familiar location for the play. I decided to identify it merely as an "Asian City," hoping to point to the orientalism of the concept and to wittily note that it was simply "not" Singapore, although a slide of downtown Singapore would dominate the backdrop of Peachum's shop for beggars. I chose a slide that caught the old shops of Singapore in the foreground with the new transnational skyscrapers rising up behind them (fig. 7.1). I hoped that the photo might situate Peachum's entrepreneurial corruption within the past, soon to give way to the "licit" transactions of transnational corporate headquarters. As Mack the Knife puts it in the final act of the play, "What's the murder of a man compared to the hiring of a man?"

We referred to the setting as "The City." I later discovered that the cast read this as a sign of my own orientalism, as if I would imagine all Asian cities to be similar to one another. Together with my co-director, Christopher Newton, we altered every locational reference in the script to signify some well-known district in either Hong Kong, Thailand, or even, sometimes, Singapore. For example, in Singapore, the Oriental Hotel is quite a grand edifice. Its name seemed to provide a perfect replacement for the Octopus Hotel in the script. It was both vague and specific. The Oriental Carpet Store also seemed a good place from whence they might have stolen the carpet for the wedding scene. Thus, most every business took the title "Oriental" as part of its name. The adjective "oriental" thus had the double valence of suggesting local places and (their own) orientalism.

Within this setting, I wanted to mark the official multiculturalism of Singapore's self-identification, by selecting elements for each costume that would mark it with an ethnic specificity. Yet the costumes also strove to look contemporary and glitzy, in order to resemble operatic spectacle. Peachum, as the shop owner, Brecht's ironic portrait of the bourgeoisie, was done up in the stereotype of the Chinese shopowner, replete with little beard. He might have lived and worked in one of the shop-houses pictured in the drop behind his stage set. His wife, played by a Sri Lankan actress, wore middle-class clothes from that culture, sporting a big purse that carried the money to be

Figure 7.1. "Singapore shophouses and transnational towers." Photo by Phua Ree Kee.

paid out for the betrayal of Mack (fig. 7.2). I hoped that an overdrawn portrait of the stereotypical Chinese merchant might mark the orientalism of the piece, cueing the audience to its distancing, self-reflexive mode.

However, the cast felt that the orchestration and the technique borrowed from Beijing Opera set up the ethnic register of the city as primarily Chinese. When asked about this by a member of the crew, I could only answer that the culture did seem primarily Chinese to me, with only a minority representation of other cultures. This is a problem in Singapore, where the Malays, for example, seem not to occupy many of the executive positions, in either business, the various ministries, or the army. The Indian population, originally Tamil, seems likewise not to be found in high places, but is instead represented there by more recent Brahmin immigrants, who are regarded as "foreign talent."

Finally, I sought some solution, if compromised, for dealing with the brothel scene and the portrait of the "whores" Brecht created. After speaking with my cast about the notion of "sex workers" who may, because of impoverished circumstances, particularly in Thailand, turn to the sex trade, we attempted to portray these women with some respect, sympathy, and dignity. We sought to make the women seem independent, mistrustful and cynical when Mack tells them his stories, alienated from the pimps who run them, but seeking some supportive relation to one another. We tried to imagine specific biographies of these women. For example, one might have come in from a Thai

Figure 7.2. Peachum, Mrs. Peachum, Polly Peachum. Photo by Phua Ree Kee.

village to make money for the family back home. Another might have been sold into sexual slavery by her family, a common practice in Thailand. We sought to create a bond among all of the women in the play as having, perforce, made their way through selling their bodies. The actress playing Mrs. Peachum, Edwina Welikande, decided that even her character, like Pirate Jenny in the song Polly sings, might have worked as a go-go dancer in a club where she met Mr. Peachum, a street type who was determined to succeed. With difficulty and through clever immigration procedures, the Peachums had found some semblance of bourgeois comfort in their shop in Singapore. These rehearsal strategies elicited real stories or imagined stories from the students about the people in the region.

I set several of the alienated *gestus*-type moments within the scenes with the whores, sounding the Chinese gong at the end of a rhythmic phrasing of sexist jokes, and turning the actresses out of the action whenever they were discounted. We opened the brothel scene on a raucous disco number, which was designed to delight the audience, but then to quickly reverse its effect by revealing the women's fatigue and disdain for the self-display demanded by the dancing. The look of the go-go bar was based upon the numerous places I had seen along Pat Pong Road in Bangkok. Open doors revealed crowded stages, with numerous women dancing to disco music, hanging on to poles. Out in front, their men lounged in chairs, or shouted through bullhorns that customers should come to watch the women pick up a Ping-Pong ball with their vagina. The members of my cast were all familiar with this notorious Ping-Pong show. We talked about the enormous success of the sex trade in young girls in Thailand and the high incidence of AIDS. We even spoke of prostitutes in Singapore, where they seemingly do not exist. Many of the prostitutes in Singapore are imported to serve the imported male workers, who come without their families to do construction work on limited contracts. One student, Suhaila Sulaiman, took photos of Singapore brothels and street sex workers, which we studied. We developed one in a grainy, blurry way to obscure the faces of the women, placing it on the cover of our program.

Yet in spite of these familiar techniques to involve the cast's imagination in the conditions of the poor or exploited in their own city, there was no accompanying sense either that they could somehow intervene in these practices or that corrupt hierarchies of power enforced them. Either that, or they were not willing or trusting enough to share these sentiments with me, an outsider and visitor, who was there for a very limited time. How could I presume to invite that trust, or more, to assume I understood the complex local conditions? Or perhaps, in a desperate attempt to retain their own prosperity and national peace, these cast members could not afford to begin imagining a necessary change in the system. Further, since feminism was not encouraged, admitting there were special problems for women would mean confronting a problem that had no form of articulation, and no form of intervention.

Finally, it seemed that global capitalism serves Singapore particularly well. With an immigrant population that could claim no indigenous traditions, and a tiny land mass that offers no natural resources, the hope of Singapore resides in the transnational investment of corporations who would use it as a base in Southeast Asia. Its promise of a controlled society, with a well-educated, English-speaking population, provides an island, a haven in a part of the world transnational capital needs but cannot afford to daily inhabit. Singapore's immediate goal is called IT 2000—a millennial project to become the digital communications center for the entire region. In other words, it will provide a nodal center for the exchange of communications through transnational links. If this is the hope of prosperity for its citizens, what role could a critique of such globalizing processes play in the imagination of its highly educated youth?

By the time the production opened, I had spent enough time in Singapore to realize that my first impressions of signifying systems there were generally misperceived. I had slowly come to realize that the subtext of occasions, responses, and even propositions were often quite different than their surface signification. However, I had not spent enough time there to understand what was actually taking place. Therefore, I do not know how the play was received

Figure 7.3. Mack the Knife at the gallows.
Photo by Phua Ree Kee.

by the general audience, how the cast really felt about their work, what they finally decided I was trying to do with all of the alterations of the text and music, or even what I thought I saw on opening night. Actually, this is quite an extraordinary condition for a director. Finally, that much-touted directorial vision was difficult to achieve and impossible to test. I am pretty certain that much of what I did was read as American and carefully deposited in that cultural vault. As Mack the Knife remarked, "What's the burgling of a bank compared to the founding of a bank?"

NOTES

1. The Singapore workforce was rated the best in the world in 1994 by Washington-based Business Environment Risk Intelligence (BERI). *Fortune* magazine voted it the "world's number one city for business" in November 1995. Official plaques in the airport announce that Changi Airport was voted best in the world in 1994. Singapore Airlines has been without accident and is rated highly for service. See *The Magic of Singapore*, p. 9.

2. As Philip Brett reminded me, the role Elisabeth Hauptmann played in the writing of this opera may be more important than the histories have credited. John Fuegi's biography of Brecht certainly makes the case for Brecht's own plundering for his own gain of the talents and labors of the women who collaborated with him. His portrayal of "whores" may well illustrate his use of the women in his own life.

3. The Necessary Stage commissioned a series of articles on Singapore theater; they have been published in a volume which has a concise history of English theater as part of the introduction. See Birch 1998.

4. My thanks to my Singaporean student Cindy Tan Ching Yee for pointing out these elements in Brecht.

5. Reported in *The Straits Times*, "Two Pioneers of Forum Theatre Trained at Marxist Workshops," February 5, 1994.

6. Thanks to my research assistant, Sharon Pressburg, for this research.

7. Adrian Tan supplied these thoughts on the orchestration.

WORKS CITED

Abbas, Ackbar. 1997. *Hong Kong*. Minneapolis: University of Minnesota Press.

Birch, David. 1998. "Singapore English Drama: A Historical Overview 1958–1985." In *10 Years of Singapore Theatre*, essays commissioned by The Necessary Stage. Singapore: The Necessary Stage Limited.

BrechtBertolt. *Threepenny Opera*. Trans. Desmond Vesey and Eric Bentley. New York: Grove Press, 1960.

Chow, Rey. 1991. *Woman and Chinese Modernity. The Politics of Reading between East and West*. Minneapolis: University of Minnesota Press.

Fook, Chew Yen. 1996. *The Magic of Singapore*. Singapore: New Holland Publishers.

Nahuijs, Col. 1996. "Extracts from the Letters of Col. Nahuijs." In *Travellers' Tales of Old Singapore*, ed. Michael Wise. London: In Print, 19–22.

PART 3.
ACTING MANLY

8. The Britten Era

Philip Brett

The following essay was conceived for an event very different from the Unnatural Acts conference but equally demanding of a sense of occasion and performance. It was the 1997 Proms Lecture, given as part of a central "Britten weekend" of the British Broadcasting Company's annual summer music festival in London, the Henry Wood Promenade Concerts. Delivered to an audience in the main concert hall of the Royal College of Music, it was also broadcast live nationwide.

I have deliberately chosen to talk today about a fiction, the Britten Era. To reduce British musical history from the mid-forties to the mid-seventies to a single expression of this kind is misleading or plain wrong on a number of counts. It would for instance ignore the second wave of the folk music movement that started in the fifties. Even more notably, it would omit the British contribution to what was arguably the most important musical development of the post-war years: if the roots of rock 'n' roll are embedded in the much-looked-down-on southern part of the United States, the vitality of that new synthesis was quickly picked up and reinterpreted in the similarly looked-down-upon northern part of England; and rock music since has been much indebted to the inventiveness, vitality, or sheer bravado of the British contingent within it.

In the world of art music with which I am concerned today, there has been a notable tendency in Britain since the late nineteenth century to focus upon a single figure representative of national musical pride. As my friend Elizabeth Wood reminds me, there has been a kind of relationship between the leading composer of the day and his British public that might be characterized as serial monogamy. The reputation of Sir Edward Elgar, she feels, queered the pitch for Ethel Smyth, whose biography she is completing. There have been grumblings of late that Ralph Vaughan Williams, generous to a fault in his dealings with other musicians of all kinds, nevertheless caused the occlusion of some notable contemporaries of his own. A feature of this singling out has been a complementary doubling which has either bolstered the prestige of the central figure or provided a safety-valve for dissenting connoisseurs: Stanford and Parry, Elgar and Delius, Vaughan Williams and Holst, and finally Britten and Tippett,[1] perhaps the last of these pairs before the onset of pluralism and postmodernism made further such constructions impossible. The challenge for the professional composer within reach of the post of head boy in this earlier situation, then, has been how to work the school rules in favor of his candidacy. This Britten set out to do.

It surely helped in Britten's case that he decided to become a composer of opera. Not only was it a genre in which for one reason or another British composers had not managed to make an impact on the standard repertory, but it also encouraged thought about self-presentation. Of course, operas have to be about something. Britten never wanted to hide behind a cloud of abstract modernism or avant-garde ideas, and would have agreed with one of his librettists, Montagu Slater, in excoriating "that monster, the work of pure art 'unmixed,' as Mr. Eliot has put it somewhere, 'with irrelevant considerations'" (Slater 1935, 364). It is one thing to reject the autonomous modernist view of art, of course, another to find stories that connect to a group beyond one's immediate friends and associates. The library shelves of opera houses are thickly populated with operas once performed and then discarded not because of any necessarily crippling defect in either musical or dramatic technique—well-known operas, after all, abound in these—but because they have very little to say to anyone in the audience. *Paul Bunyan* (1941) was a classic false start, a patronizing attempt to evoke the spirit of a nation not his own by W. H. Auden in which Britten was a somewhat dazzled accomplice—he was quite vague about the exact nature of the title role's manifestation and staging only six months before it opened.

Finding in an imported copy of *The Listener* a radio talk by E. M. Forster on the poetry of George Crabbe barely two months after the staging of *Paul Bunyan* in 1941 was a turning point. In Crabbe's poem "The Borough," and more precisely in its story of the ruffian Peter Grimes, Britten and his partner, Peter Pears, found that "something to say." It was an unlikely and unpromising tale of a rough fisherman who beat and lost his apprentices, and finally went mad and died. Christopher Isherwood, the friend they first turned to as librettist, later told the Britten scholar Donald Mitchell he was "absolutely convinced that it wouldn't work" (Brett 1983, 36). But they saw the potential of turning Grimes into a more sympathetic figure of "difference," a misunderstood dreamer, and worked on their vision as they prepared to return to England in 1942. After the plot had been further transformed by the librettist they eventually chose, the Communist playwright and journalist Montagu Slater, it worked not only stupendously well, as public response to the opening production of 1945 bears out, but also in a way that uncannily connected the

Figure 8.1. Benjamin Britten, Peter Grimes, act II, scene 1 (mm. 3–6 after fig. 17).
Courtesy of Boosey and Hawkes Music Publishers Ltd.

private concerns of a couple of left-wing pacifist lovers to public concerns to which almost anyone could relate in the late twentieth century.

The author Colin MacInnes confided to his private diary in the late 1940s that "Grimes is the homosexual hero. The melancholy of the opera is the melancholy of homosexuality" (Gould 1983, 82). Its theme of the individual who is persecuted by the community for no other reason than his difference cried out to be interpreted in this way, but could not be publicly articulated in those days. A more remarkable and far more penetrating aspect of the allegory, however, had to do with the actual social mechanism of oppression. It is the classic condition of those who do not have access to full status in society that they themselves start believing in the low opinion they perceive others to have of them. Grimes's fate is ultimately determined not simply by his isolation but by his capitulation in this way to the Borough at the climax of act 2, scene 1, a much delayed and extremely powerful cadence on to B-flat, the Borough's own key (fig. 8.1). Upon striking his friend Ellen in response to her "We've failed!" Grimes literally takes up the offstage church congregation's "Amen" in his

"So be it," proceeding to the cadence with "and God have mercy upon me," set to a musical motif (y) that dominates the rest of the opera. David Matthews points out that its "curt, emphatically cadential quality seems graphically to seal Peter's fate" (in Brett 1983, 134), and the four triadic chords that define its limits and the angry brass canon it prompts both indicate that there can be no escape once the die is cast. In this symbolic moment, therefore, Peter internalizes society's judgment of him and enters the self-destructive cycle that inevitably concludes with his suicide. In this moment, Britten may at one level have been addressing his own concerns, because in spite of a certain sangfroid about what he would have called his "queerness," there are many signs and several testimonies to point to his not being comfortable about it.

There were other private issues the opera addressed. One was inevitably the return from the irksome freedom of the America he had never fully liked to a native land about which he was also ambivalent. Since there was a war on, and he and his friends were commonly thought to have shirked their responsibilities by emigrating, he was not likely to receive a universally warm welcome. As a conscientious objector he could have faced an unpleasant term in prison. The opera contains not one but two manhunts, the second of which is one of the most terrifying episodes in modern opera. They surely owe their intensity to Britten's own sense of foreboding and victimization, and served as some sort of catharsis. Imagining the worst is a good way of dealing with a difficult situation, and if Britten's imagination was overheated in this instance, it only served the opera and his career all the better.

If I have stressed the interrelatedness of Britten and Pears's private concerns with the larger themes of Britten's music, it is not simply a matter of my own interest in exploring the stories of other gay English musicians who went to the U.S.A., but also to combat the pointed neglect of the topic. When I began writing about Britten more or less twenty years ago, the subject of his homosexuality had not been broached in relation to his music in any serious way. Here was a composer with sixteen operas, or opera-like works, to his credit, many of which, after *Grimes*, dealt at rather important levels with male relations, often with an obviously homoerotic text or subtext; yet the subject had been ignored as though it didn't exist. There were some good reasons for this. The Sexual Offences Act, which finally legalized homosexual acts between consenting adults in private, did not pass until 1967. All mention of homosexuality on the stage was specifically forbidden until 1958, and all stage material was subject to state license until 1968. Britten himself never mentioned the topic, and it was only in 1980, after Peter Pears had declared the nature of their relationship in a prime-time Easter Sunday television broadcast (of Tony Palmer's film *A Time There Was*), that others felt fully comfortable alluding to the fact.

There was a further and more significant barrier to any criticism that would include material elements, such as politics or sexuality. Art music, like poetry, had become in this century the repository of "transcendent" or "universal" values, which is almost tantamount to saying masculine and heterosexual values. This came about for a number of reasons, but one very strong cause in my estimation was the threat to its status from a widespread notion encapsulated by Havelock Ellis in a single sentence in his book on what he referred to as *Sexual Inversion:* "it has been extravagantly said that all musicians are inverts" (Ellis 1936, 295). In the aftermath of the trials of Oscar Wilde, English musicians, like other artists, cultivated images that were as distant as possible from the connection of effeminacy, aestheticism, and vice that had been discerned in those traumatic events; this cultivation of masculinity and detachment extended from their personalities to their art, and remained virtually unchallenged until quite recently.

Although the attempted separation of life and art produces protection and an honored place for the arts, as Alan Sinfield observes, "it is at the cost of limited influence, marginality, even irrelevance. Their protected status confines them to a reserve, like an endangered species insufficiently robust to cope with the modern world" (Sinfield 1987, 28). A particularly crucial misunderstanding about any relation that might exist between sexuality and music is that it will be or should be concerned exclusively with sexual attraction or with sexual acts, or alternatively with complex psychological scenarios arising from frustrated sexual drives rather than with social mechanisms. It is clear not only that *Peter Grimes* was intended to "cope with the modern world" but also that any suggestive psychological or pathological elements that might detract from its primarily *social* theme of the individual's tragic internalization of community values were steadily eliminated as the work grew to fruition. All mention of a domineering father incorporated into earlier versions of the libretto, for instance, was erased. The result was a brilliant appeal, made more palpable and convincing through music, to the alienation of every member of the audience. "In each of us there is something of a Grimes," wrote Hans Keller, "though most of us have outgrown or at least outwitted him sufficiently not to recognize him too consciously. But we do identify him, and ourselves with him, unconsciously" (Brett 1983, 105).

If it was something of a feat to get the audience to identify with an allegorical figure who could most easily be interpreted as "the homosexual," the basest member of society, and furthermore to identify the problem as one not of the "homosexual condition" but of society's vicious treatment of difference, the opera certainly offered members of its audience a plateful of related social concerns to ponder. It laid bare the paranoid nature of society's scapegoating someone who it feels to be threatening but is not; and asks the audience to consider how each of them might feel at being similarly and inexplicably scapegoated. It questioned the operation of violence, which, as Edmund Wilson saw clearly on his first journey to Britain after the war, including a visit to this opera, affects both sides: everyone is brutalized, not merely the aggressor and the victim. Coinciding with the birth of the welfare state in Britain, it also posed the (always unresolved) question of responsibility in the relation of individual and state in modern capitalistic democracies, and this is where the question of homosexuality becomes so central. The "more liberal view" espoused by the authors sees deviance in particular and criminality in general as a symptom of society's failure, and tends to want to deal with it accordingly by trying either to understand and allow for it, or, in a more problematic strategy, to control it by "medicalizing" it. The opposing view, espoused by those who resist state control in most other spheres, insists on maintaining individual conformity and responsibility, and uses institutionalization as a means of controlling deviance.

Homosexuality is deeply embedded in modern society's idea of itself. Since the trials of Oscar Wilde, exactly a half century earlier than the opera, the male homosexual in particular, as a notionally uniform but actually incoherent identity, had been foregrounded or represented in Anglo-American society and ideology as an internal enemy causing the dislocation of an otherwise ordered society—the McCarthy Era saw an extreme manifestation of this homosexual conspiracy theory. But society is in a permanent state of dislocation stemming directly from its own blockage, its own contradictions. So the dislocation, this internal negativity, was displaced and projected onto those seen ideologically as society's enemies, among whom this "homosexual" was particularly important because of the fragile nature and infinite difficulties surrounding the institutions of heterosexuality, marriage, and the family, and also because of the importance that had accrued since its invention in modern times to sexuality itself, which had replaced religion as the ultimate window into the soul. The immanent failure of the patriarchy is especially demonstrated by, and projected on, those who exercise its privilege as men but undermine the principles of sexual relation and patterns of domination on which patriarchal authority is founded in the modern world. I shall return to this point in my conclusion.

The other operas of the 1940s, *Albert Herring, The Rape of Lucretia,* even *The Little Sweep,* maintain the emphasis on oppression and internalization in different contexts and with different parameters and results. Interestingly, all except *Lucretia* also focus on working-class environments and people—though mixed in *The Little Sweep* with middle-class children with whom those in the audience who are helping to make the opera can more easily identify. (*The Little Sweep* is part of a large entertainment for children entitled *Let's Make an Opera,* and is one of several Britten works to incorporate audience participation.) And the revelation of the hypocritical nature of authority figures is powerfully continued in the person of Lady Billows and her minions in *Albert Herring* as well as in the *Beggar's Opera* realization, where the point is forcibly made that there would be no lawyers, policeman, clergymen, and politicians if there were no thieves, rogues, and whores. Peachum enunciates the lawyer's credo: "We protect and encourage cheats, 'cos we live by them."

Developments in Britten's own life and in British society made the continuing exploration of the oppression/liberation theme an unlikely way forward—the repressive atmosphere of the thirties, like so much else in British life, was swept away in the aftermath of World War II. Yet, paradoxically, Britain under a socialist government seems to have been less stimulating for left-wing idealism than those earlier days. Alan Sinfield (1989, 43–58) has shown how artists and writers responded negatively to the threat the welfare state presented to the notion of individuality they prized so highly as a condition of art. In Britten's case, there appears to have been an increasing conservatism and social assimilation in his public behavior, but I do not find in his works any amelioration of his relations to the state. His adoption of Lytton Strachey's outrageous Freudian view of Queen Elizabeth I for his coronation opera, *Gloriana,* was surely an ambivalent act of homage and aggression. On the other hand, it is true that the later operas, beginning with *Billy Budd,* focus on what might be called microcosmic politics, exploring power within relations themselves. The backdrop of society does not, of course, vanish but is localized even further into a number of small and sometimes claustrophobic worlds—the ship, the schoolroom, the family, or, in *Midsummer Night's Dream,* the wood, both literal and psychological, in which the courtiers, rustics, and warring factions of fairies encounter each other.

In all these works ambivalence tends to reign. Some of it must stem from Britten's own life. In his rueful and moving tribute to Britten, John Gill notes that the partnership of Britten and Pears did not coincide with any of the classic British models (Gill 1995, 12). These were notable for their incorporation of a discrepancy, such as the age difference emblematic of classical pederasty, or the class difference characteristic of the relations of intellectuals like Carpenter, Forster, Ackerley, and others, or the race difference nostalgically celebrated by Alan Hollinghurst in *The Swimming Pool Library,* all of which are obscurely and interestingly connected in an imperial and class-based culture such as that of Britain. Britten and Pears were not only of the same generation, class, and ethnicity, but also both active and celebrated in branches of the same field, doing their bit for the balance of payments—the model of Thatcherite citizenry but for their pacifism, politics, and homosexuality. But Britten's imagination was also caught up with boys, mostly young adolescents. Whether or not he ever acted upon his desires in this regard—Humphrey Carpenter examined the evidence and came to the conclusion he did not—he was clearly preoccupied to a great extent with the question of power which is posed by such relations. The odd stories he told his librettists about a schoolmaster's having raped him and his own father's desire for boys are tell-tale indications (Carpenter 1992, 20, 23). But stronger evidence is contained in his music. His imagination really was focused on the plight of the weaker partner, or "innocent," for which he found musical expression in work after work in terms that no one else in the twentieth century has matched. But only in *Owen Wingrave,* where the "innocent" is arrayed against the bleak and crushing might of the patriarchal family, in which the women identify with the phallic power of the Father, is there possibly a clear identification of composer and victim. In *Billy Budd* and *The Turn of the Screw,* most notably, an ambiguity surrounds the figures of power, Vere and Claggart, Quint and the Governess, that allows for the contemplation of real moral dilemmas, not easy slogans. Those increasingly powerful drumbeats that underpin and undermine Vere's final epiphany in the epilogue to the opera show (along with other musical clues) that he is so hopelessly contaminated by his role in killing other men— as the leader in battle as well as the naval disciplinarian—that his putative "salvation" must be wishful thinking.

This preoccupation with authority does not always take the same turn. The moral and tone of *The Prodigal Son* appear, for instance, to reverse the *carpe diem* anti-establishment attitudes of *Albert Herring* in favor of reconcili-ation, finally, to the law of the Father, personified as all-merciful and munifi-cent in this work in a way that suggests wish fulfillment, not like the Abraham who, in Wilfred Owen's vision incorporated in the *War Requiem,* sends his sons to destruction one by one instead of sacrificing the Ram of Pride. But the preoccupation with patriarchal characters of many kinds is never far distant.

Needless to say, it is impossible here to encapsulate an overview of the operas, and indeed one of their strengths, arising from their ambivalence and moral questioning, is that no two people will agree about their exact program. Critical thought will remain in dialogue about them for as long as they hold their place in the repertory. But the questions that are debated in them still seem in most instances real ones at the end of the twentieth century: questions of identity, of the relation of the individual to society, of power within indi-vidual human relations as a reflection of societal values, the liberal view of sexuality, and the exploration of loss and desire, all presented in music of great clarity, one that balances feeling with restraint in a way that even the conserva-tive opera audiences of our time have been able to comprehend and enjoy.

As I observed at the opening, opera was not a central genre for the British music audience, which Britten could not afford to ignore in any bid for a cen-tral position. About the time of the conception of *Peter Grimes,* Britten accord-ingly began to define his relation to the British musical tradition more clear-ly. An early manifestation was the release of his aggression toward it, which is the noteworthy feature of an article entitled "England and the Folk-Art Prob-lem" that he contributed to an American music journal in 1941. In this essay, Parry and Elgar are projected as the binary opposition haunting English com-position, the one having "stressed the amateur idea and . . . encouraged folk-art," the other emphasizing "the importance of technical efficiency and [wel-coming] any foreign influences that can be profitably assimilated." Studiously avoiding any mention at all of Holst and Vaughan Williams, Britten names Walton, Lambert, Maconchy, Berkeley, Darnton, Lutyens, Rawsthorne, and (with reservations) Ferguson and Rubbra as indicating that "since 1930 the influence of Parry has largely disappeared."

Later in the article Britten reveals his current fascination with "the nearest approach to folk-music today": this he deems to be swing and the spiritual, which, as he points out, are the result of utterly diverse ingredients. The point is to throw the authenticity of folksong of any kind into question, so that "what we call folk-music is no product of a primitive society" and that the "whole conception of folk-song as a germ from which organized music grew may prove to be a false one." The dependence on folksong as raw material is either unsatisfactory (as in *Sacre du Printemps*—Stravinsky gets better marks for its handling in *Les Noces,* and Bartók goes unmentioned), or the sign of a need for discipline which second-rate composers cannot find in themselves. Lurking behind much of the thought is the presence of W. H. Auden, a passage from whose momentous "New Year Letter" (1940) is quoted on the last page as an indication to composers to "accept their loneliness and refuse all refuges, whether of tribal nationalism or airtight intellectual systems."

Britten's few words about actual English folk tunes in this article are marked by the same ambivalence that he showed about England in a letter back to America on his return, where he celebrates the country as "unbelievably beautiful" and yet finds that "the accent is horrible and there is a provincialism & lack of vitality that makes one yearn for the other side" (Mitchell 1991, 1038). "The chief attractions of English folksongs," he writes, "are the sweetness of the melodies, the close connection between words and music, and the quiet, uneventful charm of the atmosphere. This uneventfulness however is part of the weakness of the tunes, which seldom have any striking rhythms or memorable melodic features." The ambivalence expressed here, reflected in so many aspects of Britten's life, did not prevent the composer from making considerable use of these melodies, either by arranging them for recital use or incorporating them in original works.

Ultimately, then, Britten made sure that he had a stake in folksong while emphasizing his independence of the "Pastoral School" by what means were available, largely the very different accompaniments he devised. In the exercise of arrangement, for instance, Britten understood clearly certain things that eluded Cecil Sharp and even Vaughan Williams, who tended always to assign to folksong an idealized, essential artistic quality that was somehow in Sharp's program "to exercise a purifying and regenerative effect" and produce good Englishmen (Sharp 1954, 140). Sharp apparently believed that his own anodyne arrangements preserved, as he said, "the emotional impression which the songs made upon me when sung by the folksingers themselves" (Sharp, 1915, xvi). Such blindness to the effects of changing every single parameter of performance except the notes of the tune (themselves idealized in Sharp's transcriptions, of course) is truly breathtaking viewed from this end of the century. How much more honest was Britten's recognition that the venue changed the genre and turned these songs in effect into lieder or art song.

"Little Sir William," the second song of his first published collection, may be taken as a fair example of the process. Britten's accompaniment adopts a broad narrative march-like style for the first few stanzas and then proceeds, after an almost Waltonian chord built of thirds has disrupted the mood, to portray the dead child's voice by expressive chords, one to a bar, and by creating in the accompaniment a pathetic echo of a motive from the second phrase of the tune. The song, like many in these collections, is dramatized mildly in a manner familiar to admirers of Schubert, and since it carries no obviously modal connotations it is not identifiable as a folksong at all except for its words. There is a delightful recording of Peter Pears singing it in 1946 (EMI Classics CMS 7 64727 2).

Folksong, as manifest for instance in sets of keyboard variations by the Elizabethan and Jacobean virginalist composers, had been an important ingredient of the Pastoralists' relation to English musical history. Projecting the present on to the past, Vaughan Williams wrote of "the great School of Tudor music . . . inheriting its energy and vitality from the unwritten and unrecorded art of its own countryside" (Vaughan Williams 1934, 92). For Britten, therefore, the entire Tudor period was effectively ruled out of his official English antecedents: only Dowland the proto-Purcellian songwriter, as represented by Peter Pears's remarkable artistry, merited more than cursory mention. The choice of Purcell was both rational and literally in tune with Britten's own aesthetic program as a dramatic composer. Everyone tends to pinpoint a different piece to mark the beginning of Britten's involvement with Purcell. My own candidate at present is "Let the florid music praise," the first song of the Auden cycle, *On This Island,* op. 11, of 1937, which exactly captures the quality of Purcell's rhetorical style. Whenever it began, it is no surprise that, folksong settings having paved the way, Purcell realizations should follow. The art of "realization," prominent up to the 1950s, suffered total eclipse at the hands of historically informed performance, and is now mercifully extinct. Seventeenth-century song as a whole works on the principle of vocally impassioned delivery or lyrical impulse, neither of which needs much more than a firm bass and a few chords to support it. Britten's contribution constantly vies for attention with Purcell's melodies or declamatory gestures, and the bifocal effect inevitably becomes distracting. Needless to say, Britten is at his best when Purcell's music is at its strangest: the tiny cantata, *Saul and the Witch at Endor,* for instance, is simply inspired in its use of piano sonorities to re-compose the work. The character and extent of these pieces—they number forty, far more than the demand for recital fodder might seem to require—may start us wondering whether the "realization" process is more an act of appropriation or competition than of homage, another Oedipal episode in the composer's complicated trajectory.

With a strong relation to folksong and the past, and a special investment in the comparatively neglected genre of opera, all that remained to become the national composer of the period was a clearly defined relation to the nation's choral tradition and success within it. Britten started out early on this project with his opus 3, *A Boy Was Born;* but the work seems conceived more for instruments then voices—it is difficult to perform in ways uncharacteristic of the rest the composer's choral music and may have been conceived, as Peter Evans puts it, "to break away from the rather woolly archaisms that had made such collections as the *Oxford Book of Carols* so appealing to his fellow countrymen" (Evans 1979, 86). Again, a considerable change came about with the American years, in fact precisely with the journey back to the homeland on which both *A Ceremony of Carols* and *Hymn to Saint Cecilia* were composed, as though to think of England was to think of choral music. How triumphant these pieces are, combining a secure technique and exquisite sound palette, a modernistic coolness in expression with a plentiful supply of emotional intensity, a musical language distinguished at once by its distinct character as well as its restraint—all the marks of what we think of as classicism, an attribute that cannot easily be discerned in earlier British music of the century. No less successful is the cantata *Rejoice in the Lamb,* written shortly after the return and containing at its center, framed by a Purcellian prelude and postlude and cheerful choruses and solos, a surprisingly fierce choral recitative rehearsing the theme of oppression that was about to boil over in *Peter Grimes.* A pattern was set, which could have lasted through the composer's life, of works of subsidiary importance directed not so much at the church which commissioned many of them and provided a performance venue for the others but toward a social function which appealed to the composer—he often advertised, after all, his belief in the figure of the composer as a servant of the community.

In the *War Requiem* of 1962, however, Britten suddenly seemed to become a victim of his own success simply as a result of inscribing himself into the English oratorio tradition with a major work for soloists, massed choral forces, and orchestra. This work even evoked an ingenious medievalism in its device of troping the liturgical Latin text with a vernacular commentary. The historical resonance, combined with an evocation of the sublime in the form of a bombed cathedral in the heart of Britain's industrial midlands and the metaphysical in the notion of reconciliation beyond the grave, gave the piece a portentous and grandiose character which seems oddly more of the age of Elgar than that of post–World War II. Some listeners have wondered, too, whether the evocation of the end of Elgar's *Dream of Gerontius* in the A-major conclusion ("*In paradisum*" / "Let us rest now") is sufficiently undermined by the two interruptions of boys and bells sounding the portentous augmented fourth, itself so evocative of that angst-ridden genre of the period that David Drew so wittily christened the "Cheltenham Symphony." In terms of politics, too, questions have arisen about the unilateral and unmodified application of a First World War pacifist message in a post–Second World War context as though the Holocaust were not an additional factor to be reckoned with. The integrity of Britten's homosexual politics explains a great deal here, particularly the use of fellow pacifist and homosexual Wilfred Owen's poetry as the means by which to transmit his very real anger about the fate of young men sent to their deaths by an unfeeling patriarchal system as well as his critique of empty religious forms that are in collusion with that system. And it may not be too much to suggest that a metaphorical extension of those young male bodies can be made to all innocent victims of patriarchal systems, including those who perished in the Nazi concentration camps. But the choice of a major establishment genre in which to couch these messages gives pause and leads to the connecting of several threads that I have tried to explore.

To return for a moment to the questions of folksong and realization. If one adds to the sixty-eight folksong arrangements the many folksongs and singing games, traditional or composed, in the operas, and the final *Suite on English Folk-Tunes*, op. 90, and if one adds to that the forty-three realizations and the references to historic English music (e.g., in *The Young Person's Guide to the Orchestra* and *Gloriana*), it becomes clear that Britten had as great an investment in these two linked phenomena as any bona fide member of the "Pastoral School." Furthermore, Britten's being asked to write the four sample folksong piano accompaniments for an anthology published in 1968 by Maud Karpeles, Cecil Sharp's co-researcher and successor, was surely an acknowledgment of his position as the leading English composer of the folksong movement since the death of Vaughan Williams, and therefore in some way to be accounted the latter's successor as leading national composer.

Once having distanced himself from Vaughan Williams and others, both by his "England and the Folk-Art Problem" manifesto (discreetly published abroad and not much remarked on since) and also by the very nature of his musical response to traditional musical material, Britten was nevertheless concerned to infiltrate and dominate their chosen fields of activity on his own terms. His sponsorship of the alternative Percy Grainger and his reclamation of Holst through the incorporation of his daughter into the working household at Aldeburgh were only later touches to a plan that, looked at one way, seemed from the moment of return in 1942 to be matching the ideology of the "Pastoral School" item by item. The invocation of the powerful British sea myth, again on the composer's own terms, in *Peter Grimes* and *Billy Budd*, and the substitution of Aldeburgh, Suffolk, and East Anglia for Hereford, Gloucestershire, and the West Country, a substitution formalized by the founding of the Aldeburgh Festival as the polar opposite to the Three Choirs Festival, all seem to fit the pattern, as did the co-opting of the British choral tradition along the way. "Finding one's place in society as a composer is not a straightforward job," wrote Britten in a speech, like Vaughan Williams's *National Music*, originally delivered to Americans, and sounding remarkably like the earlier document in tone (Britten 1965, 14). Perhaps, as part of returning home, Britten had even consciously understood and applied to himself Vaughan Williams's impassioned belief that younger British composers (he mentions Walton, Bliss, Lambert, and Hadley) could not expel traditional music from their systems, even though they might deny what he called "their birthright."[2] As has often been remarked, Britten certainly moderated his eclecticism during the very same period that the onset of folksong and Purcell arrangements occurred. Perhaps, then, he ultimately understood that, returning to his native country and exorcising certain fears in the cathartic score of *Peter Grimes,* he also needed to fulfill his role in ways that were laid out by Vaughan Williams in a gracious review of Britten's first published volume of folksong arrangements. The older composer, casting himself in the role of an "old fogey," welcomes the "divagations," either to right or to left, of the younger generation "so that in the end the straight line is kept intact" (Mitchell 1991, 347). The line was kept indeed, arguably to run on through Maxwell Davies.

Intact, perhaps, but not exactly straight. For what makes the crucial difference between Britten and his predecessor as a notionally "leading British composer" is the different way in which he pursued a social and political agenda itself far removed from the liberal socialism of Vaughan Williams. Along the lines of inter-war homosexual pacifist ideals, it puts personal relations above allegiance to institutions; it puts the individual before society; it tends to show institutions such as the law, the military, and the church as hypocritical, unjust, or simply evil; it favors erotic relations and exposes marriage; the patriarchal family it portrays as shallow and oppressive; justice for the victim and the victimized are passionately argued; and the difficulty of homoerotic relations is presented as a legacy of this society. In much work that has been done on the politics of marginality in recent years, it has been observed that the center needs the margin to supplement or, in other terms, to act as a symptom of, what is lacking in the center. Thus a certain contained use of the marginal is necessary for the maintenance of the center. For instance, what if Britten had been forced out of his already transparent closet by some unthinkable event? It is hard to believe that any public exposure of his homosexuality would have harmed his career greatly. When Sir John Gielgud was convicted of importuning in a Chelsea mews in 1953, I remember my mother's phrase, "idols with feet of clay," as we drove off to Stratford for yet another dose of his Prospero's vocal elixir. Even Michael Jackson does not seem to have been placed beyond the pale by his fans, and since most humans live with a sense of the complexity of gender and sexuality, it is quite likely that not only pop stars but also artists of all sorts gain from projecting their sexuality as "simultaneously provocative and reassuring," to borrow a phrase from Dave Marsh (1987, 216) quoted by Martha Nell Smith in the context of a discussion of the "blatant homoeroticisms" evident in Bruce Springsteen videos (1992, 204). Britten surely understood this, if only intuitively, since the unspoken non-mystery of a sexuality marked by his constant appearance with Peter Pears in every context (a gesture hiding the deeper complication of his sublimated pederasty) was as much part of his image as the constant presentation of his own childhood, of his pacifism, and of his regional affiliations.

In a recent book, John Champagne discerns the two critical responses to what he calls the Other, or the marginal. One, the liberal humanist response, grants the Other greater subjectivity by trying to remake it in the image of the dominant or center: this process has been at work in white responses to African American music, or in the male canon's tentative acceptance of women composers, for instance. The second valorizes or privileges the marginality of the Other, not by extending greater subjectivity to it, but by making a resistant and transgressive use of the very lack at the center which first caused the construction of the margin. These two processes are, of course, not separate but contingent on each other. I would like in my final remarks to argue for the effectiveness of Britten's own version of marginal politics—realizing full well as I try that my own effort to represent difference may already be irretrievably compromised by my appearing under the auspices of *the* Proms Lecture funded by *the* BBC. "All a poet can do is to warn" is the conclusion of the Wilfred Owen epigraph on the cover of the score of the *War Requiem*. But in order to warn, or do anything else, the poet/composer has to be heard. What North America may have taught Britten and Pears, then, was that to work for centrality at home would ultimately be more artistically and therefore politically effective than marginality abroad—as a means of articulating a message to society from that margin where Britten, at least, always imagined he lived, as countless tales of his depressions and darknesses attest. His old left friends like Slater and Auden were irritated to see him waltzing up and down church aisles on the arm of the Queen Mother; gay men like myself often have to work through a certain resentment at his exercise of privilege without disclosure; younger radicals presumably have no time for his compromised politics at all. But granted the isolated space of art music and the difficulty of any effective opposition along the lines indicated by Champagne's second option, especially in the pre-1967 conditions under which Britten lived and under which his social imagination was formed, one still needs to grant to Britten consistency and integrity in pursuing, sometimes to his friends' acute discomfort, a fairly incisive and certainly passionate line on the linked issues of pacifism and homosexuality in relation to subjectivity, nationality, and the institutions of the capitalistic democracy under which he lived. This line he maintained in his work rather than his life, where he acted out a role of charm and compliance laced with occasional brutality. The political stance of the music is all the more remarkable because it barely exists anywhere else in art music outside avant-garde circles already too self-marginalized to offer any hope of serious intervention in the status quo. And, as a starting point, it certainly wins hands down over the tired and tiring credo of the many composers today who are openly gay but vow that homosexuality has absolutely nothing whatsoever to do with their music; or those composers—composers who just happen to be gay—who ask for homosexuality to be accepted as ordinary rather than seeing it as a site from which to disrupt present notions of subjectivity and from which to imagine different organizations of power and pleasure, as I believe Britten did.

Britten's artistic effort was an attempt to disrupt the center that it occupied with the marginality that it expressed. In this it was comparable to Forster's achievement, which, though it did not specifically alleviate the persecution of his own kind, nevertheless contributed, in the novel *A Passage to India*, a good deal to the eventual downfall of the British Empire. "We are after all queer & left & conshies which is enough to put us, or make us put ourselves, outside the pale, apart from being artists as well," wrote Pears in response to a letter from Britten about "all those other dreary HRH's, you know" (Carpenter 1992, 419–20).[3] It was the achievement of the Britten Era, then—and this achievement was in no way contradicted by Britten's contemporary, Sir Michael Tippett—that British classical or art music became during those years indelibly queer and left and conshie. And instead of being instantly marginalized, Britten's music has traveled all over the world. There is no need to argue that in the process of its inevitable assimilation it may have had some transformative effect; it is enough to note that, for anyone inclined to explore beyond its deceptively "conservative" and desperately inviting surface, it offers not only a rigorous critique of the past but also the vision of a differently organized reality for the future.

NOTES

1. Sir Charles Villiers Stanford (1852–1924), Sir Hubert Parry (1848–1918), Sir Edward Elgar (1857–1934), Frederick Delius (1862–1934), Ralph Vaughan Williams (1872–1958), Gustav Holst (1874–1934), Benjamin Britten (1913–1976), Sir Michael Tippett (1905–1998); some would extend the pairing to Sir Peter Maxwell Davies (1934–) and Sir Harrison Birtwistle (1934–). The plethora of titles owes something to the fact that Queen Victoria's adored consort, Albert, was himself a composer. Britten's ending up as Lord Britten of Aldeburgh, the first composer to gain a life peerage, surely has some bearing on the argument of this essay. He would otherwise have tied neck and neck in the British honor stakes with Vaughan Williams, since both gained the more exclusive and intellectually prestigious Order of Merit (Britten took T. S. Eliot's place among the twenty-four to hold this distinction). Still, Rosamund Strode's view that he accepted the peerage not for himself, but because he "just felt it was marvellous for music," is also convincing (Carpenter 1992, 580).

2. Vaughan Williams's metaphorical evocation of jazz and neoclassicism here reflects both his passion and the different terminology of the day: "they may deny their birthright; but having once drunk deep of the living water no amount of Negroid emetics or 'Baroque' purgatives will enable them to expel it from their system" (1934, 85).

3. "Conshies" is the British abbreviation for "conscientious objectors" or "pacifists." "HRH's" stands for "His/Her Royal Highnesses."

WORKS CITED

Brett, Philip, ed. 1983. *Benjamin Britten: Peter Grimes.* Cambridge: Cambridge University Press.

Britten, Benjamin. 1941. "England and the Folk-Art Problem." *Modern Music* 18: 71–75.

————. 1965. *On Receiving the First Aspen Award.* London: Faber & Faber.

Carpenter, Humphrey. 1992. *Benjamin Britten: A Biography.* London: Faber & Faber.

Champagne, John. 1995. *The Ethics of Marginality.* Minneapolis: University of Minnesota Press.

Ellis, Havelock. 1936. *Sexual Inversion.* Vol. 2, Part 2 of *Studies in the Psychology of Sex.* 3rd ed. Philadelphia: F. A. Davis, 1915. Reprinted "complete in four volumes," New York: Random House.

Evans, Peter. 1979. *The Music of Benjamin Britten.* London: Dent.

Forster, E. M. 1941. "George Crabbe: The Poet and the Man." *The Listener,* May 29. Reprinted in Brett, pp. 3–7.

Gill, John. 1995. *Queer Noises: Male and Female Homosexuality in Twentieth-Century Music.* London: Cassell.

Gould. Tony. 1983. *Inside Outsider: The Life and Times of Colin MacInnes.* London: Chatto & Windus.

Hollinghurst, Alan. 1988. *The Swimming Pool Library.* London: Chatto & Windus.

Karpeles, Maud, ed. 1968. *Eighty English Folk Songs from the Southern Appalachians.* London: Faber & Faber. (Britten's specimen folksong accompaniments appear on pp. 11–14.)

Keller, Hans. 1952. "*Peter Grimes:* The Story; the Music Not Excluded." In *Benjamin Britten: A Commentary,* ed. Donald Mitchell and Hans Keller. London: Rockcliff. Reprinted in Brett, pp. 105–20.

Marsh, Dave. 1987. *Glory Days: Bruce Springsteen in the 1980s.* New York: Pantheon.

Mitchell, Donald, et al., eds. 1991. *Letters from a Life: The Selected Letters and Diaries of Benjamin Britten.* London, Faber & Faber.

Sharp, Cecil J. [1907] 1954. *English Folk Song: Some Conclusions.* 3rd ed., rev. Maud Karpeles. London: Methuen.

Sharp, Cecil J., ed. 1916. *One Hundred English Folksongs.* Boston: Oliver Ditson.

Sinfield, Alan. 1989. *Literature, Politics, and Culture in Postwar Britain.* Berkeley: University of California Press.

Slater, Montagu. 1935. "The Purpose of a Left Review." *Left Review* 1, no. 9 (June): 362–67.

Smith, Martha Nell. 1992. "Sexual Mobilities in Bruce Springsteen: Performance as Commentary." In *Present Tense: Rock & Roll and Culture,* ed. Anthony DeCurtis. Durham, N.C.: Duke University Press.

Vaughan Williams, Ralph. 1934. *National Music.* London: Oxford University Press.

9. A Question of Balls: The Sexual Politics of Argentine Soccer

Jeffrey Tobin

SEXUAL SUSPECTS

There is a confessional convention among intellectuals who write about soccer—a moment when the writer admits that his spirit may be willing, but his flesh is weak.[1] Eduardo Galeano, an Uruguayan intellectual, begins his history of soccer with a "confession" of his adolescent nocturnal fantasies and of his failure to realize those fantasies on the soccer field.

> Like all Uruguayans, I wanted to be a soccer player. I played so well, I was a marvel, but only at night, while I slept: during the day I was the worst player with two left feet that had been seen on the playgrounds of my country. (Galeano 1995, 1)[2]

Galeano's history of soccer is an intellectual admirer's contribution, as a writer, to the sport to which he was not able to contribute as a player or even as a true fan. Umberto Eco, an Italian intellectual, also begins one of his essays on soccer by confessing his failings as both a player and a fan. Unlike Galeano, Eco does not channel an unfulfillable desire to play soccer gloriously into a desire to glorify soccer through writing.

> Many malignant readers, seeing how I discuss here the noble sport of soccer with detachment, irritation, and (oh, all right) malevolence, will harbor the vulgar suspicion that I don't love soccer because soccer has never loved me, for from my earliest childhood I belonged to that category of infants or adolescents who, the moment they kick the ball—assuming that they manage to kick it—promptly send it into their own goal or, at best, pass it to the opponent, unless with stubborn tenacity they send it off the field, beyond hedges and fences, to become lost in a basement or a stream or to plunge among the flavors of the ice-cream cart. And so his playmates reject him and banish

> him from the happiest of competitive events. And no suspicion will ever be more patently true. I will say more. In an attempt to feel like the others (just as a terrified young homosexual may obstinately repeat to himself that he "has" to like girls), I often begged my father, a sober but loyal fan, to take me with him to the game. (Eco 1986, 167)

Eco's analogy between an intellectual boy who tries to like soccer and a homosexual who tries to like girls is not incidental. Eco recognizes a connection between compulsory soccer fandom and compulsory heterosexuality, and between non-fans such as himself and gays. Juan José Sebreli, an Argentine intellectual, makes a similar connection between an intellectual's failure as a fan and his failure as a man.

> A laborer in a factory, an employee in an office, a student in high school, or a neighbor in the *barrio* who would prefer reading or serious music will immediately suffer the quarantine decreed by his companions, and the suspicion of a dubious sexuality will weigh on him. The timid, weak, or introverted boy or adolescent male who does not play soccer is the victim of the aggression of all his companions and even his teachers. The soccer fanatics are not only hostile toward the fans of an opposing team, but principally against those who are in no way passionate about soccer, in whom they see their true enemies. (Sebreli 1981, 32)

Sebreli recognizes that working-class fans are hostile toward the fans of an opposing club, but he claims that they are even more hostile to "certain individuals—the intellectuals, the strange, the different" who are not "passionate about soccer." Thus, Sebreli's observations about soccer fandom in Argentina correspond with Eco's observations about soccer fandom in Italy. In both countries, working-class soccer fans suspect those uninterested in soccer of having a "dubious sexuality."[3]

Much as working-class soccer fans question the sexuality of intellectual non-soccer fans, Argentine intellectuals routinely question the sexuality of non-intellectual soccer players and fans. Sebreli argues that soccer players and fans tend to be "unconscious or latent homosexuals," and that the homophobia of the soccer world is a defense against repressed homosexual desire (Sebreli 1981, 93). Similarly, Marcelo Suárez-Orozco—an Argentine anthropologist located in the United States—identifies homosexual symbolism in Argentine soccer-stadium chants. Suárez-Orozco's immediate aim is to distinguish his interpretation from earlier psychoanalytic interpretations of soccer, in which the goal was read as the mother's vagina. Suárez-Orozco argues that soccer should be interpreted in terms of homosexual rather than heterosexual desire because "after one's team has scored a goal, the fans in orgasmic joy chant how their team has just put the ball 'through the asshole' of the rival team" (Suárez-Orozco 1982, 19). Eduardo Archetti—an Argentine anthropologist located in Norway—is in general agreement with Suárez-Orozco, but he also cites two stadium chants that express "the normality of heterosexuality." Both chants are anti-English. In the first chant, recorded following Argentina's defeat by England in the 1966 World Cup, Argentine fans sung about the queen that a star player *"le clava su poronga,"* that is to say, "nails her with his prick" (Archetti 1997, 210). In the second chant, recorded at the 1986 World Cup, four years after Argentina's defeat by England in the Malvinas/Falklands War, the Argentine fans sung about Margaret Thatcher that Maradona *"te anda buscando / para meterla por detrás,"* which is to say, "is looking for you / to stick it in from behind" (ibid.). For Archetti, the fact that Queen Elizabeth and Margaret Thatcher are women makes the chants "heterosexual." It is not insignificant that the queen and the former prime minister are women, and that they are women who wield political power. Nevertheless, it misses the point to classify the chants cited by Archetti as "heterosexual," just as it misses the point to classify the chants cited by Suárez-Orozco as "homosexual." What the chants cited by Archetti and Suárez-Orozco have in common is that they are sodomitical. It is relatively insignificant whether the anuses that are penetrated in these chants belong to female or male bodies.

Sodomy should not be conflated with homosexuality. To state the obvious, sodomy is not necessarily homosexual and homosexuality is not necessarily sodomitical, but as Leo Bersani observes, there is a "widespread confusion in heterosexual *and* homosexual men between fantasies of anal and vaginal sex" (Bersani 1994, 251). I believe this confusion of orifices marks both Freudian and Foucaultian theories of heterosexuality. Freud argued that in the infant imagination "sexual intercourse takes place at the anus" (Freud 1955, 78). Lee Edelman observes that this infantile belief has the effect of placing sodomy at the origin of heterosexual desire.

> Thus in the first instance the primal scene is always perceived as sodomitical, and it specifically takes shape as a sodomitical scene between sexually undifferentiated partners, both of whom, fantasmatically at least, are believed to possess the phallus. In a sense, then, the primal scene as Freud unpacks it presupposes the imaginative priority of a sort of protohomosexuality. (Edelman 1994, 180)

Note that vaginal intercourse, in this formulation, is constituted as a species of sodomy and that heterosexuality is constituted as secondary to homosexuality. Foucault made a similar observation about Plutarch, that he "borrowed from the erotics of boys its fundamental and traditional features" and used them as a model for heterosexual love (Foucault 1986, 205). I would argue, though, that the active-masculine-penetrator and passive-feminine-penetrated schematization identified by Foucault (1986, 29–30) is also borrowed from the erotics of boys. The putative logic is that being anally penetrated feminizes a man because women are vaginally penetrated in heterosexual genital intercourse. A man's anus is supposed to be read as a substitute for the vagina, but it is more accurate to read the vagina as a substitute for the anus, at least in the Argentine discourse of sexuality. In Argentina, sodomy has been routinely imagined according to the binary logic of active-dominant-masculine-penetrator and passive-dominated-feminine-penetrated. There are indications, however, that vaginal intercourse has not been so securely imagined according to this logic. Donna Guy, in her study of prostitution in early-twentieth-century Buenos Aires, notes that female prostitutes were represented as dangerous in general and as receptacles of venereal disease in particular, but that male prostitutes "were ignored as a source of illness" (Guy 1991, 86). It seems that the vagina was considered dangerous and contaminating in a way that the anus was not.[4] Accordingly, vaginal intercourse is not as consistently read according to the active-passive dichotomies of masculine-feminine hermeneutics as is anal intercourse.[5] Thus, the penetrator-penetrated schematization theorized by Foucault (1988) may fit well the top-bottom politics of homosexual anal intercourse and of the Argentine soccer stadium, but it fails to account for the politics of heterosexual vaginal intercourse which, at least in Argentina, are frequently contested.

EPISTEMOLOGY OF THE LOCKER ROOM

The opposition between active real men and passive sexual suspects informs the exchanges between fans of opposing Argentine soccer clubs. In his analysis of Argentine soccer stadium chants, Archetti argues that "what seems clear is that the fans of one team [...] are the real machos, the real men, able to force the other fans or social actors to play the homosexual" (Archetti 1997, 209). Within that general framework, however, I would like to call attention to the ways in which the fans of opposing clubs define "real men." The paradigmatic rivalry in the world of Argentine soccer is that between the fans of Argentina's two biggest soccer clubs: Boca Juniors and River Plate. Boca fans and River fans not only cast aspersions on each other's masculinity, but they do so in different, telling ways. River fans tend to accuse Boca players of sodomy, while Boca fans tended to accuse River players of effeminacy. Each soccer moiety defines its masculine ideal by paying attention to bodily skills, manners, and morals that are partially opposed to and partially outside the rival's list of optimal masculine attributes. Opposing fans often talk past each other because the contest is not only about who is a sodomite and who is a fag. It is also about which is worse, sodomy or effeminacy? Whose categorization of masculinity will be used? To a great extent, a soccer fan's answer will correspond with a particular partisan political position or a specific class consciousness. Not coincidentally, Argentina's President Carlos Menem is an avid River fan, as were most of the generals who led the juntas of 1976–1983. The historical record indicates that Juan Perón and some of his key supporters were fans of Racing Club, but Boca fans are perceived to be overwhelmingly Peronist and there is a popular/populist chant that declares *"Boca, Perón / Un solo corazón"* (Boca, Perón / A single heart). The fans of both clubs tend to be working class, but fans of River Plate are more likely to identify up, with the middle class, and to advocate rational, Menemist economic policies, while fans of Boca Juniors are more likely to identify with the working class and to advocate populist-Peronist social justice over economic rationalization.

The competing masculinities of Boca and River have been epitomized in the career of Héctor "El Bambino" Veira. Veira was a star player for River before becoming the coach of that club. His long, wavy blond hair and prolific goal-scoring made him an idol of River fans and a target for Boca fans, who often taunted him for being too pretty. By 1992 Veira was widely rumored to be Menem's pick to become the coach of Argentina's national team following the 1994 World Cup, but then he was arrested for sodomizing a twelve-year-old boy, a River fan, and was sentenced to prison. When Veira had served only a portion of his sentence, Menem intervened with the court to have the charge against Veira reduced from "violation" to "molestation." The reduction was based on the finding that there had been no penetration. Veira was not rehired by River Plate, and instead became the coach of the San Lorenzo soccer club. The team won the national championship the following season, but Veira's comeback was marred by the taunting to which he was subjected by the fans of opposing clubs, who would lower their pants and, pointing to their behinds, shout, "Here's an ass for you, Bambino." In 1996, Veira was hired to become the coach of Boca Juniors, a turn of events that would have been unimaginable four years earlier, when Veira was firmly entrenched in the River Plate family.

During my fieldwork in Buenos Aires in 1995, the Veira case was often in the news and was a frequent topic of discussion among soccer fans. Most fans said that it is common for star players and coaches to avail themselves of the boys who eagerly solicit contact with their idols. All that made the Veira case exceptional was that he was caught.[6] River fans I interviewed said that the club was better off without Veira than they had been with him. Indeed, River won several national and international championships in the years following Veira's dismissal. The club's subsequent coaches all adopted a strict code regarding players' dress (formal), jewelry (no earrings), and hair (short), perhaps in an effort to confirm the club's manliness. Many Boca fans I interviewed already called on the club to hire Veira, who at the time was still coaching San Lorenzo. It seems Veira's sodomy conviction made him an outcast among the River fans who for many years were his most devoted supporters, but at the same time, he became a favorite of Boca fans, who had long been his principal detractors. It is, however, difficult to determine whether Veira's popularity with Boca fans was because of, or—as is more likely—despite his sodomy conviction. As a rule, fans of River, San Lorenzo, and Boca all declined to label Veira "gay" or "homosexual." Gay fans, however, tended to be strongly supportive of Veira, regardless of the fans' club affiliations. They tended not to identify Veira as "gay," but still to identify him as a fellow victim of homophobia. Some argued that the boy was not innocent and that he got exactly what he wanted from the soccer star. Others worried that condemning man-boy sexual relations opened the doors to condemning man-man sexual relations. One gay

Boca fan explained to me that gays should oppose any and all instances of sexual stigmatization since gays will always be among those whom society considers sexually deviant. The only soccer fan I interviewed who adamantly condemned Veira was a straight male fan of Argentinos Juniors. He expressed disgust that Menem used his influence to reduce the charge against Veira, arguing that "it does not matter to me if it is with a boy or a girl, what is reprehensible is for an adult to exploit a child." In explaining that he had nothing against homosexuality, the fan echoed the legal decision that released Veira from prison: "When I go to the bar with my friends to watch a game, and Argentinos Juniors scores a goal, we hug and kiss. There's no penetration, but it's still homosexual."

The controversy surrounding the Veira case reveals that in addition to taunting one another about practicing sodomy, Argentine soccer fans also tend to believe, regardless of their own sexual orientation, that sodomy is common in the soccer world. Soccer players are admired as models of masculinity, and masculinity connotes a sex drive that is ultimately uncontainable, either by female resistance or by female absence. As León Gindín, an Argentine sexologist, explains, "If a guy is confined for four, five, or six years in a setting where there is an abundance of persons of the same sex, after a certain period of abstinence he will want to penetrate whatever surface is at hand" (Gíndin, quoted in Bianco 1994, 7). Sexual suspicions are inevitable because soccer is itself suspect. Fans know that their soccer-playing idols are virile—in the sense of strongly sexually driven—and that they are men who live in a world of men. In this situation, a man who practices sodomy is, as always, a sexual suspect, but so is the man who abstains—whose sex drive proves less than compelling. Fans, too, are sexual suspects because of the intensity and the depth of their fandom. "Boca is a passion" or even "my passion," according to T-shirts and bumper stickers. "Racing Club is my heart" according to a banner hung week after week at the Avellaneda stadium. And a River fan explained to me, "You can change jobs or even your wife, but never your club." Any man who does not have a club to feel that way about is a sexual suspect, but so is the man who does have a club to feel that way about—as do the millions of "real men" who are never as impassioned or excited by a woman as they are by a natural-born goal-scorer. Week after week, they go the stadium to admire strong and dexterous young men, and to accuse opposing fans of sexually suspicious behaviors.

THE NATIONAL TEAM

Soccer is, of course, a manly concern, and so is the nation (Mosse 1985). The national soccer team in particular, as Archetti observes, is a model and a mirror of male virtues (Archetti 1994, 2). As such it has been a major site for contests about Argentine masculinity. Whose style of masculinity will be exemplified by the national team? Early in the century, there were major conflicts about whether Argentina would be represented by Anglo-Argentines or Creole-Argentines (Archetti 1994). By the 1920s, upper-class Creoles had thoroughly replaced upper-class Anglos and the conflict came to be about whether working-class professional players would replace profession-class amateur players (Mason 1995). By the 1934 World Cup, Argentine (and other South American) players were changing their citizenship in order to play on the national teams of Italy and Spain. From that time until now, the relationship among ancestory, birth, residency, and citizenship has been hotly debated by fans in Argentina and much of the rest of the world. Argentines have also been hypersensitive to which region, club, or style is represented—or not represented—on the national team.

Daniel Passarella was a star player for River Plate, for Argentina's national team, and for Italy's Fiorenze soccer club before becoming the coach of River Plate in the wake of Veira's sodomy conviction. As coach of both River Plate and the national team, Passarella instigated the policies prohibiting the inclusion of players with long hair or earrings. Passarella's many critics also detected a racial bias in the coach's policies. Passarella has chosen players for his teams who are not only clean-cut and jewelry-free, but who also tend to look "European" as opposed to "*criollo.*" Passarella justified his choice of players by explaining that he had to consider the image of Argentina that the national team presents to the world when, for example, "they change planes in Frankfurt." *Sólo Fútbol*—an Argentine weekly soccer magazine—reacted to Passarella's reference to the Frankfurt airport by putting on the cover a photograph of twenty-three identical clean-cut, square-jawed, blond-haired, Aryan-looking men wearing the uniform of the national team, standing in perfectly straight rows and columns, with the title, "The National Team to Come." Note that few Argentines and very few Argentine professional soccer players resemble the model used for the *Sólo Fútbol* cover. Note, also, that Passarella's nickname is "the Kaiser" because of his tough, disciplinary style, and also because he was the captain of the Argentine national team that won the World Cup in Argentina in 1978, in the midst of the military dictatorship. The media probed Passarella's rigid comportment policies in full awareness of the nationalist, racist, masculinist, and homophobic associations those policies have in Argentine society.

On July 4, 1995, the weekly sports magazine *El Gráfico* published an interview with Passarella. The seventy-third question in the one hundred-question interview was "Would you select a homosexual?" to which Passarella answered with a simple "No" (Alegre 1995, 13). That "No" soon became the center of a debate that filled several newspaper and magazine pages and many hours of radio airtime. A week after the publication of Passarella's interview in *El Gráfico*, Carlos Jáuregui, then president of the organization Gays y Lesbianas por los Derechos Civiles, said that Passarella's policy against gay players was irrelevant since "there is in fact a homosexual player on the junior national team and on the senior team, too, though I am not sure about this last one"

(Jáuregui, quoted in *Clarín,* July 13, 1995, 43). In later comments, Jáuregui confirmed that there was, in fact, a gay man on the senior team, but that he was not necessarily a player—thereby suggesting that he belonged to the coaching staff. Despite pressure from journalists, Jáuregui refused to name names.

> It's that it seems nobody understands that there are gays everywhere. That is the reality: in the armed forces, in politics, in the art world, in the Church. They handle it with more or less hypocrisy, with more or less liberty, but we have been, are, and will be everywhere. Since yesterday morning when I said this, several journalists are pushing me to give names, but away from the microphones they know perfectly who I am talking about." (Jáuregui, quoted in *Página/12,* July 13, 1995, 18)

Jáuregui explained that the news story should not be about the identification of the players but about the fact that Passarella discriminates on the basis of sexual orientation (Jáuregui 1995a, 27). Jáuregui also deflected questions about the identities of gay players on the national team by observing that "in the two or three most important gay discos in Buenos Aires, Saturday night you always see three or four famous faces from the world of soccer" (Jáuregui, quoted in Enzetti 1995, 16).

Jáuregui's claims were supported by Cris Miró, a prominent transvestite. In figure 9.1, Miró is posed in the jersey of her favorite club, Boca Juniors. In the accompanying interview she claims, suggestively, that "there are many Boca players who have my autograph on their T-shirts" (Miró, quoted in Olivera 1996, 94). Miró was an important figure in the Argentine debate about homosexuality because of her crossover success as the only (known) transvestite to headline a straight, mainstream revue in Buenos Aires. She appeared as the principal *vedette* (female sex symbol) in a show on Avenida Corrientes, displaying her feminine charms to an audience that was in no way marked as gay. As a socially sanctioned object of heterosexual male desire, Miró blurred the bourgeois boundary between homosexuality and heterosexuality. Miró's attachment to Boca Juniors could be construed as consistent with Boca's status as the prototypical lower-class soccer club—it is very hard to imagine Miró posed in the jersey of River Plate—but Miró also succeeded as a female sex symbol for a downtown audience. Middle-class men who identified themselves as straight accepted Miró as an appropriate object of male desire. Thus, in their own ways, Jáuregui and Miró each argued that there are gays—or gay desire—"everywhere."

Despite Jáuregui's claim that many soccer players are gay and Miró's claim to have boyfriends who are soccer players, and despite the widespread belief that sodomy is common in the soccer world, very few players identify themselves as "gay" or "homosexual." Moreover, in the wake of Jáuregui's comments, almost all of the players on the national team found it necessary to deny being gay or knowing of any gay soccer players. One reading of this discrepancy

Figure 9.1. Cris Miró wearing Boca jersey.

would be that gay players are closeted. Another reading is that most of the players who are sexually active with other men do not identify themselves as "gay" precisely because they are sexually active and not passive. Justin Fashanu, a professional soccer player in England, is one of the very few professional soccer players in the world who identifies as "homosexual." He explains, however, "I'm not a 5'2" effeminate stereotype. People say football is a macho business, but I think I'm very macho" (Fashanu, quoted in Simpson 1994, 91). Mark Simpson concludes that

> The Fashanu phenomenon seems to have shown that the active homosexual (and it matters not one jot what Fashanu in fact *does* in his bedroom —something about which the public knows nothing—compared to how he *acts* on the field) who takes part in active sports, apparently disavowing "the feminine" and penetration as much as if not more than his straight pals, can now gain an honorary, if uneasy, membership of the male club (Simpson 1994, 91).

The active imperative may be even stronger in Argentina than in England. I suspect that among working-class, Argentine men, "the active homosexual" is no homosexual at all, so his membership in the male club is neither honorary nor uneasy. The "gay" label marks a man only if he is penetrated by another man. This distinction between working-class and middle-class men in Buenos Aires is analogous to the distinction between rural and urban men that Roger Lancaster finds in Nicaragua (Lancaster 1992). In both cases, lower-class men identify gayness with sexual submission, while dominant-class—urban or intellectual—men define gayness as same-sex sexual activity (or passivity).

Following Jáuregui's statements, everybody in the Argentine soccer world was asked to comment on whether or not gays were or should be allowed to be on Argentina's national team. Passarella expressed resentment that his one word answer to one question in a hundred-question interview was overshadowing issues more directly related to the national team and its performance. He explained that "it is a personal taste. Like if I did not want a player who is too tall," and he argued that "this is a democratic country" in which everyone is allowed to have his own tastes and to act accordingly (Passarella, quoted in Proietto 1995, 26). The editors of *El Gráfico*, probably in order to ensure their ongoing access to Passarella, published an article by Aldo Proietto that echoed Passarella's self-defense.

> The coach does not discriminate, he selects. And he has every right to do so. Nobody should be alarmed. He would call Blacks and Jews if they answered to the player profile that he prefers. He would not select homosexuals because *he knows that they generate problems taking into account the mentality of soccer players.* [. . .] And, in truth, Passarella's mission is limited to the management of the team and not to the sexual re-education of its members. (Proietto 1995, 27–28; emphasis in the original)

Proietto's logic—like Passarella's—is obviously strained. Proietto pretends to argue that to select is not to discriminate, yet his reassurance that Passarella would select blacks and Jews reveals that his argument is actually that it is Passarella's right to disciminate against gays, but not against blacks and Jews.[7] Julio Grondona, who as president of the Asociación de Fútbol Argentino is Passarella's boss, surprised many soccer fans by disagreeing with his coach. He said that he believed Passarella lacked tolerance because of his youth and that "if a homosexual respects the norms of the group, there would be no problems in incorporating him in the national team" (Grondona, quoted in *Clarín*, July 14, 1995, 29). Similarly, José Pekerman, the coach of Argentina's junior national teams, recognized that some players might be bothered by having an openly gay teammate, but he said he would turn to psychological and medical professionals to handle group anxiety (Pekerman, quoted in *Página/12*, July 14, 1995, 20).

As is usual in questions concerning soccer, President Menem also chose to comment. He declared that the decision to exclude gays from the national team was Passarella's to make, but it seems Menem was opposed to that decision.

> If it is that homosexuality has really become public, it would be good for those who really are in that situation to tell the truth, because in the end,

if there are homosexual marches all over the world, if there are no longer any limitations, I believe the moment has arrived in which those who are in that condition to say what their lifestyle is and what their situation is. I do not believe they will have problems. (Menem, quoted in *Página/12*, July 14, 1995, 20)

Menem's statement is—as usual—cryptic. On one level, Menem can be read as encouraging gay players to come out because "they will have no problems," but given Passarella's stated policy it is clear that openly gay players would at the least be excluded from the national team. On another level, Menem can be read as daring gay players to come out. He is saying that if it is true, as Jáuregui and others claim, that gays are now a political force to be reckoned with, they should prove it by coming out of hiding and revealing their true numbers and political stature.[8]

The most polemical response to Passarella came, predictably, from Diego Maradona. Passarella and Maradona have been archrivals since 1981, when Passarella was the leading defensive player for River Plate and Maradona was the leading offensive player for Boca Juniors. Passarella was the captain of the Argentine national team that won the 1978 World Cup, but Maradona replaced him as captain of the team that won the World Cup in 1986. Maradona responded to Passarella's anti-gay policies by saying he hoped Boca Juniors would buy Ruud Gullit, an openly gay Dutch player, widely believed to be the best player in the world in the early 1990s. Maradona asked rhetorically, "If a player is gay and he scores three goals, what is Passarella going to do?" (Maradona, quoted in Jáuregui 1995b, 17). Maradona also used the controversy to make a dramatic statement in favor of tolerance for sexual differences.

It's that in this country of snitches that we live in, if they see two guys on a bus kissing each other on the lips, they make them get off the bus, no? Then we say we have freedom. But the guys are kicked off the bus, for sure. . . . So it's simple: each goal that Cani [Claudio Caniggia] makes on an assist from me, I'll suck his face, right on the mouth. (Maradona, quoted in Arcucci 1995, 14)

Note that Argentine soccer fans routinely kiss one another on the check after scoring a goal, so what set Maradona's words apart was his vow to kiss Caniggia on the lips. From October 1995, when this statement was made, until July 1996, Maradona found few opportunities to make good on his promise, and on the few occasions he and Caniggia combined efforts to score a goal, the celebratory kiss was too perfunctory to attract much attention. On July 15, 1996, however, Boca beat River 4-1, on three goals by Caniggia. The closest Maradona came to assisting on any of those goals was when he miskicked a penalty against a goalpost and Caniggia scored on the rebound. The two took advantage of the historic victory to provide photographers with a prolonged and dramatic kiss. The caption on the photo of Maradona and Caniggia kissing that appeared in *El Gráfico* plays down the homoerotic content of the kiss, calling it "Kiss from the soul" with the explanation that "they are friends and do not have complexes, so they celebrate an unusually happy afternoon in this way" (*El Gráfico* no. 4006, July 16, 1995, 114; see fig. 9.2). By contrast, the caption from *Olé* has more fun with the homoerotic content, calling it "The pecking show" with the explanation that "The Bird [Caniggia's nickname] got wet three times. This is how Diego left his mouth sore. Love is like that. Cani leaves today for Rome [where his wife lives], also in search of kisses" (*Olé*, July 15, 1995, 3). The mention of Caniggia's wife can be read as a hasty confirmation that the player is, in fact, straight, but the mention also places the kisses Maradona shares with Caniggia on a par with the kisses he shares with his wife, Claudia.[9]

SOCCER IN THE GARDEN OF SODOM

The debates about the sexual politics of Argentine soccer that I have considered so far share a negative view of homosexuality. It is clear that working-class fans accuse the fans and players of opposing clubs of sodomy and effeminacy with the intention of stigmatizing them. I am quite sure that none of the intellectual observers I have cited—Jáuregui, Sebreli, or Suárez-Orozco

Figure 9.2. Maradona and Coniggia kissing.

—intends the attribution of homosexuality to stigmatize working-class soccer fans or players. Indeed, Sebreli is openly gay and his critique may be that soccer players and fans repress their homosexuality instead of expressing it in a healthier way. Nevertheless, each of the intellectual critics identifies a negative homosexuality, a homosexuality that is either closeted, repressed, or imposed. Jáuregui focuses attention on gay players who keep their gayness secret from journalists and fans, and Sebreli focuses attention on a player or fan who keeps his gayness secret from himself, while Suárez-Orozco focuses attention on sodomitical rape, a violent crime as opposed to a consensual, sexual act. By contrast, Jorge Azar, an Argentine visual artist, painted a series of pastels on paper in 1991, in which the relationship between soccer and homosexuality is cast in a more positive light. At first glance, the paintings depict everyday events in the soccer world. Players embrace one another after a goal, or pat one another on the behind, while the fans look on in delight (see fig. 9.3). Or the players stand naked in the locker room or the shower, on display for one another and for those privileged to have access to that inner sanctuary. On closer inspection, it becomes clear that the players not only embrace, they also penetrate one another, and the fans actively participate in the sporting festivities by masturbating as they look on (see fig. 9.4).

A short story by Adolfo Carlo titled "A Toda Pelota" (A Complete Ball) provides a complementary image of sodomy and soccer. The narrator purports to tell what happened in the popular section of the stands in Córdoba, Argentina, during a World Cup game between "Camerona" (close to the Spanish word for Cameroon) and a team of "Europingos" (close to the Spanish word for Europeans).[10] The narrator was accompanied by his friend "Clemente," which not coincidentally is the name of a cartoon character who is famous for being a fan of Cameroon. The fans in Carlo's story, like those in Azar's paintings, become sexually excited by the action on the field. Their excitement is no doubt fueled by the players. Those from Camerona take the field first, without shirts. They proceed to throw their shoes to the fans in the covered box seats ("because they were the most expensive"), their socks to the uncovered box seats, their shorts to the box seats where the government officials sit, "and of course: the jockstraps sailed into the popular section" (Carlo 1995, 24). Not to be outdone, the Europingos take the field wearing nothing but "little skirts in the colors of their flag." As their national anthem is played, each Europingo player "places one hand over his own prick and one over that of the guy next to him." The fans, too, are all soon naked—even those in the most expensive seats—with their hands "in the same position as that of the Europingo team." A helicopter flies over the stadium, but instead of dropping colorful balloons, it drops millions of condoms and tubes of lubricant. On the field, the referee is the only one still wearing a shirt, "in order to distinguish himself among so much nudity." Nevertheless, one of the blond players is sodomizing the ref, who in turn is sucking the penis of one of the black players. As the game begins, the Europingos are busy touching and kissing each other "and the

Figure 9.3. Untitled painting by Jorge Azar.

Figure 9.4. Untitled painting by Jorge Azar.

blacks take advantage of the situation to score the first goal." The fans soon get caught up in the action, engaging in an orgy of sodomy, fellatio, and mutual masturbation. The narrator explains that even after several orgasms, everyone's penis was "still hard because we were in the popular section." The game comes to an end, with all the players on the field and the fans in the stadium penetrating one another. The narrator coins a word to declare that "we were fucking *multitudinally*" (*"multitudinariamente"*; emphasis in the original). The phrase expresses the feeling of mass excitement and enjoyment shared by the multitudes of men who gather at stadiums and bars to watch soccer games together.

Carlo's story was published very soon after the infamous interview with Passarella, and it appeared in an issue of *NX*—a gay magazine—that included several articles written in opposition to Passarella's anti-gay policy. Thus, it is safe to assume that the story was written, or at least published, as part of that protest. Azar's paintings, by contrast, were completed four years before the controversy surrounding Passarella. They hung unsold from Azar's own walls until the controversy brought them new attention. Then, two of the paintings were shown by Antonio Gasalla on his popular TV show, *El Palacio de la Risa*, and Azar agreed to re-present his paintings at an exposition. At that time, I interviewed Azar about the paintings. Like the journalists who contacted Azar during this period, I sought to establish a relation between the painting and the political controversy, but interviewing Azar, I found that like many artists, he resists having his work located politically. Azar's refusal of political labeling coincides with Edelman's reflections on sodomy and the law.

> Even to name it, for instance, as pleasure, would be to sentimentalize its opacity, its resistance to cultural "meaning," by appropriating it for the order of recognizability and "truth." Let it remain, instead, the unseen and the unsaid: not as a token of its mystery or as a gesture toward its ultimate ineffabilty, but rather as a figure for the demonization of that which refuses the symbolic law of binary differentation, that which finds expression in the abjectified scene of homosexual desire. (Edelman 1994, 170)

Azar, too, advocates leaving it unsaid, though not unseen. Not surprisingly, Azar's attitude is very similar to that of his partner, the poet and anthropologist Luis Amaya, who wrote (Amaya 1996, 16):

Uno se va	One leaves
yendo de las identidades	fleeing identities
herido de creación.	injured by creation.
En esta época	In this time
de insoslayables dilemas	of unavoidable dilemmas
la medicina está en la selva.	the cure is in the forest.

Azar's paintings, like Amaya's poems, invoke a flight from Jáuregui's identity politics to a world outside history, in which the repression analyzed by Sebreli is unnecessary, and the symbolic rape identified by Saúrez-Orozco has no place. The soccer stadium for Azar, like the forest for Amaya, is a green and magical place in which men find innocent *jouissance* in the arms and eyes of one another. It is a pre-sinful Garden of Eden or, better said, a Garden of Sodom prior to the angel's vengeance, where there is no need to distinguish between homosexualities that are closeted, unconscious, or out in the open. Azar even told me that he could not understand why most of the people who viewed his paintings insisted on classifying them as gay or homosexual. The paintings, according to Azar, are about the joy of soccer, period, and they should not be expected to speak to political issues.

THE GLOBAL TRAFFIC IN SOCCER BODIES

Passarella's concern with the visual impact the national team makes "changing planes in Frankfurt" and Carlo's selection of "Cameronas" and "Europingos" for his fantasy game indicate that the sexual politics of Argentine soccer are racialized. In the Argentine soccer imagination, Germans and Cameroonians represent the two poles of soccer bodies. Germany's position was no doubt reinforced by the fact that they were Argentina's opponent in the final matches of the 1986 and 1990 World Cups. Cameroon came to occupy the dark pole following its victory over Argentina in the first game of the 1990 World Cup. In the global soccer imagination—which is not as precise as the Argentine soccer imagination—European teams in general represent the light, disciplined pole, while African and Afro-American teams represent the other, dark, creative pole.

Early in the century, the dark pole was occupied by Uruguay, which remains Argentina's nearby, familiar Other in soccer as well as in tango. Soccer was added to the Olympic Games in 1924, in Paris. Uruguay was the sole South American team entered in that competition and they surprised the European soccer fans by winning. Even more shocking to the Europeans was that Uruguay's star player, José Leandro Andrade, was black, and as Galeano observes, "Europe had never seen a black person playing soccer" (Galeano 1995, 53). European fans said that Andrade seemed to have a body made of rubber, and they observed that he stole the ball through agility, without touching his opponent, and not by the more forceful means employed by European soccer players. The fans also marveled that once Andrade had possession of the ball, he would leave defenders sprawled on the ground through the use of head and body fakes and changes of direction. The French sportswriter Gabriel Hanot contrasted the style of Andrade and his fellow Uruguayans with that of the English.

> The English professionals are excellent at geometry and [are] remarkable surveyors. . . . They play a tight game with vigour and some inflexibility. The Uruguayans are supple disciples of the spirit of fitness rather than geometry. They have pushed towards perfection the art of the feint and swerve and dodge, but they know also how to play directly and quickly. They are not

only ball jugglers. . . . They created a beautiful football, elegant but at the same time varied, rapid, powerful and effective. (Hanot, quoted in Mason 1995, 31)

The binary opposition identified by Hanot was not limited to soccer. The next year, a similar opposition prompted Jacques Charles to make last-minute choreographic changes in the Revue Nègre when it opened in Paris.

The chorus line, which was typical of black revues in Harlem nightclubs and on the Broadway stage, did not seem authentic to the Frenchman. Precision dancing, he thought, might be appropriate for German or English girls, but not for blacks, who, as everyone knew, were instinctive dancers, incapable of discipline. (Rose 1989, 5)

Whether playing soccer or dancing, black bodies were expected to be different from white bodies. Instead of the geometry and discipline demanded of white bodies, the black bodies were expected to be flexible and creative. Accordingly, an improvisational "Danse Sauvage" was added to the Revue Nègre, to be performed by Josephine Baker and her partner, Joe Alex. Andrade's triumph on the field of the Olympic Stadium preceded Baker's triumph on the stage of the Théâtre des Champs-Élysées by just fifteen months, and it is certain that Andrade's triumph contributed to the Parisian fascination with blackness that made Baker's performance bankable.[11] Andrade's triumph in Paris also kicked off a worldwide fascination with South American soccer players.

The opposition between English "geometry" and Uruguayan "beauty" that Hanot posed in 1924 has remained in effect in subsequent soccer discourse, but it has become increasingly racialized. From the 1930s through the 1980s, Brazil was the archetypal dark, exotic soccer nation, in both the Argentine and the global soccer imagination. Since then, African teams such as Cameroon and Nigeria—which defeated Argentina in the final match of the 1996 Olympics—have replaced Brazil as the soccer world's dark Other. In the meantime, Argentines, along with Uruguayans, have come to occupy a middle position, between the disciplined European teams and the creative African and Afro-American teams—such as Brazil, Colombia, and Jamaica. As a result, Argentine players are especially valued in the global soccer market. Black players from Brazil, Colombia, and several African countries have been incorporated into European soccer clubs, but they have been incorporated rather sparingly, at least compared to the incorporation of Argentine players. In European soccer, Black players tend to be limited to two or three offensive positions—as strikers or playmakers. Significantly, these are precisely the positions that are said to require the most in terms of "individuality" and "creativity." By contrast, the other eight or nine defensive and transitional positions are infrequently occupied by Black players. This racial division of soccer labor in Europe has been reproduced in Colombian soccer. In the 1994 World Cup, Francisco Maturana, then the coach of Colombia's multiracial national team, took into account "the regional characteristics of the players" when he decided that "in the

midfield the need was for hard workers and well-disciplined players, provided by Alvarez and Gabriel Gómez from the Antioquía region where such
qualities are commonplace, while the fantasy was left to Valderrama, Aspri-
lla and Rincón, people from Cali and the coast who were harder to discipline
but more creative" (Mason 1995, 140). Not coincidentally, the players from
Cali and the coast—those who are "harder to discipline but more creative"
—are black or mulatto, while those from the Antioquía region—the "hard
workers"—are *criollo*. In sum, black bodies are highly valued on the global soccer market, but in strictly limited numbers and positions. They are deployed
almost exclusively as offensive players—strikers or playmaking midfield-
ers. These are the positions in which individual creativity is expected and confined, while players in the defensive and transitional positions are required to
work more closely together, as a group.

Unlike African and Afro-American players, the Argentine players who
play in Italy and Spain are well distributed among offensive, defensive, and
transitional positions. As of August 1995, eight out of the ten Africans, Brazil-
ians, and Colombians who played in Italy's First Division were limited to offensive positions, but of the eight Argentines in Italy at the time, only three
were offensive players (all strikers), and the other five were defensive (four
backs and one defensive midfielder). As defensive players, the Argentine backs
are required to be more thoroughly integrated into the collective body of their
Italian clubs than are foreign strikers, who retain more individuality and apart-
ness. The European incorporation of Argentine players is not without anxiety,
but the anxiety is expressed regarding each individual player's capacity to pass
as the right sort of European rather than his dangerousness as an exotic. Maradona is the most famous example. His first European club was Barcelona,
where he was rejected, and his next was Naples, where he was embraced. In
neither case was Maradona judged as an exotic appendage to a collective
soccer body—the way Afro-Brazilians are most likely to be judged. Rather,
Maradona was judged as passing or failing a test of belonging integrally to a
collective European soccer body. The test is based on a complex intersection
of European and South American national, ethnic, and class identities. Barcelona, along with Real Madrid, is one of Spain's two elite clubs, and it is a
standard-bearer of Catalonian separatism (Galeano 1995, 39). It seems the
Barcelona fans rejected Maradona because they identified him as a low-class
sudaca—a derogatory Spanish term for lower-class, South American Creoles
(Levinsky 1996, 137). Naples, by contrast, is a lower-class, Southern Italian
club, and it is clear that "the Neapolitans loved Maradona because of his surprising resemblance to them or, better said, to the sub-proletarian Neapoli-
tan" (Maurizio Valenzi, quoted in Levinsky 1996, 148). So it is in general that
Argentine players have a difficult time gaining admission to European soccer
clubs, but when they are admitted, it is more often as a returning *paisano* than
as an exotic. The Argentine player—unlike the Afro-Brazilian, Afro-Colom-
bian, or African—is not essentially, eternally different from the European.

Rather, he is an exotic on the move, between the Black and the White, the South and the North, the Third World and the First. Argentine bodies are branded as Argentine, but they are more freely incorporated than are the stably exotic bodies of essentialized Others.

SOCCER IN SUNSHINE AND SHADOW

In his book *Fútbol a Sol y Sombra* (Soccer in Sunshine and Shadow), Galeano addresses the intersection of race and sexuality in global soccer politics in terms of Third World and working-class bodies joyously resisting European impositions of order. On the one hand, Galeano revels in the play that occurs out of doors, on the field, under the bright sun. On the other hand, Galeano rails against the shady business that is transacted indoors, behind the scenes. Galeano suggests that throughout this century, the pleasure of soccer-as-play has declined, while the profits of soccer-as-business have increased. He observes that "the goal is soccer's orgasm" and "like the orgasm, the goal is every day less frequent in modern life" (Galeano 1995, 9).

There are many villains and heroes in Galeano's history. Foremost among the shady villains is João Havelange, the Belgian-born Brazilian president of FIFA (the Fédération Internationale de Football Associations). Galeano's heroes are the players who overcome the discipline imposed from above, by Havelange and others, and succeed in making soccer

> a party for the eyes that watch and a joy for the body that plays. [. . .] Professional soccer does everything possible to castrate this happy energy, but it survives despite all despites. [. . .] However much the technocrats program it down to the minutest detail, however much the powerful manipulate it, soccer insists on being the art of the unforeseen. Where you least expect it the impossible leaps out, the dwarf teaches the giant a lesson and a skinny and crooked man of color makes an athlete sculpted in Greece look like a dolt (Galeano 1995, 243).

For Galeano, the history of soccer is a history of Third World dwarves conquering First World giants, and of skinny and crooked South Americans showing up Europeans; this, despite all attempts to fix it so that games will be won by the bigger, the stronger, the swifter, and the more disciplined. Accordingly, Cuba figures prominently in the margins of Galeano's soccer history, despite the fact that it is one of the few Latin American countries in which soccer is not the most important sport. Galeano gives a brief summary of global politics in his discussion of each quadrennial World Cup, and the summaries pertaining to each World Cup from 1962 to 1994 include this sentence: "Well-informed sources in Miami announced the imminent fall of Fidel Castro, who was going to tumble in a matter of hours" (Galeano 1995, 130, 139, 154, 161, 174, 183, 193, 208, and 223). Castro and the Cuban people thereby appear alongside Pelé and the Brazilian team, and Maradona and the Argentine team in Galeano's narrative, all as examples of Latin Americans who defy the odds that are biased in favor of Europe.[12] FIFA, of course, plays a major role in stacking the deck in favor of Western Europe, but there is another, subtler struggle in soccer.

It is obvious that one soccer team struggles against another and that Third World soccer associations struggle against the European domination of international soccer. What Galeano's book calls attention to is that a soccer team also resists its own coach, much as Randy Martin argues that a dance company becomes a social body in "opposition to an initial domination of language-based authority in the figure of the choreographer" (Martin 1990, 96). Even though they share an interest in producing a successful performance, there is an oppositional relationship between the dancers who move and the choreographer who speaks. It is typical for theorists of the body to invoke a natural body whose desires are thwarted, contained, and channeled by disciplinary practices such as choreography and soccer coaching. Martin, however, is careful to avoid appeals to a naturally meaningful body, arguing instead that "the body takes shape and social purpose [only] against the limits of a physical culture, that is, within a social construction of time, space, and motion" (51). The body, according to Martin, becomes meaningful within the context of a culture that disciplines it. Martin generously suggests that "the dance company could be replaced by any collective body, articulated as labor, gender, or race, against a controlling authority" (96), and, indeed, I find Martin's analysis of dance relevant to my own observations of soccer. Coaching, too, is language-based, mental labor. Coaches demand obedience and respect from their players, and they are quick to take an important portion of the credit for any victory. Almost all of the experts who comment on soccer strategy observe that good coaching is necessary to produce a solid defense. The problem for coaches is that a well-coached defense is not threatened by a well-coached offense. To score goals, it is considered necessary to have a "creative" player who is capable of "thinking with his feet": one who has mastered "the art of the unforeseen" or who has "an artistic feel for the game," in the words of soccer coach Jorge Valdano (Valdano 1996, 9). Fans go to the soccer stadium to see the individual who is able to create goals despite the plans of the opposing coach, the discipline of the opposing defenders, the skills of the opposing goalkeeper, the limits of his own coach's offense, the offside rule, the rule that denies him the use of his hands, the boundaries of the playing field, the penalty area, and the goal itself.

"Even if it is a *golcito*," a little goal, as opposed to a big goal *golazo*, Galeano observes that "it always comes out 'gooooooooooooooooooooal' in the throat of the radio commentators" (Galeano 1995, 9). This cry is comparable to what José Limón, observing *mexicanos* in South Texas, calls "the *gritos*, long cries of celebratory approval, coming from the men sitting or standing at the bar, as they watch a particularly artful execution on the [dance] floor" (Limón 1994, 163–164). An important difference is that the Mexican American men Limón describes celebrate the virtuosity of women and men on the dance floor, while the virtuosity celebrated by Argentine soccer fans is exclusively male. Nevertheless, there are similar class politics in Argentine soccer and Mexican dance, despite the very different politics of gender and sexuality. Drawing on Martin's work, Limón explains that "to hear the sharp, well-formed class-consciousness of the *grito,* is to realize that, for a moment, some measure of artful control over [the forces of hard, working-class labor, substance use, and sexual desire]—some measure of victory—has been achieved in the never-ending struggle against the choreography of race, class, and, one has to say, gender" (ibid., 165). A soccer goal is certainly a blow against the rival team, but it is also a bodily blow against the mental strategies, rules, and regulations that conspire to make the goal every day less frequent. As such it is celebrated by the working-class, male fans, who take political pleasure in witnessing the creative capacity of a fellow male, working-class body.

NOTES

1. For my part, I confess that in the soccer games I participated in during my fieldwork, I was repeatedly damned with the extremely faint praise that I did not play so badly "for a yanqui."

2. All quotes from Spanish-language sources are my translation.

3. Reading Sebreli's comments on the sexual stigmatization of intellectuals it is relevant to consider Sebreli's position as an openly gay man as well as an intellectual. At a conference on sports and society held at the University of Buenos Aires in August 1996, all the members of a keynote panel on soccer agreed that Sebreli's 1981 *Fútbol y Masas* was seriously flawed because Sebreli "is not a soccer fan" and "does not have a real feeling for the game." *Fútbol y Masas* is without a doubt one of the most intellectually rigorous Spanish-language studies of soccer, so it impossible to escape the suspicion that the work was dismissed because of its author's "dubious sexuality," or at least that its author's "dubious sexuality" was used to dismiss the work.

4. Thus, the current fin de siècle discourse of AIDS inverts last century's fin de siècle discourse of syphilis. As Bersani (1994) argues, it is now the anuses of gay men that are constituted as infinitely dangerous, while the vaginas of straight women are represented as safe.

5. Roger Lancaster makes the important observation that there is no natural basis for the association of penetration with activity. "By what necessity is the penis 'active' and the anus (or vagina) 'passive' in sexual intercourse? Intercourse could just as easily be imagined the other way around. Or any participant in any position could be seen as an 'active' partner in intercourse" (Lancaster 1992, 273). Andrea Dworkin (1987) offers an example of imaging heterosexual intercourse the other way around.

Remarkably, it is not the man who is considered possessed in intercourse, even though he (his penis) is buried inside another human being; and his penis is surrounded by strong muscles that contract like a fist shutting tight and release with such a force that pushes hard on the tender thing, always so vulnerable no matter how hard (Dworkin 1987, 64).

Rather than imagine the penis as penetrating the vagina, it is possible to imagine the vagina as invaginating the penis, just as it is possible to imagine the anus as "analating" the penis. Because it is possible to imagine each penetrative act "the other way around," how each act is imagined should be considered motivated and interpretable.

6. There have indeed been many indications that man-boy love is common in the world of soccer. The Brazilian star Pelé, for example, "confessed that he had been sexually initiated by a homosexual and that the majority of the players on Santos in that time period had done the same" (Bianco 1994, 4). The suggested scenario is that older players on a club's First Division squad routinely sodomize the younger players, who repeat the practice with the next generation when they themselves advance to the First Division. Similarly, Jorge "El Indio" Solari, an Argentine soccer coach, asserts that "there are some coaches in the younger divisions who are not what we call real men [*muy hombres*] and who take advantage of the boys" (Solari, quoted in Bianco 1994, 4).

7. In fact, one of Passarella's most surprising early selections for the national team was Juan Pablo Sorín, who is Jewish, though it is worth noting that Sorín had already been "discovered" by the coach of Argentina's junior national team, José Pekerman, who is also Jewish.

8. I also find it interesting that Menem's statement constitutes gayness as a "condition" or "situation." To my ears, at least, it sounds as though Menem might be conflating homosexuality with pregnancy. My hunch is that Menem is thinking back to his youth when pregnancy and homosexuality were each conditions that had something to do with sex and that were supposed to be kept private. Now, however, homosexuality, like pregnancy, "has really become public" so "those who are in that condition" can say "what their situation is."

9. The substitution of Claudio Caniggia for Claudia Maradona is a recurring theme in reports about Diego Maradona. Their substitutability is facilitated by the coincidence that they have similar first names and similar blond hair (though Claudio's is natural and Claudia's is dyed). As this paper goes to press, there are reports that Caniggia's wife is suing Caniggia for divorce, and that she is using photos of Maradona and Caniggia kissing to sue Maradona for alienation of affection. The alienation of affection suit locates Maradona in the position of Caniggia's mistress, who is liable for stealing Caniggia's heart away from Caniggia's wife.

10. At the risk of being too literal, I observe that the fictional game might have been inspired by the 1978 World Cup game between Tunisia and West Germany played in Córdoba, though that game ended 0-0.

11. Andrade himself was a well-known performer in the carnival of Montevideo, and after the games, he remained for several months in Paris, where he earned a living as a tango dancer—a combination of performer, instructor, and gigolo (Puppo 1969, 42).

12. Galeano's location as an Uruguayan is also essential since Uruguay is by far the smallest country to have won the World Cup.

WORKS CITED

Alegre, Alfredo. 1995. "Passarella cien por cien." *El Gráfico* no. 3952 (July 4): 10–13.
Amaya, Luis. 1996. *Como Tres Veces el Mundo para Curar los Males*. Buenos Aires: Editorial El Borde Cultural Lola Montes.

Archetti, Eduardo P. 1994. "Masculinity and Football: The Formation of National Identity in Argentina." In *Game without Frontiers: Football, Identity and Modernity*, ed. Richard Giulianotti and John Williams. Aldershot, England: Arena.

———. 1997. "Multiple Masculinities: The Worlds of Tango and Football in Argentina." In *Sex and Sexuality in Latin America*, ed. Daniel Balderston and Donna J. Guy. New York: New York University Press.

Arcucci, Daniel. 1995. "Volvió para siempre." *El Gráfico* no. 3965 (October 3): 4–22.

Bersani, Leo. 1994. "Is the Rectum a Grave?" In *Reclaiming Sodom*, ed. Jonathan Goldberg. New York: Routledge.

Bianco, Marcelo. 1994. "No al miedo, sí a la prevención." *Goles* 35, no. 1801: 3–7.

Carlo, Adolfo. 1995. "A toda pelota." *NX: Periodismo Gay para todos*, no. 22 (August): 24–26.

Dworkin, Andrea. 1987. *Intercourse*. New York: Free Press.

Eco, Umberto. 1986. *Travels in Hyperreality*. Trans. William Weaver. San Diego: Harcourt Brace Jovanovich.

Edelman, Lee. 1994. *Homographesis: Essays in Gay Literary and Cultural Theory*. New York: Routledge.

Enzetti, Daniel. 1995. "Entrevista a Carlos Jáuregui." *Humor*, no. 456 (July 26): 15–17.

Foucault, Michel. 1986. *The Care of the Self*. Trans. Robert Hurley. Vol. 3 of *The History of Sexuality*. New York: Vintage Books.

———. 1988. "Sexual Choice, Sexual Act: Foucault and Homosexuality." In *Politics, Philosophy, Culture: Interviews and Other Writings of Michel Foucault, 1977–1984*, ed. Lawrence D. Kritzman. New York: Routledge.

Freud, Sigmund. 1955. "From the History of an Infantile Neurosis." In *The Standard Edition of the Complete Psychological Works of Sigmund Freud*, ed. James Strachey, vol. 17. London: The Hogarth Press.

Galeano, Eduardo. 1995. *El Fútbol a Sol y Sombra*. Buenos Aires: Catálogos.

Guy, Donna J. 1991. *Sex and Danger in Buenos Aires: Prostitution, Family, and Nation in Argentina*. Lincoln: University of Nebraska Press.

Jáuregui, Carlos. 1995a. "En el fútbol tambien hay homosexuales." *El Gráfico*, no. 3954 (July 18): 27.

———. 1995b. "Verdad y consecuencia." *NX: Periodismo Gay para todos*, no. 22 (August 1995): 17.

Lancaster, Roger N. 1992. *Life Is Hard: Machismo, Danger, and the Intimacy of Power in Nicaragua*. Berkeley: University of California Press.

Levinsky, Sergio. 1996. *Rebelde con Causa*. Buenos Aires: Corregidor.

Limón, José E. 1994. *Dancing with the Devil: Society and Cultural Poetics in Mexican-American South Texas*. Madison: University of Wisconsin Press.

Martin, Randy. 1990. *Performance as Political Act: The Embodied Self*. New York: Bergin and Garvey Publishers.

Mason, Tony. 1995. *Passion of the People? Football in South America*. London: Verso.

Mosse, George L. 1985. *Nationalism and Sexuality: Middle-Class Morality and Sexual Norms in Modern Europe*. Madison: University of Wisconsin Press.

Olivera, Daniel. 1996. "Diego es muy especial. . . ." *Noticias* 19, no. 1024 (August): 92–94.

Proietto, Aldo. 1995. "La polémica rosa." *El Gráfico*, no. 3954 (July 18): 26–28.

Puppo, José César. 1969. "Una vida excepcional: Andrade." In *El Fútbol (Antología)*. Montevideo: Centro Editor de América Latina.

Rose, Phyllis. 1989. *Jazz Cleopatra: Josephine Baker in Her Time.* New York: Doubleday.

Sebreli, Juan José. 1981. *Fútbol y Masas.* Buenos Aires: Editorial Galerna.

Simpson, Mark. 1994. *Male Impersonators: Men Performing Masculinity.* New York: Routledge.

Suárez-Orozco, Marcelo Mario. 1982. "A Study of Argentine Soccer: The Dynamics of Its Fans and Their Folklore." *Journal of Psychoanalytic Anthropology* 5, no. 1: 7–28.

Valdano, Jorge. 1996. "Un mal de ausencias." *Clarín* (June 8), deportivo (sports section): 9.

10. Music at Home, Politics Afar

Timothy D. Taylor

On October 21, 1996, the computer company Packard Bell unveiled a sixty-second television ad that showed real/retouched—hyperreal—people waiting in line at a big city bank which looks like a library. They wait and wait and wait, hardly moving in this impossible queue. The weather is dark, moody, awful, post-nuclear. We see a young woman age suddenly. No one talks to anyone. Storm troopers march and intimidate. A bureaucrat inside the bank laughs evilly. A little girl peeks, frightened, out from behind a copy of *Paradise Lost*. The scene is a post-apocalyptic vision of modernity gone terribly wrong. Then, after exactly three-quarters of the ad has elapsed, cut to a cartoon house, inside of which is a bright (real) study with a shiny new Packard Bell computer, sitting alone on a table. "Wouldn't you rather be at home?" a suave male voice asks. Indeed.[1]

This spot illustrates some of the changes being wrought by technology in contemporary America: public spaces are becoming increasingly uninhabitable, intolerant and intolerable, even monstrous; being in public is like being in prison, or in a police state. And even if our home lives are problematic or unreal—indicated by the idealized cartoon house in a cartoon green valley—there is one pleasant, real reality, brought to you by Packard Bell computers. The music used in the ad is electronically generated, save for a male voice that wails wordless vocals above the mix. But when we pan to the idyllic cottage in the country, the music shifts, brightening up, changing from the minor mode to major, and a chorus replaces the single voice. The musical message is that in public you're alone, but when you're alone with your computer, you're not alone at all.

Packard Bell's ad is part of an American public culture that is fast disappearing; more and more people are seeking the solitary pleasures of their home computers, where they can now conduct all sorts of household business, such

Figure 10.1. Stills from Packard Bell television ad.

as banking or information gathering. And musicking. But in this Packard Bell ad, while there are people in the post-apocalyptic, untechnological "before," in the bright, shiny, and technological "after," there is only the computer alone sitting on a desk: there is no person in front of it. As I will discuss below, what the computer and the retreat from the public seem to be resulting in are new configurations of identity, as individuals who are separate from groups, while at the same time making affiliations with new delocalized groups or causes. And since the musicians in this digital technoculture are makers of cultural forms that sell, there are representations of selves that we need to think about. So in this paper I want to examine the retreat into a personal world of musicking and the concomitant contraction of public cultural space and what this has meant for music and musicians in a certain group of musics called collectively techno or electronica that are made solely by computers, samplers (devices that make exact digital copies of pre-recorded sounds and music), and drum machines. Some of these musics have achieved a modicum of mainstream popularity, so that bands such as the Prodigy or the Chemical Brothers are fairly well known among rock fans.[2] The bands I will focus on in this article —Muslimgauze and Banco de Gaia—are, however, much more on the fringes.

Last, in this introductory space, a brief word on the use of the term "public." For a word that does as much cultural work as this one does in contemporary American life, the various contrasting and conflicting uses of it have, interestingly, never been teased out. This isn't my task here, though; instead, I would like to examine a few variations and how the insights they offer bear on this study.

Nowadays it is practically impossible in academic circles to use the word "public" without invoking—intentionally or not—the work of the German philosopher Jürgen Habermas. Over the years, Habermas has provided clear-cut characterizations of what he means by "public sphere": "The bourgeois public sphere may be conceived above all as the sphere of private people come together as a public."[3] Elsewhere he writes, "[W]e mean first of all a realm of our social life in which something approaching public opinion can be formed."[4] Habermas is interested in the space in which the "public" hashes over the crucial issues of a democratic polity; for him, the public sphere is the space of an idealized democratic process. All well and good, but this formulation isn't without problems; most importantly, as Nancy Fraser and others have argued, Habermas's formulation is highly gendered, and exclusive.[5] Habermas never really asks what for Fraser and others is the crucial question: Public sphere for whom?[6]

Another "public" that might shed some light on the issues here is the term "public culture" as outlined by Arjun Appadurai and Carol Breckenridge in the inaugural issue of the journal of that title. For them, the term "public culture" designates an "arena . . . in which . . . emergent cosmopolitan cultural forms . . . shape each other."[7] "Realm" in Habermas's words; "arena" in Appadurai and Breckenridge's. Yet all these scholars are less interested in processes than results, or the forms that result from processes. I am interested in these, too, but at the same time neither formulation of these "publics" refers to what I mean by the word here, which is more of a street sense of the term. I use the word "street" on purpose, for I am using "public" to refer more than anything else to the "modernism in the streets" written about so vividly by Marshall Berman in *All That Is Solid Melts into Air*.[8] This is an urban phenomenon, to be sure, a "primal scene" as Berman describes it, made possible by the construction of wide boulevards in Paris in the second half of the nineteenth century and first chronicled by Baudelaire. In this new Paris of the 1860s and 1870s, for the first time everyone could see everyone else and at the same time be unnoticed in this new flux of people. So the use of the term "public" here refers to space more than anything else, in keeping with Berman and others, such as Mike Davis and Edward W. Soja,[9] who study the ever-changing geography of urban areas.

ELECTRONICA, TECHNOLOGY, AND EFFACED SELVES

The decreasing cost of technology to the average consumer has resulted in the last decade in entirely new kinds of musics that rely heavily on personal computers, synthesizers, drum machines, samplers, and other electronic gear. These new musics are performed live, but they are just as frequently never heard live at all; the musician sits alone in her studio cranking out tunes. These new technologies aren't solely used in these marginal musics, however; I think it is safe to say that there is virtually no contemporary music that does not make use of some kind of electronic technology, whether or not listeners can discern it. Before the advent of recording technology and radio, people made their own music most of the time, but what is radically different today is that it is now possible to create entire worlds of sound all by yourself with your computer; there is no longer a necessary social aspect to musicking. It may well be, however, that one of the reasons that sampling has itself become an art form (and some musicians now call themselves "sampling artists"[10]) is that it provides aural glimpses of the social, condensed into fragments of acoustic musicking, but in their new contexts of electronically generated music these glimpses are historicized: music as social activity is becoming a thing of the past for many of these musicians.

While technology is involved in a dynamic that helps musicians and others create new kinds of subject positions, these musicians have different modes of self-representation that are caught up in the collective aesthetics of their subgenres. It is common in the dance musics part of electronica musics to hide or obscure the names of the musicians; insiders know, but it is a ploy to ensure that these musics are not co-opted into the mainstream: If you're an A&R (artist and repertoire) person from a major label and an outsider to the scene, it's very hard to track down the people who make this music.[11] So many of these bands use names that cover up their membership; many change their names frequently; many use different names simultaneously; some change their name for every album; many use different names for the different kinds of music they make. The two electronica bands that I'll talk about in detail below are called Muslimgauze and Banco de Gaia, two groups that are pretty marginal and far from the attention that has been given to more mainstream electronica bands, such as the Chemical Brothers, the Prodigy, Underworld, Aphex Twin, and Orbital. Like some of these better-known groups, Muslimgauze and Banco de Gaia are also not "bands" at all but individuals, for each band consists of only one person.

This use of names that hide rather than reveal—or celebrate—the individual musician is partly what I want to point out: that in this moment in which public culture seems to be waning, it is not necessarily waning in favor of a new or heightened individual. Just as that Packard Bell ad showcased the computer alone, not a fictionalized user, so these bands draw attention to themselves not as individuals but as hidden, mysterious creators. I have never seen an album in these genres that shows a recognizable picture of the musician, and I have never seen an album that uses the musician's real name anywhere in it, except occasionally in the copyright fine print (even this happens only when the band is reasonably well known and wants to protect itself from being sampled or remixed without permission). Some of these musicians have web pages and give interviews, but even if these include pictures, as they occasionally do, the pictures are so obscure that it is often difficult or impossible to tell much about what the person actually looks like. For example, *The Wire*, the British new music monthly, featured Muslimgauze's Bryn Jones in an interview and published a self-portrait of Jones obscuring his face in a way that is reminiscent of a Muslim woman's veil, obscuring all of his face save his eyes, and a bit of his nose and forehead.[12]

Like Bryn Jones, Banco de Gaia's Toby Marks conceals his identity, though not quite to the same degree; his web pages on the Internet offer a few photographs that are reasonably clear, though still highly manipulated: They're fuzzy, colored, hazy. At the same time, though, perhaps the most extensive part of his web site is a series of pages devoted to a quiz about his biography; he provides many paired statements that you can click on to proceed to the next pair, but there's only one answer that tells you when you're right—

> In 1995 I released my second album on Planet Dog Records.
> Yes, you made it—it's all true![13]

But of course, the pairs before this one can't all be true. And for this one entry, there are ten that tell you you're wrong, and fourteen others than pose paired statements only, without giving any clue to the correct answer. So for the most part, we never know what's true, though some of the multiple choice answers given are improbable and we can occasionally surmise what's *not* true.

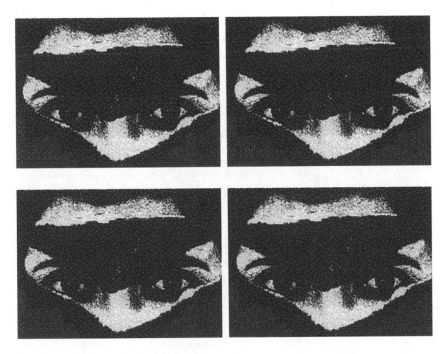

Figure 10.2. Self-Collage by Bryn Jones of Muslimgauze.

For example:

In 1989 I completed my training and got my first job on a building site.	In 1989 I gave up carpentry after an unfortunate gardening accident.

Both could be true or untrue and we are never told.

So while Marks has fun with his biography, it appears that he is thus partly hiding behind the name of the band, which he claims in interviews is the title of an obscure Puccini opera about an accountant that contains long passages in the libretto about accountancy; Marks said that

> it's a very little known fact . . . that Puccini actually wanted to be an accountant, but he wasn't very good at math, so he had to learn to be a musician, to be a composer instead.
>
> *That's strange. That's kind of backwards. You usually expect it to be the other way around.*
>
> You'd be surprised how many frustrated accountants there are [. . .] and I should know.
>
> *You're a frustrated accountant too?*
>
> Yeah. I really do want to be an accountant.
>
> *You're kidding me, right?*
>
> Yeah, I might be.
>
> *Don't mess with me like that.*[14]

As a diligent musicologist, I should point out that there is no obscure or unfinished opera by Puccini called *Banco de Gaia*; this is a fabrication as well.

On the Banco de Gaia web page, there is this "information":

> Banco de Gaia was a 16th century Spanish missionary in South America who came across a small tribe in the jungle somewhere. Whilst trying to convert them to Christianity he learned a lot about their own spiritual system and they ended up being known as the "Gaians," practising a mixture of Virgin Mary worship and pagan earth magic.[15]

Near as I can tell, this isn't true either.

It will help to illuminate this practice of deliberate self-effacement—either through concealment or obfuscation—among these fringe techno/ambient bands if I contrast it to another genre, and I do this not only by way of comparison, but to point out also that there is a good deal of overlap between all these musics, though the practices around them can be quite different. People on the Internet newsgroups alt.music.ambient, alt.music.techno, and others, argue all the time about what makes their music different from another genre. The biggest split among these musics occurs between New Age music and everything else, mainly because New Age is now a mainstream genre that works through the normal channels in the music industry, but, like all musics, it has its margins, and these are blurred with ambient, techno, and other electronica. New Age has a chart in *Billboard,* it has a Grammy award, it has stars who can make fortunes (though who don't sell as much as musicians in the rock category).[16]

But one of the biggest differences between New Age and other musicians who make electronic musics is that New Age musicians usually foreground themselves as selves. New Age musicians almost always include pictures of themselves on the material accompanying their recordings; they use their real names, or perhaps just their first names (such as Yanni or Enya) but there is never any doubt as to who they are. Yanni and Enya are big stars, but even the New Age musicians on the margins never let you forget who they are. So, for example, Tobias de la Sarno goes by the name "Tobias" only, but if you open up the booklet accompanying his CD *Rainforest Rhapsody in the Key of Bali,* you find his full name listed as the producer.

New Age music practices are related in a way to more mainstream electronica musicians such as Deep Forest and Enigma. It seems to be the case that if one of these groups wants to try to enter the mainstream, they will hit on a name and exploit it. One prominent example in this genre is Deep Forest, which is now a band, but in their first album, *Deep Forest,* the two musicians involved weren't named as a band at all. But with the astonishing international success of this recording (which has sold at least 2.5 million copies worldwide since its release in 1993), the two Belgian producers who made the album decided to go by the band name Deep Forest on their next album.[17]

While there are active electronica dance music scenes in many urban areas, most of these electronica musicians I am concerned with here don't participate, even though their music and practices have various features in common with these scenes. The fans of ambient and techno musics are more dispersed. But one of the more interesting features of this music is that its reliance on technology means that the fans as well as the musicians are competent with computers. There is a vast amount of information on these musics available on the Internet; in fact, Yahoo's guide to music genres has more entries for electronica (more than three hundred at this writing, plus more than one hundred in the "Industrial" category, which overlaps with electronica) than any other genre save, first, rock, and second (strangely enough), march.[18] There is usually comparatively little on individual musicians, except for the most famous of these, but the newsgroups devoted to these musics are legion, and they are extremely active. A good deal of arcane technical information also floats around, information about equipment, how-to guides, and more.

But I should also note that, while there are many conversations about this music, there are few places where the fans gather together; this is largely though not exclusively post-concert and post-social music, if in using the word "social" I am permitted to refer to face-to-face (or "f2f" as these Internet users write) interactions in both the production of the music and its consumption;

conversations about it occur primarily on the Internet, not face-to-face. Information is spread mainly through the Internet and zines rather than in the public space of concerts or clubs, or, for that matter, the mainstream media. So this music, in its sound and use of samples, and in its reception, is largely delocalized, deterritorialized, though musicians and fans are united by the Internet.

ONE-CAUSE WONDERS

Even as these musicians efface their identities, they redirect their identity-function in other ways. A few of these electronica musicians take on overt political causes, and it is to this that I now want to turn my attention. Despite the great differences in approach, presentation, discourse, and, to a lesser extent, music, it's interesting that the techno/ambient crowd tends to be more overtly political than the New Agers—or at least, it wields more conventional signifiers of the political. I have found a number of bands devoting entire albums to political causes, such as Muslimgauze, which was formed to project an Islamic point of view to counterbalance what its sole member Bryn Jones saw as a news media dominated by pro-Israel coverage. Banco de Gaia's *Last Train to Lhasa* includes in the notes a plea to help get China out of Tibet.

Even so, the electronica musicians' ideas of the political are by no means conventional or common. Some of the statements of these musicians, as well as their music, are enough to leave one breathless.

Muslimgauze

Muslimgauze, for example, was formed in direct opposition to Israel after that country's invasion of Lebanon in June of 1982. The band's sole member, Englishman Bryn Jones, possesses a fair amount of knowledge about the political situation in the Middle East, but he has never been there and says he has no ambition to go, is not a Muslim, and doesn't know Arabic. Moreover, it is not clear how his politics are received by any Middle Eastern people, or Muslims in general; Jones gets no feedback from any Palestinian, Islamic, or Arab-ic sources, and says that "we don't look for it, it's not important" (and Muslimgauze is virtually never discussed on any Islamic/Middle Eastern/political newsgroups on the Internet). Jones does say that he gets "abuse" from Jews and other supporters of Israel.[19]

Jones's rhetoric is marked by an incredible passion and vehemence equaled only by its inflexibility. When asked by *Village Voice* interviewer about the October 1994 bombing of a Tel Aviv bus by Hamas which had been criticized by Edward Said as "criminal" and "stupid," Jones replied: "They're doing what they think is right. They're fighting for the people. I don't think you can criticize them from the outside." Continuing, the interviewer asked,

Didn't you find the attack at the very least counterproductive?

I don't think so. Those people have got absolutely nothing. They're working from zero. They can't vote.

There must be other forms of resistance.

There isn't.[20]

In another interview, when asked if he had "complete animosity toward the state of Israel" and if he would "exempt certain Israelis that [he] might consider good people," he replied: "I wouldn't talk to any of them, the whole people are disgusting so no, I wouldn't."[21]

Jones's music strikes the listener as being as compromising as his rhetoric is uncompromising; there's little about it that could be considered a political polemic (though some fans occasionally describe it as aggressive or angry, it is unclear if they are hearing this in the music or reacting to Jones's rhetoric and packaging). The only sign of his political position is in the artwork accompanying the recordings, and in album and song titles; his first LP was called *Kabul* (from 1983), forming a critique of Russia's invasion of Afghanistan; other albums have been more explicit: *Hajj* (1986, referring to the major Islamic pilgrimage to Mecca); *The Rape of Palestine* (1988); *United States of Islam* (1991); *Vote Hezbollah* (1993); and *Betrayal* (1993), which featured a photo in the booklet of Yasser Arafat shaking hands with Yitzhak Rabin in 1993. These are just album titles; song titles convey more comments, as does the cover art. For example, the cover to *Hamas Arc* (1993) shows Iranian women shooting handguns.

For Jones, who never plays live, all these politics are largely distinct from the music. "The music can be listened to without an appreciation of its political origin," says Jones, "but I hope that after listening the person then asks why it's called what it is and from this finds out more about the subject. It's up to them. Go out and discover."[22] Elsewhere, in an answer to a request to sum up Muslimgauze, he said, "Every piece of music is influenced by a particular fact, be it Palestine, Iran, or Afghanistan, the whole Middle East is an influence to Muslimgauze. From the political situations I am influenced to create music, endless music."[23]

Muslimgauze, however political it is, nonetheless samples music and sounds from all over the place but seemingly without any overriding aesthetic or rationale. One interviewer asked:

> You have a strong rhythmic base to your music and a heavy emphasis on percussion, does that come from some aspect of Islam?

> No, it's just what interests me, percussion sounds working with other sounds as well, it's whatever interests me really. We don't aim to be pigeonholed into any musical category, that's one thing that I hope Muslimgauze can't be, you know, put into a specific box; we do this or that or the other. Personally, when people ask me what it's like, I can't really explain.[24]

Figure 10.3. Muslimgauze: *Hamas Arc*, cover.

Some fans of Muslimgauze seem a bit put off by Jones's political views. For them, it gets in the way of the music. One wrote to rec.music.industrial that "unfortunately, the stratifying political propaganda that the group puts out will always keep me at arm's length from embracing the music." Others seem to feel that Jones's output is becoming derivative; he is too prolific, and his music is beginning to sound the same. Sometimes, the discourse of art is invoked to critique Jones's music; an e-zine reviewer of one album wrote that "I hate politics, and I think art should not demean itself by letting itself be used for political manipulation."[25]

Banco de Gaia

Like Muslimgauze, Banco de Gaia, another English "band," is the work of one person, Toby Marks, of Leamington Spa, England, who formed the "band" in 1992. One important difference between Muslimgauze and Banco de Gaia is that Banco de Gaia occasionally appears live, so it is closer to the dance music roots of his electronica than Muslimgauze. This is partly an accident of geography: Leamington Spa is not exactly an urban center teeming with dance clubs, but it is fairly near what has become one of the most active and influential clubs in England, Whirl-Y-Gig, the brainchild of DJ Monkey Pilot. The success of Whirl-Y-Gig brought Marks and other musicians to national prominence, and since so many of these bands sample "ethnic" musics, they were ultimately noticed by Peter Gabriel, who created a Whirl-Y-Gig tent at the WOMAD (World of Music and Dance) festival in 1995.

Even though Banco de Gaia does play an occasional live gig, Marks conceives his music in terms of recordings, not as dance music.

> I generally write albums, I don't really think in terms of 12s [LPs] and singles and DJs; I write for albums that I envisage people sitting at home and listening to, with maybe the odd DJ playing the odd track, but on the whole not writing dance-floor music. So the idea of actually trying to release something which was aimed specifically at DJs and at the dance floor appealed to me quite a lot.[26]

So Banco de Gaia, like Muslimgauze, depends on DJ remixes to turn his music into dance music. Oliver Lieb and Speedy J, "hardly the usual suspects in the area of global ambiance," writes one reviewer,[27] were brought in to make dance versions of "Kincajou," a track from *Last Train to Lhasa*. "It was deliberately aimed more at the dance floor than what I normally do, the idea was to emphasize the more techno side of it, the more dance friendly side of it."[28] Marks recalls that hiring DJs to make dance remixes of his music was probably his record label's idea, but he supported it.[29]

Marks, in the one instance I have known him to take a political position at all, advocates a single mega-cause, as does Bryn Jones. "The one thing I find difficult is there's so many causes and so many fights in the world, that sometimes it feels very strange just to be highlighting one above all the others. But, one thing at a time—this album's called *Last Train to Lhasa*, so it was the obvious thing to mention."[30] Marks has made it clear that he decries the Chinese occupation of Tibet and its treatment of Tibetans, and speaks in strong radical terms about it.

> The Chinese have been very brutal about the way they've gained control of Tibet: torturing, killing, destroying the culture. This goes on everywhere, even our countries have done it. In this day and age there's no reason this should be allowed to happen, the rest of the world can stop it. They won't, though, because China is such a big trade market, which is a perfect example of the way governments work these days. Countries would have to take a moral stance that China has no right to invade Tibet, but they won't because they don't want to lose all those wonderful trading dollars from China. Governments have become big banks, or corporations.

But Marks's political views are as reluctant as Bryn Jones's are vehement. In answer to the question following the one just quoted, he says, "I'm not into political music, I don't have slogans chanted over the top of my music or anything."[31]

So Marks explains the album's title this way:

[W]hen I was putting this album together I wasn't writing a concept album, it wasn't supposed to be about Tibet or anything in particular, apart from the track *Last Train to Lhasa*, which was very loosely inspired by the thought that it would be shit if they built a railway, that would really do it, that would really finish it off, 'cause at the time I had no idea there was going to be a railway, it was just theoretical.

So then I'd written all the tracks and the album needed a title, and someone said, "Oh, Last Train to Lhasa, that'd make a good name for an album," and I thought, yeah, okay, that'll do. It was no more than that. Then I started thinking about it. . . . well, if you're gonna call it this, maybe I could do something useful here, 'cause people read sleeve notes, and it is in effect an advertising space, so why not write something on there just highlighting what's going on in Tibet, and what it's all about, and who to contact if people wanna do something about it.

Unfortunately, what's happened, in retrospect, and I should have realised it, is a lot of people approached the album as a concept album about Tibet. I saw one review where it was saying "this is a really nice album, but I really can't see what this is supposed to have to do with Tibet. I'm disappointed, I thought it'd be more obvious." I never said it was about Tibet! Don't tell me I've failed on that score![32]

Yet inside the liner notes to the CD there is a photograph of the Potala, the Dalai Lama's historical main residence in Lhasa; the note accompanying the CD booklet gives a brief history of the Chinese invasion and genocide in Tibet, and concludes with information on how to contact the International Campaign for Tibet. The Banco de Gaia web pages for a time featured a series of pages called "Why Bother? Reflections on Tibet," with film clips of Chinese soldiers beating Tibetans, but these pages were later removed.[33]

Like Muslimgauze, Banco de Gaia's cover art is one of the important sites of political positioning. The cover to *Last Train to Lhasa* features a photograph of a locomotive with a red star, behind which are the Potala and the Himalayas; Tibetan people, some of whom are monks, appear near the train.

In contrast, New Age and other mainstream electronica musicians such as Deep Forest and Enigma by and large eschew the kind of politics and advocacy I have been discussing here. New Age musicians construct their identities as modern, bourgeois subjects, even hyper-subjects: They position themselves as creative individuals and seem to want their creativity recognized. Anything that might seem to be political might compromise their artistic autonomy and prevent their achieving a wide audience or major hit. New Age musicians, when they identify themselves with a particular cause, tend to espouse cuddly

Figure 10.4. Banco de Gaia: *Last Train to Lhasa,* cover.

ones, the We're All One Big Happy World kinds of causes. For example, Alain Eskinasi's recent *Many Worlds, One Tribe.* He appears (along with several un-named "natives") on the front cover, and there are three more pictures of him inside the CD booklet and on the back page. There may be many worlds and one tribe, but only one person in this tribe has power of representation here. This cover also illustrates a difference between New Age musicians and fringe electronica such as Muslimgauze and Banco de Gaia: the latter never appear in a recognizable fashion in or on their albums, which is rarely the case with New Age musicians.

SAMPLING: AESTHETICS AND PRACTICES

Like Jones and most of the people who make this kind of music, Toby Marks has clear views about sampling as a practice and art, and possesses a high-modernist idea of how to treat sampled material: as extremely aestheti-cized bits of sound. Marks's descriptions of what he's doing can be at odds with the effects.

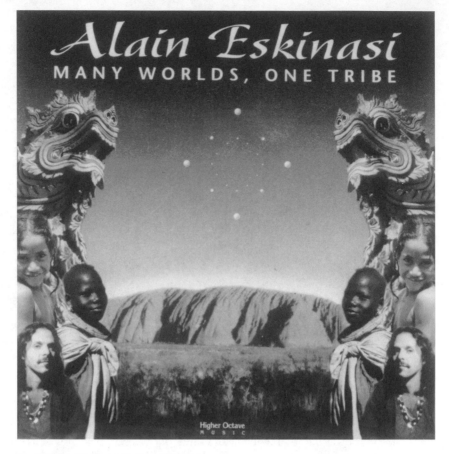

Figure 10.5. Alain Eskinasi: *Many Worlds, One Tribe*, cover.

There's about three ways to go about it. First, you can get it cleared by the rights holder of the original piece you sampled. That can be a complete nightmare, and be quite a bit more expensive. The second way is you distort the sample to such an extent that it's not recognizable. As far as I understand it, under UK law, that's legitimate. If its not recognizable as the original, then you're clear and your piece is considered a new artistic work. The third way is to use really obscure samples, which probably no one is ever going to know where it's come from.

It's this next portion I would direct your attention to in particular.

A lot of my samples come from all over the world, and I don't want to rip people off and not give them any credit. For instance: I find a Chinese sample which is lovely, but I can't track down where it came from—I'm going to use it anyway.

This "for instance" is an example of ripping someone off and not giving them credit, not of his unwillingness to do so.

Yet I would maintain that there is a difference between a modern aesthetic idea of the sample, and a different, newer, technological result. Jones and Marks view their samples not just as material, but as reified, digitized bits; modernist composers, no matter how much they hid their appropriated musics, both with their discourse and with their musical procedures, nonetheless tended to choose music to which they had some sort of connection, or to which they wanted to attach some kind of meaning. So, for example, the Russian Igor Stravinsky (1882–1971) took Russian folk music; Hungarian Béla Bartók (1881–1945) Eastern European folk music, and American Charles Ives (1874–1954) American music.[34] Later composers, after World War II, didn't necessarily possess an ethnic or national connection to the music they appropriated, but they nonetheless tended to establish long-term relationships to it, whether Olivier Messiaen (1908–1992) and his "Hindoo Rhythms," which pervade his *The Technique of My Musical Language* of 1957, or Henry Cowell (1897–1965) and his lifelong study of musics from many parts of the world.[35] It was meanings they were after, and they both found and constructed them in these other musics. It wasn't until the late 1960s that the kind of pastiches now common arose, and even these would be put to a larger idea, much like the New Age musicians discussed earlier. Karlheinz Stockhausen's (1928–) *Hymnen* (1966–67), for example, pulls together national anthems from all over the world; and *Telemusik* (1966), he tells us, is an attempt to realize an "old and ever-recurrent dream: to go a step further towards writing, not 'my' music, but a music of the whole world, of all lands and races."[36]

In hip-hop, the popular music that first used samplers as musical instruments and not just shortcuts or cost-cutting devices, sampled material to this day tends to be used either as homage to musical forebears, such as Parliament/George Clinton, and James Brown, and/or it's used as a way to establish a kind of musical community; hip-hop musicians sample music of their own past, music they like, music from their parents' record collections.[37] As Prince Be of P.M. Dawn told an interviewer,

> I love listening to records, I love feeling vibes from other people, I love being influenced by everything. I guess that's why music takes the turns that it does because there are no boundaries in who we want and who we listen to; we can take a Sly Stone sample, we can take a Joni Mitchell sample, we can take a James Brown sample, we can take a Cal Tjader sample. It doesn't really make a difference, it's just all vibes and how everything feels and how everything emotes itself, you know.[38]

Or this from De La Soul's Posdnuos:

> We don't exclude anything from playing a part in our music. I think it's crazy

how a lot of rappers are just doing the same thing over and over—Parliament/Funkadelic/James Brown—and all that. I bought Steely Dan's *Aja* when it first came out, and "Peg" was a song I always loved, so when it came down to making my own music, that was definitely a song I wanted to use. . . . It doesn't make any difference whether a sample is from James Brown, Cheech and Chong, Lee Dorsey, or a TV theme; if there's something that catches my ear, I'll use it.[39]

Some African American musicians view sampling as a more political act, as does Public Enemy's Chuck D: "Our music is filled with bites, bits of information from the real world, a world that's rarely exposed. Our songs are almost like headline news. We bring things to the table of discussion that are not usually discussed, or at least not from that perspective."[40] No matter the discourse, or the result, almost all hip-hop sampling practices are involved with making meanings, meanings that make sense to the musicians and to their fans.[41]

But these ethnic, national, or political, and community connections— meanings—are gone with these electronica musicians who are the subject of this paper; affect—as Fredric Jameson famously diagnosed—seems to have waned.[42] They can digitally manipulate the music they sample as well and as complexly as art music composers, but their manipulations don't necessarily have anything to with their discourse and their messages about the music. Toby Marks samples and manipulates both Chinese and Tibetan musics (among others) in the tracks on *Last Train to Lhasa,* and doesn't seem to notice that it might be possible to interpret his tampering with Tibetan music as not unrelated to Chinese treatment of Tibet and Tibetans. Marks has said that "people need to see that it's just other traditions which I'm taking."[43] Yet, this "taking," as I and many others have written, isn't completely distinct from the European colonial project generally, and in particular the Chinese imperial project that Marks is supposedly critiquing.[44]

Marks says that he gets his samples from all over the place.

I don't have any particular method of even finding them. I just sort of come across things, like when I'm traveling I've heard people play and recorded a bit, I've picked up tapes, heard things here and there. It's something that I can't be too specific about for obvious reasons.

Do you usually have samples you want to use first, or musical ideas?

It varies. Sometimes I'll just come across something I think is amazing and I might be able to imagine a tune built around it. Other times I stockpile stuff and when I'm working on a tune if I need a male Arabic vocal to fit a section I'll see if I have anything which would be suitable. But it tends to vary. Sometimes a sample will suggest the whole tune to me, but not very often unfortunately. It would be far too easy if that happened all the time![45]

Note the kinds of categories Marks uses: "male Arabic vocal," for example; it is clear that he possesses a very different idea about what music is: it's something that can be sampled, and neatly categorized.[46]

Once he has his samples, Marks's use of them is completely and arbitrarily free: He manipulates them any way he wishes.

> [I]t's pretty rare to [sample] something straight. Usually I'll find a starting point, I'll filter it, reverse it, slow it down or something so that it's different from the original. On one of my songs, "Amber," the vocal is actually backwards. It actually sounded more natural backwards. It was from this really weird language. I just slowed it down a bit, reversed it, and thought: "that sounds fucking gorgeous!" Played forward it sounds fucked up; played backwards it sounds like someone is singing it. It's weird.[47]

Natural to whom? Weird language to whom? I played this vocal backwards (that is to say, as it originally sounded) and it didn't sound much different (or any more recognizable); neither did Marks's synthesized music.

Again, this discourse is far different from similar practices in more mainstream musics. Steven Feld writes in a recent article that one of the four primary narratives through which western digital sampling practices operates is a discourse that always professes admiration for the appropriated music. "Everyone—no matter how exoticizing, how patronizing, how romanticizing, how essentializing in their rhetoric or packaging—declares their fundamental respect, even deep affection for the original music and its makers."[48] In fact, however, not all musicians professes this deep respect; this discourse is common in the New Age and/or mainstream market—which is mainly what Feld is considering, and where declarations of love, appreciation, and professions of small-worldness are de rigueur. But on the fringes, which is where most electronica musicians work, musicians' attitudes toward the samples are frequently more circumspect, and more informationalized. In other words, these New Age/mainstream musicians haven't abandoned meanings; their samples are there to do some work.

Another more tentative reason for the New Age/mainstream discourse may be that this music can become popular enough so that people whose music has been sampled will demand their fair share, as is happening with increasing frequency.[49] Very small labels and bands out of the mainstream, on the other hand, can sample with relative impunity. I have yet to see any sample clearance information on any of these albums, or even any discussion on the albums of what the samples might be. When samples and influences are discussed it is in the most general terms, such as "ethnic percussion" or "Chinese vocals," or, as we saw above, "male Arabic vocal."

WHAT'S UP?

Now that I have outlined some of the ideas and musical practices and political stances of these musicians, let's move to a discussion of how we can understand them in a larger cultural framework. There are several interrelated issues. One is the lack of a public projection of self, while at the same time the public connection with political causes; another concerns attitudes toward sampling; and the last concerns a postmodern theoretical concern with the "objectal form" (as Jameson calls it) of contemporary cultural production at the expense of the practices in which such forms are caught up.

Digitization of the Self and the World

If there seems to be a certain detachment or disjuncture between these auto-self-effaced electronica musicians and their causes, the vehemence with which Bryn Jones expresses his anti-Israeli stance is a little startling. Lawrence Grossberg has commented on the display of emotion—affect—as a display for its own sake, and offers the examples of Jack Nicholson, the quintessential male actor of the 1970s who convinced us of his characters' sincerity, and Dennis Hopper, the quintessential male actor of the 1980s, whose characters seem to display anger for no apparent reason other than effect. This observation is part of a larger argument about various kinds of affective authenticities and inauthenticities.

> Postmodernity refers to the changing nature of the articulation between the different planes of life. However cynically, the contemporary formations of ideology and desire remain committed to their own systems of difference and to the fact that these differences matter. On the other hand, without the anchor of affective investments, such differences cannot matter. Without these articulations, it doesn't matter what matters for, in the end, nothing matters.[50]

I would agree with Grossberg, but I'm not sure I would put it in the same way; and it may be that it isn't necessary to invoke the overused-into-obfuscation term "postmodernity." Clearly, though, in the face of the increasing penetration of extremely sophisticated technology into everyone's everyday lives, we are transitioning into some kind of new historical moment, but one in which, at the same time, older ideologies and practices haven't been eclipsed. They're still available, but not in an across-the-board, monolithic way, just as these new technologies and post-social worlds don't necessarily apply to everyone. Not everyone can afford the kind of music-making technologies I have been talking about, for example.

The forcefulness with which Jones expresses his political opinions may be part of a larger transition contemporary developed societies are undergoing, whether we call it post-industrial, late modern, postmodern, or whatever. Taking off from Grossberg's remark, I think it is possible to make a case for an increasingly separate, digitized, contemporary culture in which everything, every "plane of life" is more particularized and detached than ever before. Sociologist Manuel Castells writes in a recent study of technology and its relationship to contemporary culture:

Social movements tend to be fragmented, localistic, single-issue oriented, and ephemeral, either retrenched in their inner worlds, or flaring up for just an instant around a media symbol. In such a world of uncontrolled, confusing change, people tend to regroup around primary identities: religious, ethnic, territorial, national.[51]

But in the absence of religion—which, after all, many Western Europeans and Americans have abandoned—alignment with mega-causes can serve some of the same functions. Castells allows for this a little later when he writes that "the distinctive social and political trend of the 1990s is the construction of social action and politics around primary identities, either ascribed, rooted in history and geography, or newly built in an anxious search for meaning and spirituality."[52]

Castells identifies the central dynamic of the late twentieth century as the increasing distance between globalization and identity, between what he calls "the net and the self." It seems to me that in this late modern or postmodern era of computers, this process of splitting, fracturing, is becoming highlighted and emphasized and at the same time more particularized, so that new kinds of juxtapositions and combinations are possible, resulting in even greater contradictions and paradoxes than we saw in modernity. This same process is the digital process.

Digitization is busily colonizing everything, turning everything into information that can be disseminated instantly if one is affluent enough to own or have access to the proper technology. Paul Virilio writes that information "nowadays [is] outstripping the notions of mass and energy";[53] then, with the advent of Tele-action—that is, telecommunications transport of data—"information comes to the fore as an entirely separate form of energy: *sound and image* energy, the energy of long-distance touch and contact" (emphasis in original).[54] This is information as the digitized bit, which has the power to imperialize everything and everywhere, while at the same time it effaces our sense of where everywhere is.

Despite these newer, smaller, looser bifurcations and splits, at the same time, it is beginning to be possible to posit a new larger binary opposition between Castells's "the net and the self," where the net isn't only the Internet, but the network of communications, trade, and information that more and more of us increasingly inhabit.

If we return to an examination of Jones and Marks and their music, it's clear that they seem to want to be political and non-political at the same time. Rather than pursuing a local politics, they advocate faraway causes (and it may not be a coincidence that these two British subjects have chosen to protest imperialist regimes). The samples in their music may or may not have anything to do with their rhetoric about the music. They make a kind of music derived from dance music and the English dance club scene, but Marks seems to owe his fame not to his few live appearances but his CD sales, and Muslimgauze doesn't appear live at all; CD sales seem to be his main source of income. And both bands make music for albums, not dances, and so their music is remixed by DJs to make it danceable.

It is also possible to make an argument that electronica musicians such as Marks and Jones eschew the club scene in favor of a more aestheticized musicking; this is Sarah Thornton's argument in *Club Cultures,* in which she writes that ambient musicians attempt to aestheticize the music and make a bid for it as art by distinguishing it as a music to be listened to rather than danced to.[55] This would not be unrelated to these musicians' adoption of a starving-poet-in-the-garret mode of production, one of the deepest Western cultural myths about artistic production.

So there seem to be many contradictions and paradoxes, but the point is that, from a more digital and digitized perspective, these aren't contradictions and paradoxes at all; contemporary life for these and many other people has simply assumed some new structures.

Sampling

Nothing better exemplifies musically the split between the micro-self and the espousal of macro-causes than the use of samples in this music. Andrew Goodwin has labeled the kind of sampling practices I have been examining here as "postmodern," in which samples are "juxtaposed materials in a network of 'texts' which refuse any position of judgment on them; the listener has only a tissue of fragmented references which exemplify a culture saturated with sounds but which prevent interpretive fixities or certitudes."[56] I should point out, though, that one cannot know if interpretations are prevented without talking to interpreters, and, as usual, an ethnographic perspective is almost always lacking in such discussions. Some people do make meanings out of this music, and for these musicians themselves, while nonetheless hearing their samples more as information than affective signifiers, it appears to be also the case that affect isn't entirely absent, either, as I will illustrate in a moment.

It is clear that fans listen to this music in different ways than most musicians or musicologists; they often possess astonishingly arcane knowledge of what is sampled in the music.[57] But it's not just specialized knowledge or skill: it's a different set of conceptions about how the music works as music. Here's an example. The Germany-based band Enigma, a hugely successful, more mainstream example of the kinds of musicians I'm talking about here, sampled aboriginal Taiwanese folk music in their *Return to Innocence* of 1993.[58] There was a good deal of discussion about this song on the Enigma mailing list on the Internet, but what interests me is that, while for musicologists the most salient feature of the song is the nature of the sample, and sampling in general, what Enigma fans seem to find most remarkable about the song is its form. Enigma experts and fans have commented on the simple formal structure of the song; the keeper of one of the Enigma web pages calls it their most traditional song—a verse-chorus arrangement (with the sampled Taiwanese music as the chorus). Some fans like this simplicity, but others think is too simple, or traditional.

For these fans, this music isn't necessarily depthless, or mere pastiche; they don't often hear the samples as decontextualized or aestheticized, but as things that contribute to the meaning of the songs. For the listeners of the bands on the fringes such as Muslimgauze and Banco de Gaia, fans' discourse is harder to come by, and also tends to speak more to the aestheticized nature of the music and sampling. Fans tend to speak in fairly technical terms, though there are some at the same time who say simply that they love the music. Early in 1997, one wrote in to the Enigma mailing list (which often considers Enigma-like music) that "the title song of this album [*Last Train to Lhasa*] is a very attractive track, at 12 minutes it has a well-made buildup starting initially with the sound of a steam train. This forms the rhythm frame to which the percussion and drums add. Later on a Tibetan chant is used to good effect as the singing part." These Enigma fans almost always note that Banco de Gaia's music is "a bit more techno" or "a bit more ambient" than Enigma, but that they still like it. And I should note that they often speak of Enigma's music (and that of other more mainstream acts) in extremely emotional terms.[59]

Outside of the Enigma mailing list, however, fans speak mainly in technical terms. One fan wrote into rec.music.ambient in March 1996:

> *Izlamaphobia* [Muslimgauze's 1995 album] is 30 or so (still shortish) rythmic [*sic*] ejaculations, most of which don't bother with the mundane concepts of introduction or theme development, dropping you in abruptly to some nerve-crushing loop space, with no linear beginning, middle or end. Most of the cust are in the three minute range (with some as long as 8 or 9 minutes (and some only 1.5 minute specks), which ordinarily bothers me, as ususally sound needs some chronic space to develop its groove. However, the music here is so nasty and aggressive and intense, the lengths are just fine.[60]

And so forth.

The electronica fans of Banco de Gaia and Muslimgauze are clearly more concerned with technical issues than the fans of related but more mainstream musics, but at the same time it is evident that they possess an aesthetic and a kind of affect about this music.

POSTMODERNISM; OR, BENJAMIN DEFENDED AGAINST HIS DEVOTEES

So far so good: everything I have written about this music, the musicians, and their fans seems to jibe pretty well with the postmodern world described by Fredric Jameson, Jean Baudrillard, and others: cultural production in this historical moment—at least on the margins I have been examining—is nothing but a sea of floating signifiers, ungrounded in anything real, much less original or authentic; all forms are pastiches, blank parodies, statues without eyeballs; affect has waned; a new depthlessness seems to be the order of the day.[61] And I have used some of these terms in my discussion thus far.

But concentrating on what these new cultural forms are like, or on sampling not so much as a practice per se but as a practice that results in musical objects, seems to me to be too focused on these forms as objects or products, rather than as always/already incomplete results of an ongoing process. In discussions of mechanical and, now, electronic and digital (re)productions of cultural forms, Walter Benjamin's 1935 essay, "The Work of Art in the Age of Mechanical Reproduction," is almost always discussed.[62] Given the high visibility of this article, it is probably not necessary to outline his argument here beyond saying that for Benjamin, the increasing mechanical reproduction of artworks signaled the end of the "aura" of the artwork—that which made it original, unique, authentic. Benjamin lamented this end, but at the same time was aware of the liberatory possibilities raised by mechanical reproduction, partly because this would make artworks available to the masses as never before.

I find this essay cited with growing frequency, to the extent that I think we are at present in the midst of a Benjamin renaissance. And yet, I think Benjamin's argument is actually quite limited in helping us understand the materials I've presented here, or popular culture in general. It's clear from Benjamin that he is talking about art, and even though it is common today to refer to popular musicians as artists—and that, more broadly, the hegemony of art as a discourse is waning—I would still argue that Benjamin's conception of aura simply does not apply to popular musics, never did, and that extensions of his argument into the realm of the popular are ignorant of audiences, reception, and ethnographic perspectives generally, perspectives that Benjamin himself did not seek out either.

But Benjamin is invariably invoked in discussions of popular music and technology—there is undeniably a specter of aura haunting popular music studies. Benjamin turns up in Andrew Goodwin's "Sample and Hold," for example (and if I seem to be picking on Goodwin here it is only because his arguments are better than most).[63] Goodwin writes that "*everyone* may purchase an 'original,'"[64] even though I would counter that this was never an issue to musicians or fans—again the lack of an ethnographic perspective causes problems. Goodwin accounts for the attendance at live concerts as a way to soak up the aura of live performers, but I would say that this might be the only time this term should apply, and that, more importantly, it may be the communal aspect of going to concerts, and the cultural capital acquired in doing so, that provide the more compelling motivation. Besides, people go to sporting events and attend speaking engagements of public figures for the same reason; if this is aura, it is not restricted to art. Goodwin is also right to tackle "the postmodernists" who insist on viewing sampling as a new and depthless practice, not noticing how much it is tied to earlier ways of musicking, and not paying enough attention to actual music.

I am sure that some would argue that the distinction I am making be-tween popular culture and art is too facile, too binarized, and is ignoring what some have viewed as a crucial feature of postmodern cultural production gen-erally: that there is an increasing communication across the "great divide" of high and low in terms of cultural production.[65] There is a little crossing down (more like "slumming"), I think, and there are some subgroups that listen a little more adventurously than they might have in the past (particularly those groups with high amounts of educational capital). But nonetheless, I would argue that, ethnographically speaking, this great divide is still with us; the same audiences go to pretty much the same concerts, and the consumption of cul-tural forms is as linked to cultural capital as it ever was, as Pierre Bourdieu so memorably taught us.[66]

In rejecting the Benjaminesque aura in considerations of popular music (and popular culture in general), I am not jettisoning ethnographic concerns of authenticity, originality, or creativity, which are often discussed as related to conceptions of aura. But if we want to find something resembling aura that is talked about in the terms of authenticity or creativity or what have you, and if we pay attention to where the fans and musicians are, it is possible to view this set of practices from another perspective. As I have written elsewhere, if one has one's ear to the ground, that is, if you cultivate an ethnographic perspec-tive, there are meanings being made all over the place.[67] The point I would like to emphasize here, though, is that not only are fans making meanings, but that there is also another way of looking at this kind of cultural production. Sam-pling and music technology are being put to a variety of different ends, as I have already discussed with regard to New Age music and hip-hop. More gen-erally, many who write about the rise of new technologies speak of the so-called democratization of musicking—electronics makes musicking easier than ever—though this point is curiously never elaborated by anyone: aura always receives the first, and usually only, consideration.[68]

For example, Simon Frith writes in "Art versus Technology,"

> Technology, the shifting possibility of mechanical reproduction, has certain-ly been the necessary condition for the rise of the multinational entertain-ment business, for ever more sophisticated techniques of ideological ma-nipulation, but technology has also made possible new forms of cultural democracy and new opportunities of individual and collective expression.[69]

And this is the sole extent of his treatment of this issue of "cultural democ-racy."

But what does this "cultural democracy" mean? Alan Durant outlines three different way the term is used, without really taking a position on any of them. One meaning, he writes, refers to democracy as "something which results from cheapness of the equipment"; the second refers to a democracy "as something which results from an input into definition of the technology"—that is, every-one can have a say in the development of music technology; and third, democracy refers to "something which results from a low or easily attainable skills-threshold for using the technology."[70]

I would like to try to move this discussion away from its emphasis on the "objectal form" of the technology-involved work—with its qualities of pastiche, bricolage, depthlessness, and others—and toward the arena of process, of Durant's first meaning of "democracy"; we have already seen how meanings can be made by both musicians and fans from technological musics and sampling. And Benjamin wrote about this, too, though this part of his essay has not been nearly so influential in considerations of popular music and technology. Rather than fetishizing or reifying "aura," I would rather draw attention to the possibility for authorship, as does Benjamin:

> [T]oday there is hardly a gainfully employed European who could not, in principle, find an opportunity to publish somewhere or other comments on his work, grievances, documentary reports, or that sort of thing. Thus, the distinction between author and public is about to lose its basic character. The difference becomes merely functional; it may vary from case to case. At any moment the reader is ready to turn into a writer. As expert, which he had to become willy-nilly in an extremely specialized work process, even if only in some minor respect, the reader gains access to authorship.[71]

But as that Packard Bell ad showed, the "basic character" of the distinction between the author and her public is not only blurred; at the same time, the public in the era of digital reproduction is decreasingly a realm in which there is significant discourse or interchange.

While I would not celebrate the decline of the public, this phenomenon might at least be mitigated if one result is that more people make music for themselves. In *Noise,* Jacques Attali posits a fourth stage of musicking that he calls "composition," in which people make their own music for the own reasons and pleasure. While this argument is often cited in discussions of music and technology, I think it has not received the attention it deserves because most scholars are too focused on the resulting musical object rather than the processes that produced it, as noted above.

Attali writes:

> We are all condemned to silence—unless we create our own relation with the world and try to tie other people into the meaning we thus create. That is what composing is. Doing solely for the sake of doing, without trying artificially to recreate the old codes in order to reinsert communication into them.[72]

And later:

> Composition thus leads to a staggering conception of history, a history that is open, unstable, in which labor no longer advances accumulation, in which the object is no longer a stockpiling of lack, in which music effects a reappropriation of time and space. Time no longer flows in a linear fashion; sometimes it crystallizes in stable codes in which everyone's composition is com-

patible, sometimes in a multifaceted time in which rhythms, styles, and codes diverge, interdependencies become more burdensome, and rules dissolve.[73]

This excerpt describes reasonably well the kinds of music I have been discussing.

It is no accident that fans of Muslimgauze, Banco de Gaia, and ambient, techno, and industrial music in general tend to speak more in technical terms than affective ones, since many of them are already involved in making this music. In order for ordinary people to make this music, however—in order to be "democratic"—the technology involved has to be affordable. By and large, it isn't, but these fringe dance electronica musicians have cultivated a do-it-yourself ethic that advocates using cheap and old equipment, thus deliberately avoiding the newer-is-better, faster-is-better ethic of most technologists.

Some musicians/fans argue that this is how the music came into existence in the first place, as does this Australian musician:

> However, the reason [techno] came about was because the kids who invented the form, were locked into it by economics. There was a time in the late 80s when no-one wanted those old analogue synths. They wanted the new gleaming digital stuff. It was a time when TB-303s [Roland analogue synthesizers] were given away. Sold at garage sales . . . for a fiver. A time when, if a pot [knob] became scratchy or broke all together on a synth, you'd probably throw it away rather than replace it. Or at most sell it for 50 bucks to someone who you considered a fool for buying it at any price. Whatever happened, it meant that people didn't place much value in these "old buckets."

> The kids were no fools. Unlike vintage synth collectors . . . the kids needed to get into it at what ever level they could. They'd most likely look at the gleaming digitals and aspire to own them but they could afford bucket loads of cheap, hand-me-down analogues. Then they discovered, more as novelties, the weird and wonderful sounds they could make. I remember them well and I remember my attitude. "Oh that's cute but we *real* musicians have progressed somewhat." Man was I wrong. This stuff became "Thee Shit."[74]

By insisting on using relatively inexpensive, easy-to-find equipment, electronica musicians are ensuring that anyone who wants to make their music can. This is not just an aesthetic, or a fetishization of the cheap; according to German musician Pete Namlook (whose real name is Peter Kuhlmann; "Namlook" is "Kuhlmann" backwards spelled phonetically; "Namlook backwards is "koolman"), "The aim is for everyone to make a living, to bring music forward, to make innovation in music. Not to stand still. To achieve this what has happened is a social revolution where musicians are now helping each other to release music."[75] "Forget about talent," says "How to Become a Techno God," a guide to making your own techno music; "talent just gets in the way."[76]

The efforts of the music industry early in 1997 to try to mainstream some electronica musics will no doubt succeed to some degree, as the history of the industry suggests. At the same time, the musicians' DIY ethic, their refusal to be co-opted into the industry (which means that they make and sell their own cassettes, or in the case of Banco de Gaia and Muslimgauze and other bands who don't usually appear live, make small numbers of compact discs for small, independent labels), the dissemination of information about these bands through word of mouth, zines, and the Internet rather than the mainstream press, the continued espousal of affordable equipment—all of these factors indicate that Attali's moment of composition is here, at least, on the fringes. Perhaps the day will come when our shiny new Packard Bell personal computer comes equipped with not only a CD-ROM and sound card, but a drum machine and a sampler so we can make our own music instead of just buying it.

NOTES

This is a revised version of a paper presented at Unnatural Acts, at the University of California, Riverside, on April 11, 1997. I would like to thank Deborah Wong for inviting me to participate. I would also like to thank Deborah and the other Unnatural Acts participants for their insightful comments that helped improve this paper, in particular Philip Brett, Sue-Ellen Case, George Lipsitz, René T. A. Lysloff, and the respondent to our panel, Christopher Waterman. Finally, thanks, as usual, go to Sherry B. Ortner, who always helps more than she knows.

1. Packard Bell is proud of this spot, and on its web site offers eight different still photos from it, as well as downloadable versions of the entire ad. The first page of their web pages features a new logo that asks their trademark question, "Wouldn't you rather be at home?" They also promise an eventual trio of thirty-second ads that will "expand on the commercial's main ideas." See www.packardbell.com/ads96/television.asp. (*Note:* I am including all URLs for the sake of documentation, but many are no longer available, such as this one at Packard Bell. Defunct URLs will be indicated.)

2. This is a fast-growing genre, currently being touted as The Next Big Thing by the sales-depressed music industry. See Brett Attwood, "Electronic Music Poised for Power Surge in States: Radio, Video Offering Mainstream Exposure," *Billboard,* February 15, 1997, 1; Larry Flick and Doug Reece, "Electronic Music Poised for Power Surge in States: Rising Interest Sparks Excitement, Concern," *Billboard,* February 15, 1997, 1; Karen Schoemer, "Electronic Eden," *Newsweek,* February 10, 1997, 60–62; and Neil Strauss, "The Next Big Thing or the Next Bust?" *New York Times,* January 26, 1997, H36. MTV has also begun a new program, *amp,* devoted to this music, though it's significant that this show airs at one o'clock on Sunday mornings.

3. Jürgen Habermas, *The Structural Transformation of the Public Sphere: An Inquiry into a Category of Bourgeois Society,* trans. Thomas Burger and Frederick Lawrence (Cambridge, Mass.: MIT Press, 1991), p. 27.

4. Quoted by Geoff Eley, "Nations, Publics, and Political Cultures: Placing Habermas in the Nineteenth Century," in *Culture/Power/History: A Reader in Contemporary Social Theory,* ed. Nicholas B. Dirks, Geoff Eley, and Sherry B. Ortner (Princeton, N.J.: Princeton University Press, 1994), p. 297.

5. Nancy Fraser, *Unruly Practices: Power, Discourse and Gender in Contemporary Social Theory* (Minneapolis: University of Minnesota Press, 1989). See also Eley, "Nations, Publics, and Political Cultures."

6. In setting aside Habermas, I am merely doing so because he doesn't help much with the issues at hand. There are a growing number of scholars who are expanding Habermas's ideas to argue that the revitalization of the democratic process will happen with the increasing influence of the Internet. See, for example, Howard Rheingold, *The Virtual Community: Homesteading on the Electronic Frontier* (New York: Harper-Perennial, 1993) which explicitly builds on Habermas (in pages 282–85). A recent article in the chronicle of cyberlife, *Wired*, tackles issues directly relevant to Habermas: Jon Katz's "The Netizen: Birth of a Digital Nation," *Wired*, April 1997, 49, as does Mark Poster's earlier "The Net as a Public Sphere?" *Wired*, November 1995, 135–36. For academic treatments of similar issues, see Robert Bledsoe, "The Sentimental Culture of the Internet: Transformations of the Publics [*sic*] Spheres in the Eighteenth and Twentieth Centuries," paper delivered at the Modern Language Association, 1995, formerly archived on the Internet at http://www.humnet.ucla.edu/projects/netcrit/rsb_mla95.html, no longer available; Robin Datta and Cynthia West, "The Citizen as Cyborg: An Exploration of New Information Technologies, Interactive Spectatorship, and the Shifting Concept of the Citizen," paper delivered at the Western Political Science Association, San Francisco, California, 1996, formerly archived at http://www.ssct.ucsb.edu/~datta/wpsa96.html; and Mark Poster, "CyberDemocracy: Internet and the Public Sphere," at http://www.hnet.uci.edu/mposter/writings/democ.html.

7. Arjun Appadurai and Carol Breckenridge, "Why Public Culture?" *Public Culture* 1 (Fall 1988): 5.

8. Marshall Berman, *All That Is Solid Melts into Air: The Experience of Modernity* (New York: Penguin, 1988).

9. Mike Davis, *City of Quartz: Excavating the Future in Los Angeles* (New York: Vintage, 1992); Edward W. Soja, *Postmodern Geographies: The Reassertion of Space in Critical Social Theory* (London and New York: Verso, 1989).

10. Prince Be, for example, in an interview with Terry Gross, said that about 35 percent of his album *Jesus Wept* (1995) "is musicians and the rest are samples. I'm a sampling artist, what can I tell you?" (National Public Radio, *Fresh Air*, November 29, 1995).

11. See Sarah Thornton's *Club Cultures* (Middletown, Conn.: Wesleyan University Press, 1996) for a discussion of the dance music underground in the United Kingdom and the naming practices of the bands.

12. Just as this article was going to press, I learned that Bryn Jones had died of a rare fungal infection on January 14, 1999. See Neil Strauss, "Bryn Jones, 38, Musician Known as Muslimgauze," *New York Times*, January 28, 1999, C23.

13. http://www.banco.co.uk/

14. http://www.hallucinet.com/asylem/asylem4/bdg.htm

15. http://www.banco.co.uk/

16. In *Billboard* 's recent list of the top-selling albums of 1996, only one New Age musician, Enya, appeared. There were no electronica groups (Ed Christman, "Indies No. 1 in Total Album Mark Share for First Time; WEA Is No. 1 in 'Current' Share," *Billboard*, January 18, 1997, 60).

17. See Carrie Borzillo, "U.S. Ad Uses Adds to Commercial Success of *Deep Forest*," *Billboard*, June 11, 1994, 44, and "Deep Forest Growing in Popularity; 550's World Music-Dance Hybrid Climbs Charts," *Billboard*, February 19, 1994, 8; Steven Feld, "Pygmy POP: A Genealogy of Schizophonic Mimesis," in *Yearbook for Traditional Music*, vol. 28 (1997); Andrew Ross, review of *Deep Forest*, *Artforum* 32 (December 1993): 11; and Al Weisel, "Deep Forest's Lush Lullaby," *Rolling Stone*, April 21, 1994, 26.

18. This is probably the result of the many high school and college students who participate in marching bands.

19. http://www.compusmart.ab.ca/tbennett/html/musarticles.htm, now gone

20. Richard Gehr, "Muslimgauze: Beyond the Veil," *The Village Voice*, October 28, 1994, 67.

21. http://www.compusmart.ab.ca/tbennett/html/Muslimgauze/.

22. From a media release by Extreme, http://www.xtr.com/extreme/muslimg.htm.

23. http://www.compusmart.ab.ca/tbennett/html/musarticles.htm

24. http://www.compusmart.ab.ca/tbennett/html/musarticles.htm

25. http://www.compusmart.ab.ca/tbennett/html/muspress.htm

26. http://www.demon.co.uk/london-calling/mbanco1.html; but this site lacks these older pages.

27. Ibid.

28. Ibid.

29. He expressed reservations in another interview, however, where he questioned this process: "But to me that always seems a bit like saying well here's the proper one and this remix album is stuff we played around with and some of it's alright and some of [it] isn't. I really want to do it that way" (http://www.nettfriends.com/~pop/banco-ten.html, no longer available). Clearly there is some tension between dance-related electronica such as Marks and Jones produce, and dance music for clubs, but that is the subject for another paper.

30. http://www.demon.co.uk/london-calling/mbancocov.html. This newer Banco de Gaia site does not contain these older pages.

31. http://www.outerbass.com/resonance/banco/indexF.html

32. http://www.demon.co.uk/london-calling/mbanco3.html

33. The Banco de Gaia web site is http://www.banco.co.uk/.

34. For writings on these composers and their uses of other musics, see Lawrence Morton, "Footnotes to Stravinsky Studies: *Le Sacre du Printemps*," *Tempo* 78 (1979): 9–16; Richard Taruskin, "Russian Folk Melodies in *The Rite of Spring*," *Journal of the American Musicological Society* 33 (1980): 501–43; Benjamin Suchoff, "Ethnomusicological Roots of Béla Bartók's Musical Language," *World of Music* 29 (1987): 43–65; and J. Peter Burkholder, *All Made of Tunes: Charles Ives and the Uses of Musical Borrowing* (New Haven, Conn.: Yale University Press, 1995).

35. Olivier Messiaen, *The Technique of My Musical Language*, trans. John Satterfield (Paris: A. Leduc, 1956).

36. Karl H. Wörner, *Stockhausen: Life and Work*, trans. and ed. Bill Hopkins (Berkeley: University of California Press, 1973), p. 58. See also Karlheinz Stockhausen, "World Music," trans. Bernard Radloff, *The Dalhousie Review* 69 (1989): 318–26; and *Towards a Cosmic Music*, sel. and trans. Tim Nevill (Longmead, Shaftesbury, Dorset, England: Element Books, 1989).

37. For discussions of sampling in hip-hop, see Andrew Bartlett, "Airshafts, Loud-speakers, and the Hip Hop Sample: Contexts and African American Musical Aesthetics," *African American Review* 28 (Winter 1994): 639–52; and Tricia Rose, *Black Noise: Rap Music and Black Culture in Contemporary America* (Middletown, Conn. Wesleyan University Press, 1994).

38. Interview with Terry Gross, National Public Radio, *Fresh Air*, November 29, 1995.

39. Quoted by Mark Dery, "Tommy Boy X 3: Digital Underground, Coldcut, and De La Soul Jam the Beat with Audio Junkyard Collisions," *Keyboard*, March 1991, 70.

40. Quoted by Mark Dery, "Public Enemy: Confrontation," *Keyboard*, September 1990, 93.

41. See Sarah Thornton's *Club Cultures* for a discussion of "black" and "white" approaches to dance music in the United Kingdom.

42. In the influential opening essay that lends its name to the title of the book, in Fredric Jameson, *Postmodernism; or, The Cultural Logic of Late Capitalism*, Post-Contemporary Interventions, ed. Stanley Fish and Fredric Jameson (Durham, N.C.: Duke University Press, 1991).

43. Quoted by Dominic Pride, "U.K.'s Nation of 'Ethno-Techno,'" *Billboard*, October 28, 1995, 52.

44. See, among others, Feld, "Pygmy POP"; Deborah Root, *Cannibal Culture: Art, Appropriation, and the Commodification of Difference* (Boulder, Colo.: Westview Press, 1996); my *Global Pop: World Music, World Markets* (New York and London: Routledge, 1997); and Marianna Torgovnick, *Gone Primitive: Savage Intellects, Modern Lives* (Chicago: University of Chicago Press, 1990).

45. http://www.nettfriends.com/~pop/bancosamples.html, no longer available.

46. Philip Brett suggests that this kind of categorization may have originated among musicians with the work of Brian Eno, who himself is generally credited with inventing the genre "ambient."

47. http://www.outerbass.com/resonance/banco/indexF.html

48. Feld, "Pygmy POP," p. 26.

49. Ibid.

50. Lawrence Grossberg, *We Gotta Get Out of This Place: Popular Conservatism and Postmodern Culture* (New York and London: Routledge, 1992), 224.

51. Manuel Castells, *The Rise of the Network Society* (Cambridge, Mass., and Oxford: Blackwell, 1996), p. 3.

52. Ibid., p. 22.

53. Paul Virilio, *The Art of the Motor*, trans. Julie Rose (Minneapolis and London: University of Minnesota Press, 1995), p. 125.

54. Ibid., p. 138.

55. Thornton, *Club Cultures*, p. 71.

56. Goodwin's argument in "Sample and Hold: Pop Music in the Digital Age of Reproduction," in *On Record: Rock, Pop, and the Written Word*, ed. Simon Frith and Andrew Goodwin (New York: Pantheon, 1990), is summarized here by Alan Durant, "A New Day for Music? Digital Technologies in Contemporary Music-Making," in *Culture, Technology and Creativity*, ed. Philip Hayward (London: John Libbey, 1990), p. 186.

57. See, for example, the "The Top 531 Sampling Groups" compilation, a list of the top 481 sample sources, contained on the Internet at http://phobos.astro.uwo.ca/~etittley/top_samples/grouplist.html

58. See my "A Riddle Wrapped in a Mystery: Transnational Music Sampling and Enigma's 'Return to Innocence,'" in preparation.

59. Ibid.

60. Original spellings have been retained in all newsgroup and mailing list postings.

61. See, most importantly, Baudrillard's *In the Shadow of Silent Majorities* (New York: Semiotext(e), 1983) and *Selected Writings,* ed. Mark Poster (Stanford: Stanford University Press, 1988); and Jameson, *Postmodernism; or, The Cultural Logic of Late Capitalism.*

62. Collected in *Illuminations,* ed. Hannah Arendt, trans. Harry Zohn (New York: Schocken Books, 1969).

63. See John Mowitt, "The Sound of Music in the Era of its Electronic Reproducibility," in *Music and Society: The Politics of Composition, Performance and Reception,* ed. Richard Leppert and Susan McClary (Cambridge: Cambridge University Press, 1987); T. G. Schumacher, "'This Is a Sampling Sport': Digital Sampling, Rap Music and the Law in Cultural Production," *Media, Culture & Society* 17 (1995): 253–73; and many others.

64. Goodwin, "Sample and Hold," p. 259.

65. Andreas Huyssen, *After the Great Divide: Modernism, Mass Culture, Postmodernism,* Theories of Representation and Difference, ed. Teresa de Lauretis (Bloomington and Indianapolis: Indiana University Press, 1986).

66. Pierre Bourdieu, *Distinction: A Social Critique of the Judgement of Taste,* trans. Richard Nice (Cambridge: Harvard University Press, 1984). See also Andrew Goodwin's "Popular Music and Postmodern Theory," *Cultural Studies* 5 (May 1991): 174–90 for a useful critique of the idea of the breakdown of distinctions between high and low.

67. Taylor, "A Riddle Wrapped in a Mystery."

68. See Alan Durant, "A New Day for Music? Digital Technologies in Contemporary Music-Making," in *Culture, Technology and Creativity,* ed. Philip Hayward (London: John Libbey, 1990), especially pp. 193–95.

69. Simon Frith, "Art versus Technology: The Strange Case of Popular Music," *Media, Culture & Society* 8 (July 1986): 278.

70. Durant, "A New Day for Music?" p. 193.

71. Benjamin, "The Work of Art in the Age of Mechanical Reproduction," in *Illuminations,* ed. Hannah Arendt, trans. by Harry Zohn (New York: Schocken Books, 1969), p. 232.

72. Jacques Attali, *Noise: The Political Economy of Music,* trans. Brian Massumi (Minneapolis: University of Minnesota Press, 1985), p. 134

73. Ibid., p. 147.

74. http://www2.gist.net.au/~aek/batz/paradigm.txt, no longer available. Thanks are due to Susana Loza, who gave me this URL. See also David Toop's *Ocean of Sound: Aether Talk, Ambient Sound and Imaginary Worlds* (London and New York: Serpent's Tail, 1995), pp. 212–14, for a discussion of the importance of cheap equipment.

75. Quoted by Mark Prendergast, "The Chilling Fields," *New Statesman & Society* 8 (January 13, 1995): 32.

76. From the Internet newsgroup alt.rave. I have left the original spelling intact.

REFERENCES

Discography

Banco de Gaia. *Last Train to Lhasa.* Mammoth/Planet Dog MR0115-2, 1995.
Eskinasi, Alain. *Many Worlds, One Tribe.* Higher Octave Music HOMCD 7089, 1996.
Muslimgauze. *Hamas Arc.* Staalplaat ST CD 051, 1993.
Tobias. *Rainforest Rhapsody in the Key of Bali.* Malibu Records MR -09920-DA, n.d.

Webography

Note: All URLs are accurate as of September 1999.
http://phobos.astro.uwo.ca/~etittley/top_samples/grouplist.html
    The Top 531 Sampling Groups" compilation
http://www.compusmart.ab.ca/tbennett/html/Muslimgauze/
    Muslimgauze page
http://www.london-calling.co.uk
http://www.hallucinet.com/asylem/asylem4/bdg.htm
http://www.nettfriends.com/~pop/bancoten.html
    Pages devoted to Banco de Gaia, no longer available
http://www.banco.co.uk
    Banco de Gaia home page
http://www.outerbass.com/resonance/banco/indexF.html
http://www.packardbell.com/ads96/television.asp
    Packard Bell's television ad site, no longer active
http://www.synthcom.com/cgi-bin/gear
    Neil Bradley's USA Used Gear Price List
http://www.xtr.com/extreme/muslimg.htm
    Extreme, the label of Muslimgauze
http://www.tqmcomms.co.uk/uk-dance/
    UK-Dance page, no longer active

Unpublished Materials

Bledsoe, Robert. "The Sentimental Culture of the Internet: Transformations of the Publics [*sic*] Spheres in the Eighteenth and Twentieth Centuries." Paper delivered at the Modern Language Assocation, 1995.
http://www.humnet.ucla.edu/projects/netcrit/rsb_mla95.html, no longer available
Datta, Robin, and Cynthia West. "The Citizen as Cyborg: An Exploration of New Information Technologies, Interactive Spectatorship, and the Shifting Concept of the Citizen." Paper delivered at the Western Political Science Association, San Francisco, California, 1996.
http://www.sscf.ucsb.edu/~datta/wpsa96.html, no longer available
Poster, Mark. "CyberDemocracy: Internet and the Public Sphere." http://www.hnet.uci.edu/mposter/writings/democ.html

Prince Be. Interview with Terry Gross. *Fresh Air.* National Public Radio. November 29, 1995.

Taylor, Timothy D. "A Riddle Wrapped in a Mystery: Transnational Music Sampling and Enigma's 'Return to Innocence.'" In preparation.

Bibliography

Appadurai, Arjun, and Carol Breckenridge. "Why Public Culture?" *Public Culture* 1 (Fall 1988): 5–9.

Attali, Jacques. *Noise: The Political Economy of Music.* Trans. Brian Massumi. Theory and History of Literature, ed. Wlad Godzich and Jochen Schulte-Sasse, no. 16. Minneapolis: University of Minnesota Press, 1985.

Attwood, Brett. "Electronic Music Poised for Power Surge in States: Radio, Video Offering Mainstream Exposure." *Billboard,* February 15, 1997, 1.

Bartlett, Andrew. "Airshafts, Loudspeakers, and the Hip Hop Sample: Contexts and African American Musical Aesthetics." *African American Review* 28 (Winter 1994): 639–52.

Baudrillard, Jean. *In the Shadow of Silent Majorities.* New York: Semiotext(e), 1983.

———. *Selected Writings.* Ed. Mark Poster. Stanford, Calif.: Stanford University Press, 1988.

Benjamin, Walter. "The Work of Art in the Age of Mechanical Reproduction." In *Illuminations,* ed. Hannah Arendt. Trans. Harry Zohn. New York: Schocken Books, 1969.

Berman, Marshall. *All That Is Solid Melts into Air: The Experience of Modernity.* New York: Penguin, 1988.

Borzillo, Carrie. "Deep Forest Growing in Popularity; 550's World Music-Dance Hybrid Climbs Charts." *Billboard,* February 19, 1994, 8.

———. "U.S. Ad Use Adds to Commercial Success of Deep Forest." *Billboard,* June 11, 1994, 44.

Bourdieu, Pierre. *Distinction: A Social Critique of the Judgement of Taste.* Trans. Richard Nice. Cambridge: Harvard University Press, 1984.

Burkholder, J. Peter. *All Made of Tunes: Charles Ives and the Uses of Musical Borrowing.* New Haven, Conn.: Yale University Press, 1995.

Castells, Manuel. *The Rise of the Network Society.* The Information Age: Economy, Society and Culture, vol. 1. Cambridge, Mass., and Oxford: Blackwell, 1996.

Christman, Ed. "Indies No. 1 in Total Album Mark Share for First Time; WEA Is No. 1 in 'Current' Share." *Billboard,* January 18, 1997, 60.

Davis, Mike. *City of Quartz: Excavating the Future in Los Angeles.* New York: Vintage, 1992.

Dery, Mark. "Public Enemy: Confrontation." *Keyboard,* September 1990, 81–96.

———. "Tommy Boy X 3: Digital Underground, Coldcut, and De La Soul Jam the Beat with Audio Junkyard Collisions." *Keyboard,* March 1991, 64–78.

Durant, Alan. "A New Day for Music? Digital Technologies in Contemporary Music-Making." In *Culture, Technology and Creativity,* ed. Philip Hayward. London: John Libbey, 1990.

Eley, Geoff. "Nations, Publics, and Political Cultures: Placing Habermas in the Nineteenth Century." In *Culture/Power/History: A Reader in Contemporary Social The-*

ory, ed. Nicholas B. Dirks, Geoff Eley, and Sherry B. Ortner. Princeton Studies in Culture/Power/History, ed. Nicholas B. Dirks, Geoff Eley and Sherry B. Ortner. Princeton, N.J.: Princeton University Press, 1994.

Feld, Steven. "Pygmy POP: A Genealogy of Schizophonic Mimesis." In *Yearbook for Traditional Music*, vol. 28 (1997).

Flick, Larry, and Doug Reece. "Electronic Music Poised for Power Surge in States: Rising Interest Sparks Excitement, Concern." *Billboard*, February 15, 1997, 1.

Fraser, Nancy. *Unruly Practices: Power, Discourse and Gender in Contemporary Social Theory*. Minneapolis: University of Minnesota Press, 1989.

Frith, Simon. "Art versus Technology: The Strange Case of Popular Music." *Media, Culture & Society* 8 (July 1986): 263–79.

Gehr, Richard. "Muslimgauze: Beyond the Veil." *The Village Voice*, October 28, 1994, 67.

Goodwin, Andrew. "Popular Music and Postmodern Theory." *Cultural Studies*, May 1991, 174–90.

———. "Sample and Hold: Pop Music in the Digital Age of Reproduction." In *On Record: Rock, Pop, and the Written Word*, ed. Simon Frith and Andrew Goodwin. New York: Pantheon, 1990.

Grossberg, Lawrence. *We Gotta Get Out of This Place: Popular Conservatism and Postmodern Culture*. New York and London: Routledge, 1992.

Habermas, Jürgen. *The Structural Transformation of the Public Sphere: An Inquiry into a Category of Bourgeois Society*. Trans. Thomas Burger and Frederick Lawrence. Cambridge, Mass.: MIT Press, 1991.

Huyssen, Andreas. *After the Great Divide: Modernism, Mass Culture, Postmodernism*. Theories of Representation and Difference, ed. Teresa de Lauretis. Bloomington and Indianapolis: Indiana University Press, 1986.

Jameson, Fredric. *Postmodernism, or, the Cultural Logic of Late Capitalism*. Post-Contemporary Interventions, ed. Stanley Fish and Fredric Jameson. Durham, N.C.: Duke University Press, 1991.

Katz, Jon. "The Netizen: Birth of a Digital Nation." *Wired*, April 1997, 49.

Messiaen, Olivier. *The Technique of My Musical Language*. Trans. John Satterfield. Paris: A. Leduc, 1956.

Morton, Lawrence. "Footnotes to Stravinsky Studies: *Le Sacre du Printemps*." *Tempo* 78 (1979): 9–16.

Mowitt, John. "The Sound of Music in the Era of Its Electronic Reproducibility." In *Music and Society: The Politics of Composition, Performance and Reception*, ed. Richard Leppert and Susan McClary. Cambridge: Cambridge University Press, 1987.

Poster, Mark. "The Net as a Public Sphere?" *Wired*, November 1995, 135–36.

Prendergast, Mark. "The Chilling Fields." *New Statesman & Society*, January 13, 1995, 32–33.

Pride, Dominic. "U.K.'s Nation of 'Ethno-Techno.'" *Billboard*, October 28, 1995, 1.

Rheingold, Howard. *The Virtual Community: Homesteading on the Electronic Frontier*. New York: HarperPerennial, 1993.

Root, Deborah. *Cannibal Culture: Art, Appropriation, and the Commodification of Difference*. Boulder, Colo.: Westview Press, 1996.

Rose, Tricia. *Black Noise: Rap Music and Black Culture in Contemporary America*. Music/Culture, ed. George Lipsitz, Susan McClary, and Robert Walser. Middletown, Conn.: Wesleyan University Press, 1994.

Ross, Andrew. Review of *Deep Forest. Artforum,* December 1993, 11.

Schoemer, Karen. "Electronic Eden." *Newsweek,* February 10, 1997, 60–62.

Schumacher, T. G. "'This Is a Sampling Sport': Digital Sampling, Rap Music and the Law in Cultural Production." *Media, Culture & Society* 17 (1995): 253–73.

Soja, Edward W. *Postmodern Geographies: The Reassertion of Space in Critical Social Theory.* London and New York: Verso, 1989.

Stockhausen, Karlheinz. *Towards a Cosmic Music.* Sel. and trans. Tim Nevill. Longmead, Shaftesbury, Dorset, England: Element Books, 1989.

———. "World Music." Trans. Bernard Radloff. *The Dalhousie Review* 69 (1989): 318–26.

Strauss, Neil. "Bryn Jones, 38, Musician Known as Muslimgauze." *New York Times,* January 28, 1999, C23.

———. "The Next Big Thing or the Next Bust?" *New York Times,* January 26, 1997, H36.

Suchoff, Benjamin. "Ethnomusicological Roots of Béla Bartók's Musical Language." *World of Music* 29 (1987): 43–65.

Taruskin, Richard. "Russian Folk Melodies in *The Rite of Spring.*" *Journal of the American Musicological Society* 33 (1980): 501–43.

Taylor, Timothy D. *Global Pop: World Music, World Markets.* New York and London: Routledge, 1997.

Thornton, Sarah. *Club Cultures.* Music/Culture, ed. George Lipsitz, Susan McClary, and Robert Walser. Middletown, Conn.: Wesleyan University Press, 1996.

Toop, David. *Ocean of Sound: Aether Talk, Ambient Sound and Imaginary Worlds.* London and New York: Serpent's Tail, 1995.

Torgovnick, Marianna. *Gone Primitive: Savage Intellects, Modern Lives.* Chicago: University of Chicago Press, 1990.

Virilio, Paul. *The Art of the Motor.* Trans. Julie Rose. Minneapolis and London: University of Minnesota Press, 1995.

Weisel, Al. "Deep Forests's Lush Lullaby." *Rolling Stone,* April 21, 1994, 26.

Wörner, Karl H. *Stockhausen: Life and Work.* Trans. and ed. Bill Hopkins. Berkeley: University of California Press, 1973.

PART 4.
    TALKING VULVAS AND OTHER BODY PARTS

11. Looking like a Lesbian: Yvonne Rainer's Theory of Probability

Catherine Lord

Our unconscious is not the willful product of an impossibly perfect, perfectly neurotic, Eurocentric, property owning, procreative, heterosexual family, but hovers, as unfocussed as sexuality really is, ever changing and ever present: a filmy fabric thrown over and made one with the entire social field. It is out in the open air and everywhere around us and between us, holding us together and keeping us apart.

—MARTHA FLEMING AND LYNE LAPOINTE[1]

I dreamt I crossed the Rubicon carrying a large suitcase. On the far shore I opened it and found there was room for several more objects. I picked up some stones and put them in. They fit perfectly.

—MILDRED DAVENPORT, DANCING CLOSE WITH HER LOVER, DORIS SCHWARTZ

I make up very little.

—YVONNE RAINER[2]

It's never easy coming out.

About five years ago, when I served on the board of a large gay and lesbian film festival, I remember arguing into the evening about whether or not it would be appropriate to open with Yvonne Rainer's *Privilege*. True, the festival had never opened with a lesbian film. There were still so few and they weren't—the "therefore" went without saying—so good. True, the festival desperately needed to program feature films made by people other than white guys. True, *Privilege* featured a lesbian character. True, the director was now a lesbian, but we had never been in the business of screening films about queers by heterosexuals and Rainer had not been a lesbian when she made the film.

The festival opened with . . . well, I forget, but I'm sure the guy who made it was thrilled. And times have changed. Maybe life is better now that a full house of dykes can cheer the babes in *Bound*, even and perhaps especially because it was made by two straight guys, now that m-to-lesbians have a certain cachet, now that fags can sleep with straight girls and still be fags. Maybe this *is* post-essentialism and we're riding that perfect wave.

So I loaned a rough cut of Rainer's new film, *MURDER and murder*, to a friend on the other side of the country, not a close friend, but a woman with whom I share a political commitment to feminism and a woman of my age, that is to say, easily old enough to be her students' mother. She had been wanting to see *MURDER* not particularly because it was a lesbian love story, or even because it was a lesbian love story with a happy ending, but because she had had a mastectomy and breast cancer is one of the murders of the title. She didn't much care for it. "I could handle it when all those young bodies were decorating the theory in Yvonne's films," she said. "There was a kind of pleasure in the margins for me then, but I can't take theory in middle-aged bodies."

These stories, I think, begin to suggest the conundrums in which Rainer has landed herself with *MURDER and murder*, that self being among other things a feminist with a chronic antipathy to party lines, a onetime (long-time) heterosexual, and a (very) political lesbian. It's the sort of situation that stretches reception theory to its limit. If you queer a coming-out story by being old enough (sixty-something) to make it interesting—that is, if you've had a lot of experience with the architecture that sustains closets and plenty of opportunity to see what sort of spaces lie on the other side of their doors—it's unlikely to be an easy read. Or, if you decide to be a lesbian in the middle of a queer marketing nirvana embodied and visualized through the young, imagine making things as complicated as they actually are: embed the sexiness of two smart middle-aged dykes in a critique of essentialist beliefs about identity formation and a disquisition on the politics of environmental pollution.

The love story, then. Doris (Joanna Merlin) loves Mildred. Mildred (Kathleen Chalfant) loves Doris. Doris is a part-time teacher, a performance artist, a former copulator, and a grandmother. Doris is sixty-something. Mildred, a professor of women's studies, is a high-minded WASP whose fling with heterosexuality was way back and way brief. Mildred is in her early fifties. Doris is often broke and doesn't have a credit card. Mildred has tenure. Doris wasn't a lesbian. Mildred was. Doris is the enthusiastic convert. ("There are lesbians everywhere!") Mildred, the expert on matters lesbian, is skeptical of everything but Doris. ("This is serious business!") The seduction happened at the Clit Club. Doris asked Mildred out. Mildred wore the socks Doris gave her. Doris, after years of inconclusive biopsies, has one that uncovers a small tumor. Mildred moves into Doris's loft. They see shrinks. They get a cat. They have interesting sex, often. Doris has a mastectomy. Doris won't let Mildred take care of her. They fight, about subways, laundry, money, of course, who gets to make love to who, and English muffins. They make up. Doris plays at being an exhibitionist with her new unsexed chest. Mildred is horrified. Doris eats turnip greens and tofu. She slurps her soup straight from the bowl. Mildred smokes and drinks. She eats delicately, reading at the dinner table.

It's a lesbian love story, all right, the ordinary lives of remarkable women, the extraordinary lives of ordinary survivors. We know these stories. Many of

Figure 11.1. Joanna Merlin (*left*) and Kathleen Chalfant. Photo by Esther Levine. Production still from Yvonne Rainer's *MURDER and murder*. Courtesy of Yvonne Rainer and Zeitgeist Films.

us live them. We never see them at the movies. That I can write the outline so simply, even sweetly, however, is an indication that *MURDER* is a shift of orientation for Rainer that far exceeds the sexual. There are characters. There is no putting off the viewer by having more than one actor play a single character. There is a narrative, and it is no longer being murdered for those old feminist causes, like interrupting desire, or deconstructing realism, or exposing the apparatus of visual pleasure. Homicidal impulses are, after all, a luxury when representations are scarce. Middle-aged dykes, in love and in lust, not with a younger woman but with each other, are absolutely invisible to mainstream film, or, for that matter, to independent film. We are phantoms on the symbolic screen. When we appear, we must appear singly to invoke and to contain the specter of deviance. One of us can be useful. Two of us is out of the question.[3]

An interruption, a little murder of the critical narrative. When I first saw a rough cut of *MURDER*, I felt nothing so clearly and immediately as gratitude at seeing for the first time in my life a story in which I could recognize myself. More slowly came the realization that I was experiencing a visual pleasure that was not in most fundamental ways illicit, that it is simpler and easier and altogether more delightful to watch a film without having to engage in the usual spectatorial acrobatics of disavowal, splitting, and doubling in order to find pleasure across those deep chasms of sex, gender, age, sexual preference, race, and political conviction. There's more pleasure in reading with the grain. There's more pleasure in seeing a representation that puts you and your kind center stage. Not to be hyperbolic, but perhaps I finally *got* the concept of entertainment.[4]

To tell the love story, however, perhaps runs the risk of making it sound like Rainer has become yet another casualty of queer chic. No, she has not gone Hollywood. She at once seduces with a graphically non-platonic, wonderfully cantankerous liaison between two older women and asks a thousand disruptive questions about the romance, using all the help she can drag in to speculate about why it took so long to get there and who in the hell she is now. As in the past, she pushes genre over the edge, in this case expanding the coming-out story to the point where it collapses as the defining moment of queer identity.

Consider the ghosts. They open the film, playing Frisbee on a wide deserted beach. To the soundtrack of *Jaws*, the camera hunts them down, only to avoid them when it realizes what it has found. The ghosts feint and dodge to stay in the frame as speaking subjects. They are the Young Mildred (Catherine Kellner), barely eighteen, a cool and beautiful blond with the gift of prophecy, and Jenny (Isa Thomas), Doris's mother, an ex-seamstress with a mouth. Long dead of Alzheimer's, in the film she is the same age as Doris. Young Mildred leans to 1950s tomboy drag; Jenny spends the entire film in a 1915 bathing dress. We marry our father, or our mother, or both. The child is mother to the woman. We know these clichés by heart. Why not put them to work telling the story? Invisible to Mildred and Doris, the ghosts will haunt the rest of the film, partners in entertaining each other, audience to the spectacle of the love they have engendered, buddies in curiosity about the outcome of the story they have together conceived.

In the very next scene, Doris, sitting on that same beach, is in the middle of an indispensable element in the classic coming-out story, the scene where the queer explains herself tactfully to the sympathetic but uninformed heterosexual friend (e.g., "I'd wanted to tell you, but . . . ," or "I love her just as you love him"). She sits straight and proud. She takes off her sunglasses and looks her friend squarely in the eye. Never losing for a moment the cadence of her byzantine syntax, in fact barely restraining herself from smacking her lips, she gets off what must be the most gloriously perverse declaration in the history of lesbian film: "You know, Alice, never in my wildest dreams, my most far-out fantasies, did I ever come close to imagining that I would one day be able to say—with the utmost conviction—I *love* eating pussy."

Go girl!!!! Any familiar construction of the lesbian stands not a chance against this combination of triumphantly sexual old woman (now that's *much* harder to say than "lesbian") and the antics of family histories that won't shut up (think of the ghosts of lover and mother as the PFLAG of the representational apparatus). Indeed, much of the project of the film is to question the placement of every single brick in the edifice of political identity. Undertaken by an earnest academic, the result could be . . . well, murder, but the dumb-founded incredulity of Rainer's questions drives this film in staccato fast-for-ward, through slapstick, through theory, through statistical tables, through melodrama, through lovely little morsels of naturalistic interaction. Today I'm a lesbian. Yesterday I was a heterosexual. Today I have cancer. Yesterday I wasn't at risk. How can this happen? What does it mean? What's the connec-tion? What's the dis-ease about this body?

From Doris's declaration Rainer takes us in rapid sequence to the places where the trouble begins for queers, that is, to the streets and to the bedroom. A series of people stand at a public phone booth (a trope that will reappear), handing off to each other as they gossip about Doris's motivations. "I think Doris loves being a lesbian even more than being with Mildred." "Now Doris can be the oppressed person she's always wanted to be." Then, in a nicely cho-reographed shift of theoretical weight from the public to the private, we move to the bed, or in this case the couch, upon which Mildred reclines with her shirt unbuttoned. The camera pans down her breasts and her belly. Doris leans toward her. Mildred's expression, though the viewer who listens closely may imagine her to be making slight moans, is a triumph of femininity-as-enigma. From the movement of Doris's clothed arm, we can infer that she is finger fucking Mildred, off camera, with slow assurance. "When you get dressed up in a butch way," murmurs Doris, "I'm utterly thrilled. I think, 'My lover is an unabashed dyke.'" Replies Mildred, "You have to be an unabashed dyke to be thrilled by one."

This is theory not just embodied but wet, and it reminds us of all that actually can be brought to bear on the questioning of sexual identity. Every-thing goes: really bad jokes,[5] tender buttons, illustrations of heterosexism, fan-tasy, a bit of psychoanalysis, excursions into the history of sexuality. The ghosts, for example, do a great deal of educational work about the historical condi-tions that enable or prohibit female pleasure, let alone claiming a lesbian iden-tity. Young Mildred, sitting naked in the bathtub of Doris's cold-water apart-ment, asks Jenny why she has to get married if she's going to turn out lesbian in the end. "What else can you do?," says the ever sensible Jenny. "You're still in 1960. How many lesbians do you know? No woman is coming out of the woodwork to sweep you off your feet." In another scene, Young Mildred and Jenny are on vacation with Doris and Mildred in a small cottage by a lake. Mildred is smothering Doris with solicitude. Young Mildred and Jenny es-cape to the water's edge, and Young Mildred, ever inquisitive, asks Jenny if she were ever attracted to women. "I dunno," Jenny replies. "I love my girlfriends. I guess I just never thought much about it."[6] And later in the film—much water under the narrative bridge about breast cancer, about Doris, and about Mildred—a close-up of a laptop computer screen shows a paragraph on an un-named, unmoored "she" (who by that point could be Doris, someone Mildred is describing, or Rainer herself) and her high school friends.

Back then it seemed, and still seems, so obvious to her that they were no different from her. Attracted to each other, enjoying each other's bodies, loving female physicality. Now many when they're older and divorced and their children are grown, some of them will become lesbians. But they sure didn't, they sure couldn't, when they were younger.

Sexual identity is queered, methodically, by various strategies. Rainer weaves through *MURDER* various moments—wry, ironic, sometimes slapstick—that visibly and vividly make heterosexuality strange, suggesting how homosexuality functions as the pathologized other that enables the fiction of a prior and "natural" heterosexuality. Mildred and Doris, following a few (literally) animated squabbles about the nonfunctioning New York subway system, sit on an unmoving train watching the heterosexual couple on the opposite bench. The girl has entwined herself over the boy. "What if *we* did that?" Doris muses. Mildred's very femme hairdresser asks whether she and Doris are looking for a two-bedroom place. Mildred gulps and dodges. The hairdresser, without missing a snip, delivers all it takes to suggest the homophobia was Mildred's: one Marxist sentence on the relation of property to the nuclear family. Best of all are the scenes of Doris's daughter and her husband. A hopelessly homophobic brace of yuppies, they can barely bring themselves to utter the word "lesbian," and they remain deeply in the closet to their friends about the queering of the family they thought they had. Over a leisurely lunch in an uptown restaurant, against the backdrop of a couple of homeless old women who stand outside the window pointing and gesticulating and in general having a grand old time making a spectacle of the nuclear family in distress, the yuppies try to defend themselves against Doris's gentle scorn. They dig themselves deeper as they go. "[My parents] were talking about my sister Cathy," says the husband. "They're afraid she might be a lesbian. She's stopped shaving her legs and she's going to Hampshire College. I just couldn't bring myself to mention your situation . . . "

Gender is likewise rendered precarious. In one memorable scene, a sort of dream sequence played to Mildred and the ghosts, Doris has a fling with an Asian man who turns into a German. (A bad joke on turning Japanese?) She is, however, in drag as a gay man, GQ style, who tries to avoid anal penetration by proffering the vagina she "may or may not have had, or once had, or might have again." And finally, Mildred and Doris destabilize sexual identity by the unsettling tactic of eroticizing essentialism. Bantering about who was the straight woman and who did the corrupting, who first put the moves on whom, is one of the ways they seduce themselves into the love they wish to live. Naked in bed, in an obvious state of rumpled bliss, they make identity politics a kind of pillow talk. "I was straight when you got involved with me," protests Doris, tickling Mildred's breasts with her toes. "No, you weren't," Mildred counters. "A straight woman wouldn't have behaved the way you did."

About a third of the way into the film Rainer begins to introduce her other subject, the main murder, the wrench that will twist familiar theoretical questions on their end, bring the musings about essential versus constructed identities back home to the body. Shortly after the couch scene, and directly after a scene in which Mildred and Doris stroll home chatting about a dog named Emma Goldman, Rainer cuts to a black screen that fills with a list of words reminiscent of one of Felix Gonzalez-Torres' early photostats: "frisbee, Raquel Welch, bandolier, Lady Chatterley's Lover. . . ." We have scarcely time to read the words before they vanish one by one, leaving center screen only "metastasize." We cut back to Mildred and Doris, cooking dinner together. Across the bottom of the screen crawls the first set of the statistics that will multiply: "There are 1.8 million women in the U.S. who've been diagnosed with breast cancer. One million others have the disease and do not yet know it." Like the phone gossip that creates the apparition of Doris's lesbianism at the beginning of *MURDER*, breast cancer is then made manifest and simultaneously ghosted through small talk, specifically—in another deft link with the architecture of homosexuality—a conversation between two unseen women in the stalls of a public toilet. While Doris washes her hands, they chat about their bowling scores and a friend's lumpectomy. As the film moves, breast cancer remains strategically and consistently disembodied, discussed in voice-overs, deployed in statistics, or invoked in absentia, as when Mildred complains in front of the ghosts she cannot see about Doris's stubborn secrecy.

In the pivotal scene of the film, the lesbian title bout, the big fight, various pathologies converge. It's in a boxing ring, complete with a cheering audience

Figure 11.2. Kathleen Chalfant (*top*) and Joanna Merlin. Production still from Yvonne Rainer's *MURDER and murder*. Courtesy of Yvonne Rainer and Zeitgeist Films.

(or audiences) of thousands, borrowed from 1930s Hollywood fight movies. We see Mildred and Doris in full regalia, trunks, gloves, and high socks. It is couples' therapy writ large, and they are under orders from the referee (Novella Nelson, in skirt and heels) to have a good clean fight. Doris, in fact, is under orders from her shrink/trainer not to fight at all. They dance around, doing fancy footwork back and forth across a ring covered with the statistics on breast cancer that have been punctuating the film. Periodically, they clinch and fight about the usual—the muffins, the laundry, the loft. They move from fighting to wild desire, and go down for the count to make love, beginning delicious moments of pleasure before the wildly cheering crowd and continuing when Rainer jump-cuts them—in the same positions, fully clothed—onto their kitchen table. Somewhere in the middle, they get that cat.

The big fight, appropriately intertitled "SHRINKAGE," is also the point at which Rainer, as a character in the film, makes her move. Not that she hasn't been there all along. On the contrary, she has been unforgettably in evidence from almost the very beginning, ever since she strolled into Doris's tiny kitchen, dressed in the tuxedo that will be her uniform, to interrupt Young Mildred and Jenny and introduce herself. Standing at a phone booth, she has translated a fight between Mildred and Doris into therapese. She has crammed herself into Doris's apartment to watch them cooking, taken the subway with them, waited while they crossed the street, hovered over Doris at her computer, and leaned against the wall during that first long moment when the camera stayed on Doris while we read statistics about breast cancer. She has railed against Pat Robertson, homophobia, Stanley Kubrick, and whatever else she pleases. She has been not just a faithful master of ceremonies, but voyeur, flaneur, and provocateur. She has been everywhere, invisible to Doris and Mildred, invisible to the ghosts, invisible to everyone in the film, but to us a spectacularly *visible* ghost, the feisty, stubborn, awkward embodiment of the apparitional lesbian.

At ringside for the big fight, Rainer sits next to Young Mildred and Jenny, dressed for the occasion in her own flashy robe, like the fighter she is. "All right, I've been putting this off," she confesses. While the referee introduces the noncombatants, she slips off the left side of the robe to reveal her mastectomy scar and her very flat chest. She makes a spectacle of herself. She flaunts her lack of breast. Staring straight at the camera, she summarizes her various biopsies and surgeons' recommendations: "He wanted to take 'em both off. No breasts, no breast cancer." She considers risk: "'You're more likely to die in a car accident,' Susan Love had said." She puzzles: "Since I didn't own a car, I didn't know quite what to make of that." Still in the robe, she stuffs a cigar in her mouth and grabs two cardboard signs that she brandishes to explain the difference between homophobia, a toxic environment, breast cancer (MURDER) and repression, stigma, fantasy (murder).

In fact, though she puts her tuxedo back on after this scene, Rainer keeps her mastectomized chest emphatically center frame by wearing a shirt with the

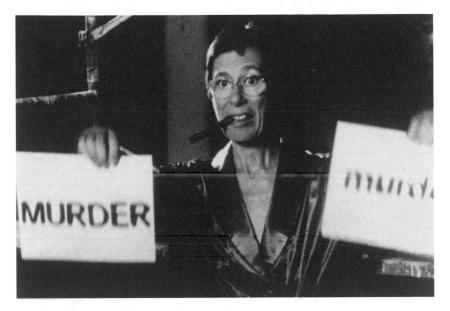

Figure 11.3. Yvonne Rainer. Production still from Yvonne Rainer's *MURDER and murder.*
Courtesy of Yvonne Rainer and Zeitgeist Films.

left side cut away for the remainder of the film. With calculation, she lays bare femininity as masquerade.[7] As statistics on breast cancer punctuate the film more frequently, the intensity of her appearances builds. She takes over entirely, as somehow we knew she would, playing court jester in the grand finale. In an elaborate KeystoneCops "number" on environmental pollution, she wheels a shopping cart full of carcinogenic household products and covers her naked chest with a very large, very white prosthetic breast. We last see her locked in a passionate stage kiss with a large, very black drag queen, shading the performance of gender she has created.

It becomes clear, as Rainer insists upon herself as a spectacle, that the disease she is making visible, embodying for us, is not a matter of biological certainty but of statistical risk. It is here where the "shrinkage" becomes evident, the parallel between the themes of "getting cancer" and "coming out," between disease and desire, between one pathologized identity and another. There is no precise moment when one changes objectively from a person without cancer to a person with cancer. It's possibility and probability, bowling scores and poker, something very much like turning into a lesbian.[8] *MURDER's* extended meditation on identity and causality lays one set of questions against another, entangling them until they eventually implode. Was I always a lesbian? When did it begin? How do I look like it? When did I get cancer?

What caused it? Could it possibly be too much peanut butter? Or fucking a woman?[9]

The play in *MURDER* lies in the space between abstraction and individual, between cipher of identity and intractable materiality of lived experience, between actors and author, between performance and the performing body. Perhaps because of the lightness of the love story and the heaviness of the science, that play comes to rest squarely on Rainer's own body as it oscillates between the bearer of information and the woman very much in question. In one scene, in fact, Rainer repeatedly crosscuts, with virtually the effect of a strobe, between herself as master of ceremonies in a tuxedo providing statistics ("Breast cancer is the leading killer of women between the ages of 35 and 45") and herself as an individual who intersects those statistics ("At first you feel a tremendous tautness across that area").

Autobiography has never been far from Rainer's work. She has always played the ham in her films, using her body to disrupt her production, to distance the viewer, to foreclose the seduction of identification. But in *MURDER,* I would argue, there is a qualitative change: as some viewers are pulled inexorably into the pleasure of a more naturalistic narrative, Rainer's becomes a spectacularly disruptive, profoundly unnaturalized presence. She declines to *act,* declines to offer us the seamless magic of a coherent identity, providing instead an untutored reading of her lines and the artifice of her own altered body. The effect is clumsy, often comic, even painful. It is, literally, halting. It produces Rainer as the other who refuses to disappear into oblivion, pathology, or even her own cozy romance. She will be a victim of neither disease nor love nor film. She is, as Mildred foretold much earlier, the court jester. In that role, she neither achieves "natural" dignity as male nor plays the fool as female. She is a dyke, and that story is altogether different. Though Rainer never makes a spectacle of the lovers that represent her in *MURDER,* just as she never asks them to break character to speak her theory, she puts her own middle-aged body on display for all sorts of purposes: to invent gender or to invert it, to use theory or to mock it, to bestow narrative pleasure or to take it away, to comply with the apparatus that ghosts her or to insist on her visibility.

Rainer's performance of herself as character relocates her body to the center of a different, complex, set of pleasures: jester for an audience who will get the joke. As always, the butt is desire, narrative, that unstoppable need for coherence, for someone who can explain it all. We want the author, but we'd settle for a good voice-over.[10] The pleasures Rainer offers seem abstract, but they are merely unfamiliar: detachment, knowledge, power, a delight in ambiguity, relief at not being jerked around by the same old Oedipal strings.

This, however, is vintage Rainer: she's never been interested in seducing her spectators.[11] The difference in *MURDER* revolves around the spanner in the filmic works, that insistently and consistently disruptive force, the figure who shouldn't be there, who should be dead already, safely ghosted—that body doubly and triply diseased, the aging female, the woman who lacks a breast,

Figure 11.4. Kathleen Chalfant (*left*), Joanna Merlin (*center*), and Yvonne Rainer (*right*). Photo by Esther Levine. Production still from Yvonne Rainer's *MURDER and murder*. Courtesy of Yvonne Rainer and Zeitgeist Films.

the grotesque, the Amazon, the unwoman, the lesbian. For a particular kind of spectator, I think, the spectator who is herself or himself dis-eased in at least some of the same ways, the spectacle Rainer makes provides an unprecedented pleasure. It's not simply the visual satisfaction of watching a very handsome dyke turn up wherever she can, far less the (allegedly simplistic) political comfort of seeing an image from which one does not recoil. It's the perverse pleasure of seeing a deeply unnatural act, the ghost working the machine. Instead of seeing the apparatus of representation disappear the woman who is its dis-ease before our eyes, we see her in command, operating the big machine, showing us not just her presence but the way in which the contraption has ghosted her and ghosts us. Rainer displays herself bumped from center stage into the wings, from flesh and blood into twilight girl, and then puts herself back into the action, re-embodies herself before our eyes. She gives us the pleasure of paradox, playing the ghost that must increasingly irritate because no one wants to admit to seeing her.

This is the coming-out story, representationally speaking, which can best be grasped by considering the sea change that lies between *Privilege* and *MURDER*. It's not that the latter was made by a woman who regularly has sex with a woman and the former wasn't, but that the lesbian is figured so differently. In *Privilege*, the lesbian character—and there is only one allowed into that narrative—is for all practical purposes a cipher, her sexual preference standing for and heightening her credibility as an innocent victim of a (near) rape. To be lesbian is, presumably, better to eradicate any hint of heterosexual desire, any suspicion of female complicity, from the scene of the crime. In *Privilege*, the lesbian is ghosted in order to foreground the questioning of certain privileges: skin, class, and femininity constructed and naturalized by heterosexual desire. Race and gender are denaturalized, albeit unevenly.[12]

MURDER, in contrast, puts the lesbian at the center of various structural stages: Rainer as a character, the romance of Mildred and Doris, the backdrop of lesbians at parties, in bars, on the street, and in the delicious lesbiana that suffuses the film.[13] Too, the film abounds in the tropes of spectacle, slyly and hilariously embodied in the material world: classrooms, theatrical stages, film screens, televisions, arenas, roller coasters. High queer squabbles about performativity as well as low queer conversations about outing are thus nicely put in their place, which is to say positioned within a structure designed to shift the "conditions of the visible," in Teresa de Lauretis's prescient phrase, for the lesbian.[14] Race, it will be said about this film and shall be noted here, fades to the edge of the frame: of the characters who aren't white, there's Jeffrey, the friend with AIDS, the referee, the gynecologist, and that drag queen. There's one of the trainers at the big fight. There are a couple of young dykes in a bar discussing the rapid aging of a menopausal ex. In the various statistics Rainer invokes about environmental pollution and women's health, there is a heavy emphasis on structural racism. And race could, of course, have been embodied in the relationship between Mildred and Doris by coloring one of them something other than white, but then it wouldn't have been the story Rainer in fact has to tell. *MURDER* is not simply about homosexual visibility (which as we know all too often means visibility only for those bodies that happen to be male as well as white), but about the lived conditions of visuality for a particular, unpopular, difficult, even dowdy lesbian body. It's a coming-out fiction that refuses to tell tales about beauty, or authenticity, or transformation, a story "about" lesbians and breast cancer told with the same perverse intransigence that drives the story about menopause and race in *Privilege*.

It's all in the "about."

———◆◆◇———

My middle-aged lover and I are lying in bed one Sunday morning, alternately reading the magazine section of the newspaper, which happens to be on aging,[15] watching *MURDER,* and arguing, as we have for weeks, about how big the bed should be and where to put it. The latter is a way to displace anxiety about her moving in, and I am resorting to *murder* in the hope that representation will do something for our decision-making process. It helps. "Aging won't be the same for us baby boomers," I say eventually. "There isn't a single lesbian in that magazine," she counters.

NOTES

This essay is a revised version of a talk first presented under the aegis of the Unnatural Acts series at the University of California, Riverside and later published in *Documents.* My thanks to both for the opportunity to develop these ideas.

1. Studiolo (Windsor, Canada: Artextes and the Art Gallery of Windsor, 1997), p. 51.

2. In conversation with the author, 1997. Yvonne realized that I'd assumed she simply made up a line she delivers in the *MURDER and murder:* "Statistics show that lesbians are chronic late returners of library books." "Oh no," she said, "I got that from Paula Treichler."

3. I borrow this line of reasoning from Terry Castle, *The Apparitional Lesbian: Female Homosexuality and Modern Culture* (New York: Columbia University Press, 1993). Mildred quotes her too, standing in a classroom lecturing about queer theory to her sleeping students, herself at eighteen, and her lover's mother: "Why is it so difficult to see the lesbian—even when she is there quite plainly, in front of us? In part because she has been 'ghosted'—or made to seem invisible—by culture itself."

4. In one of our conversations, Rainer told me that it was precisely because of the erasure of lesbians that she felt she had to tell the story, at least this part of her story, in the conventional way. The richness of the relationship warranted naturalism, she said, and she had already done all the other stuff.

5. Jenny and Young Mildred are playing Punch and Judy puppets. Jenny is the straight man, so to speak. Young Mildred gets the jokes.

How is a tumor different from a lesbian?

One ages well, the other doesn't.

6. Jenny, in fact, teaches us a great deal about the circumstances of pleasure in working-class female culture during the early part of this century, suggesting the limited opportunity for any pleasure given long work days, the casual pragmatics of extramarital heterosexual encounters, and the erotics of female friendships.

7. And she will have Doris interpret the strategy later on, when Mildred asks her not to exhibit her mastectomized chest at the masquerade party Rainer will hijack. "But I'm legal," Doris explains in an atypically theoretical moment. "It isn't as though I'd be exposing a sexual part of my anatomy. And besides, if femininity itself is something we can put on and take off, like a prosthesis, why can't I show a breastless side of myself?" Mildred, in case you were wondering, has already covered Joan Riviere with her students.

8. Young Mildred, late in the film, looks out the window and daydreams possibility to her buddy Jenny: "Just think of it: if in one year only one girl from every graduating class in every high school in the country becomes a lesbian, that would be 33,000 lesbians. In a decade that would add up to 330,000. In thirty years, it would be a million."

9. The statistics on breast cancer get more dismal near the end of the film, as they are delivered in voice over by Rainer over a shot of Doris on the gynecologist's table: "Lesbians have a 1 in 3 risk of developing breast cancer. That's a 2 to 3 times higher risk than heterosexual women. . . . Lesbians with breast cancer have a mortality rate of 30 percent, compared to a 25 percent rate for heterosexual women." Mildred, wise in this as in other things, sorts it out for us in a voice-over as the credits roll, explaining that economic discrimination and medical homophobia makes it more likely that lesbians will seek and receive treatment at a later stage of the disease.

10. "Rather than repositioning ourselves as spectators in response to cues that indicate we are being multivocally *addressed* and not just worked on by the filmic text," Rainer wrote about *The Man Who Envied Women* (1985), "we still attempt to locate a singular author or wait for a conclusive outcome. The Master's Voice Syndrome all over again." Yvonne Rainer, "Some Ruminations around Cinematic Antidotes to the Oedipal Net(les) While Playing with De Lauraedipus Mulvey; or, He May Be Off Screen, but . . . ," *The Independent*, April 1986, p. 22.

11. Writing after the script of *MURDER* was completed, but before the film went into production, Rainer says: "As for accessibility in the sense of intelligibility, I still believe in the necessity of certain kinds of narrative 'distanciation,' a belief that may lack the polemical fervor that characterized my espousals of ten years ago, but which nevertheless continues to inflect many of my decisions. The goals remain the same: to jar the spectator out of comfortable identification into critical detachment, to complicate and compound the spectator's relation to the original scene with additional information, analysis, or emotional effect, and for comic relief. . . . My latest rationale is that real life does not wait for polite introductions or recognizable opportunity before making an appearance." "Skirting," unpublished manuscript, 1994.

12. Heterosexuality, however, is not itself a privilege under scrutiny. What if Yvonne Washington, Rainer's alterego in *Privilege,* the one who puts the hard questions to the menopausal Jenny (or Jennys, since the main character is played by more than one actor) had been played not only by an African American woman, but an African American woman who played a lesbian, thus unsettling the complacency of Jenny's white-

ness *and* her heterosexuality? On questionings of some privileges and blind spots about others, see Michele Wallace, "Multiculturalism and Oppositionality," *Afterimage,* October 1991, for a critique of Rainer's marginalization of women of color in *Privilege* and my "Journeys to the Other Side: Yvonne Rainer's Privilege," *Afterimage,* February 1991, in which I foreground the question of white skin privilege without discussing the marginalization of lesbians.

13. *MURDER* is deliberately redolent of lesbian history; Anne Lister, Janet Flanner, Audre Lorde, Susan Love, and Diana Fuss all get one kind of cameo or another.

14. Teresa de Lauretis, "Sexual Indifference and Lesbian Representation," *Theatre Journal* 40, no. 2 (May 1988), as well as "Film and the Visible," in *How Do I Look? Queer Film and Video,* ed. Bad Object-Choices (Seattle: Bay Press, 1991).

15. "Funny, We Don't Feel Old," *The New York Times Magazine,* March 9, 1997.

12. Structure, Size, and Play: The Case of the Talking Vulva

B. J. Wray

Open it up, it gets pretty scary.

—Shawna Dempsey, *We're Talking Vulva*

UNNATURAL ORIGINS

The lesbian body has always been unnatural. Physical deformities and irregular mannerisms have characterized the female homosexual since her emergence as a subject within the official discourse of late-nineteenth-century sexology. Indeed, as lesbian historians such as Lillian Faderman have aptly demonstrated, the solidification of lesbian identity as a legal, social, and political reality was coterminous with the denaturalization of her bodily appearance. Broad shoulders, narrow hips, and a deep voice were unmistakably coded as sexually deviant traits, thereby marking the lesbian body as an improper female form and, not incidentally, functioning simultaneously to re-entrench a normative feminine physique. Richard von Krafft-Ebing's 1888 description of the female homosexual typifies the discourse: "She had coarse male features, a rough and rather deep voice, and with the exception of the bosom and female contour of the pelvis, looked more like a man in woman's clothing than like a woman."[1] Crucially, then, the circulation of lesbian identity within phallocentric economies of knowledge was predicated on the concomitant invocation of a degenerate female body; by definition, lesbians in Krafft-Ebing's formulation do not inhabit their female bodies properly. The masculinization of the lesbian secured her ontological placement within a visual logic that regulated how and in what form bodies may appear. The trope of drag that Krafft-Ebing cites serves to enforce the unnatural status of this body through the reiteration of taken-for-granted somatic differences and, therefore, guarantees the perpetuation of those very differences.

Given the seemingly inevitable recuperation of lesbian identity into a phallocentric representational matrix, it should come as no surprise that challenges to this imperative have frequently coalesced around the (dis)appearance of female genitalia in representational forms. In an attempt to disrupt what theorist Donald Morton has described as "the easy trafficking of meaning in culture,"[2] lesbian and feminist artists and theorists alike have sought repeatedly to rework the notion of female "lack" and the viselike control that it wields over the terms of women's appearance in traditional visual economies. As one of the primary structures that has determined how female identification and desire are constituted, "lack" has consistently haunted women's attempts to enter a representational economy in which our only mandated positions are either invisibility or being the object rather than the subject of the gaze. As the Krafft-Ebing comments indicate, this dilemma becomes particularly acute in the realm of lesbian representation where the only possible sites of identification and desire are doubly bound within both phallocentric and heterocentric pre-scripted narratives. It is no wonder, then, that psychoanalytic notions of "lack" and their subsequent regulation of representation have been soundly denounced in lesbian and feminist texts for several decades. Protesting that lesbian identity and desire cannot be contained within the boundaries of conventional understandings of phallic lack, oppositional representation tactics have often sought to shore up the stability and coherence of lesbian subjectivity through recourse to the depiction of so-called positive images. In these counter-discursive frameworks, invisibility is replaced with visibility and absence is countered with presence in the hope of creating an alternative to the erasure and elision of gay and lesbian bodies, narratives, and desires.

THE PARADOX OF THE MATTER

This logic of substitutions (visibility for invisibility, etc.) is, of course, necessarily predicated on the very system of representation that it seeks to undermine and is heavily invested in maintaining the parameters of the binaries that it takes up. Australian performance artist and writer Anna Munster discerns this investment in her comment that "queer performance is literally saturated by a desire to understand and pose the body as raw material, the body unmediated by the form and consumption of spectacle."[3] Although the notion of an "unmediated" performance has been substantially critiqued by postmodernist understandings of representation, Munster touches on the seemingly unassailable drive toward visibility and recognition that permeates gay and lesbian identity politics. Or, as Lynda Hart describes it in her 1995 piece on "The Queer Real," "[T]here is still an overwhelming urge (is it indeed a 'drive,' something like an instinct?) to mark a stationary place, to appeal to a referent, to have recourse to a/the 'real thing.'"[4] This recourse to the "real thing" requires that we perpetuate existing divisions between representation and the real and that we set aside what Munster terms the "form and consumption of spectacle." In doing so, oppositional strategies of representation must ignore their own complicity with taken-for-granted paradigms and proceed as if the trans-formation from invisibility to visibility is a seamless one that is open to all bodies equally.

What interests me, then, is the destabilization of this seamless substitu-tion by tactics of representation that consistently foreground their paradoxi-cal relationship to visual and discursive economies. The urge to re-stabilize the referent is queerly suspended in lesbian texts that both desire to estab-lish the coherence of lesbian subjectivity *and* to remain cognizant of current deconstructions of the speaking subject. The tension inherent in this ambiva-lent desire is reconceptualized by the employment of an "aesthetics of lack" in Shawna Dempsey and Lorri Millan's performance/film *We're Talking Vulva*.[5] It is an attentiveness to, even an absolute reliance on paradox that characterizes the performance of lack in this text. Clearly, resignifications of lack can only occur within the paradoxical situation of inhabiting a construction in order to critique it. To represent lack, to speak of lack, to perform lack, to theorize lack is to embark on a labyrinthine journey through the maze of presences and absences that are at the heart of figurations of lesbian identity and desire.

LIPPING OFF

Originally created as a costume-centered performance piece in 1986, the five-foot talking vulva was adapted for film by Dempsey and Millan in 1990 as part of the National Film Board of Canada's *Five Feminist Minutes*. Set within the framework of the NFB's feminist undertaking, *We're Talking Vulva* may be viewed as a sort of celebratory teaching text earnestly determined to extol the pleasures and powers of female genitalia to an undereducated audience, or, as the vulva cum Dempsey tells us: "I'm here to say hello / Show ya around down below." To a certain extent, this film, which has played all over the world to an estimated audience of over one million viewers, accomplishes precisely that: five minutes of in-your-face vulva action is a wickedly funny corrective to the general invisibility and disgust traditionally associated with female anatomy.[6] A costumed Dempsey says as much while pointedly gazing into the camera during the film's opening rap: "The vulva is something men have feared / Looks innocent enough, a bit like a beard / On the outside it's fuzzy, it's fluf-fy, it's hairy / Open it up it gets pretty scary." Given the regulation of women's entry into a phallocentric visual culture, it should come as no surprise that the Manitoba Film Classification Board sought to (re)cover vulvic knowledge with an R rating.[7] It is to this ongoing erasure of women's "private" parts that *We're Talking Vulva* does, indeed, direct its information-oriented lyrics. Dempsey raps through a litany of vulva functions, including the merits of pubic hair ("Pubic hair is a good place to begin / It keeps dust out, it keeps warmth in"); the existential properties of the labia ("Labia, too, exists for a reason / To keep us warm in the cold of the season / Also erectile they fill up with blood / When a hand or tongue shows them some love"); the finer points of urinating ("This

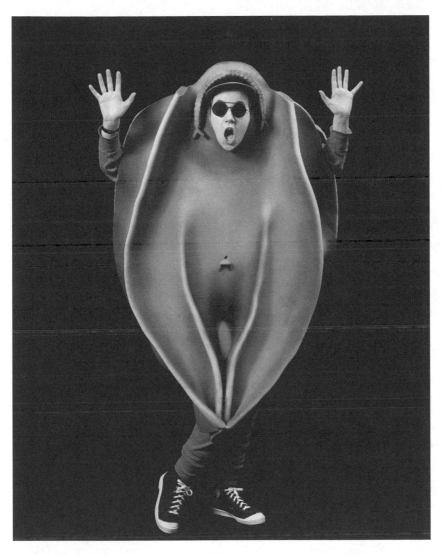

Figure 12.1. Shawna Dempsey as the Talking Vulva. Photo by Sheila Spence.
Courtesy of Shawna Dempsey and Lorri Millan.

is the hole, this is the place / from which our urine does escape / A lot when it's
wanted and a little when it's not / When we sneeze or laugh or fuck or cough").
And, finally, the lyrics turn to the pleasures of clitoral stimulation. Accompanied by increasingly frenetic music and the visual overlay of the vulva engaged
in a mocked-up aerobic workout ("And four more / And three more / And two

more / And one more"), the vulva orgasms and the film ends having accomplished its "down below" tour de force.

But our vulvic education has only just begun, and it is to the situation of Dempsey and Millan's performance within a larger representational matrix that I would like to direct my analysis. The talking and acting vulva, in one respect, rehearses a rather tired polemic on the primacy of women's sexual difference while, I will argue, it concurrently demonstrates the impossibility of · such an essential reliance on what does or does not constitute a body. The obvious shock value of Dempsey's costume and its equally obvious play on the regulation of women's sexuality in contemporary cultural representations to a large extent resist lapsing into a gimmicky liberationist text because the performance itself foregrounds its own uneasy relationship to such ur-narratives. The cinematic composition of *We're Talking Vulva* presents us with a work whose multiple narrative levels and generic parodies endeavor to interrogate the "knowingness" that often circulates around identity-based representational forms.[8] Engorged with large dosages of parodic play, the talking vulva opens into a number of existing generic paradigms: notably, the aforementioned institutional sex-education/community service films; rap music phrasing and rhythm; and early versions of the rock videos produced for Canada's music television station, Much Music. In citing these models, particularly rap and the rock music format, *We're Talking Vulva* calls on the reiterable properties of popular culture to provide the necessary currency and contextualization for its hyperbolic spectacle. In addition to a catchy aesthetics, rap lends a thematics of self-celebration, self-aggrandizement, and self-promotion,[9] while the rock music video structure furnishes *We're Talking Vulva* with its distinctive visual transitions between shots of the vulvacious band performing onstage and various scenes of the vulva herself rapping in the "real" world. That Dempsey's white-girl rap resembles a camped-up infomercial taxonomy of genital functions much more than an Ice-T or Public Enemy commentary of defiance, and that her rock band features a mascotlike giant vulva as its lead singer undoubtedly secure the playful humor and parodic intentions of this performance. Ultimately, it is this twisted take on generic codings and its concomitant interrogation of representational forms that enable *We're Talking Vulva* to queerly inhabit the interstice between discursive production and bodies that matter.

As this brief introduction to the film's format indicates, *We're Talking Vulva,* and indeed all of Dempsey and Millan's performances, insist on the incongruous, the "unlikely," and the paradoxical as their modus operandi. Their pieces tend to proceed, both narratively and visually, through a series of juxtapositions that disrupt the signification of the familiar, the normative, and the conventional across a broad spectrum of discursive registers.[10] An aesthetics of lack, then, requires that certain conventions not only be present as a component of transgressive narratives, but that these narratives be foregrounded as the territories under contestation. As Elizabeth Grosz instructs in "Re-figuring Lesbian Desire," "All sexual practices are made possible and function with-

Figure 12.2. Dempsey and the Vulva Band. Photo by Lorri Millan.
Courtesy of Shawna Dempsey and Lorri Millan.

in the constraints of heterosexism and phallocentrism, but this indeed is the condition of any effective transgression of them."[11] The success of parodic interruptions and displacements paradoxically relies on the temporary invocation and restabilization of the paradigms subject to critique. Dempsey's hyperbolic rendering of lack in the form of her vulva suit succeeds in its destabilization of the "naturalness" or "authenticity" of dominant psychoanalytic models precisely because of the juxtapositioning against the normative that Dempsey herself invokes. As I have mentioned, the talking vulva re-articulates for her audience, in the opening seconds of this film, the conventional narrative of castration: "The vulva is something men have feared." The talking vulva exploits this fear—this is castration complex writ large, for as Freud observes, it is the "sight of the genitals of the other sex"[12] that provokes anxiety—as the site of her comic intervention into the discourse.

The seemingly impossible display of lack hinges, in *We're Talking Vulva,* on the spectacular focus on sites of female lack. The hyperbolization of existing modes of knowing and the representational forms that they generate is crucial as a marker of the parodic interventions these artists initiate. Marking the performance as a performance seems crucial to any discussion of the campy refigurations of female lack that Dempsey and Millan play with. As signifiers of the tensions inherent in any articulation of subjectivity that is mindful of contradictions, the parodic performances of lack in this piece foreground the complex relationship between "real" lesbian bodies and their entry into a phallic representational economy. Whether or not lack may be successfully recuperated from its historical baggage of oppression is perhaps a less useful consideration than how, precisely, lack is used as a strategic disruption of the "easy trafficking of meaning in culture." I am hesitant to link this text or the notion of an aesthetics of lack to a renewed lesbian-feminist revisionist project and am more concerned with exploring the necessary tensions inherent in any resignification. In what ways, then, does the exploitation of lack in these works fulfill what Teresa de Lauretis describes in her 1991 article "Film and the Visible" as a project of "redefining the conditions of vision, as well as the modes of representing"?[13] Does this performance, again in the words of de Lauretis, "produce modes of representing that effectively alter the standard frame of reference and visibility, the conditions of the visible, what *can* be seen and represented?"[14] Finally, how does an aesthetics of lack represent the problem of representation?

GENEROUSLY (DIS)PROPORTIONED

As the most visible marker of excess in the film, the vulva costume functions as the focal point for our viewing attention. Its gigantic proportions not only command the bulk of the cinematic frame but literally appear to overwhelm Dempsey's body-made-miniature. The partial disappearance of Dempsey's body, encased within the giant vulva, serves to endow the vulva itself with agency status. Dempsey's protruding appendages (head, legs, and arms) exist as accessories to the vulvic "subject" and are themselves accessorized with accouterments that properly belong to the realm of the everyday (sunglasses, running shoes, and a watch). The strategies of transgression figured in Dempsey's larger-than-life performance initiate a kind of terrorization of the sign system that subsequently recasts the position and power of female lack. Susan Bennett observes, in her article on the performance art of Dempsey and her collaborator Lorri Millan, that "[i]f the body is bound as a medium of culture, then the question of who gets the opportunity to direct such a powerful medium is an obviously crucial one."[15] Dempsey's vulva-skin ruptures the assigned codings of a phallocentric visual field and occasions what Judith Butler calls "a repetition of the law into hyperbole, a rearticulation of the law against the authority of the one who delivers it."[16] The effect of these representational tactics, as well as the central premise of a speaking organ, is to recuperate the always already lacking vulva as a signifying entity. That is not to say that this vulvic signification may be conceptualized along an oppositional trajectory of absence made presence. Indeed, such a first-degree level of reading fails to account for the ways in which this part cast as the (w)hole calls into question the very materialization of all bodies. This spectacular vulva not only "makes[s] explicit the 'naturalized' roles of women's bodies/sexuality,"[17] but also begins to unravel the boundaries which hold the natural/unnatural dichotomy in its representational place. As the film progresses and the "lifelike" qualities of the vulva are enhanced through a series of hilarious, mundane appearances—the vulva buys groceries at the supermarket, chats with the produce manager, and amazes fellow shoppers; the vulva toboggans down snow-covered Winnipeg Hill; the vulva demonstrates for equal rights in front of the Manitoba legislature buildings; the vulva visits a construction site; the vulva has her pubic hair styled and dyed in a beauty parlor—we are confronted by the extent to which our comprehension of meaningful bodies is produced within the parameters of discursive registers. The incongruity evidenced by these unlikely scenes remarks the familiar as a site of bodily materialization and, in doing so, points toward the crucial role of reiteration in the constitution of the "natural."

Dempsey's hyperbolic reiteration of women's essential lack fully depends on the conditions of phallocentric vision to discern a certain distance between her actions and those very conventions she seeks to erase. If the conflation of the phallus with the penis adheres around a visual economy that privileges presence (here I am thinking of Rosalind Minsky's take on Lacan: "It is because it is so easy to confuse the most obvious sign of difference for the child— the visible, physical penis—with the phallus, the cultural sign of power, that the construction of femininity can never be on the basis of anything other than lack, of 'not having' and therefore 'not being'"[18]), then the talking vulva reenacts entry into the symbolic with a certain twist. The most radical potential of Dempsey's performance inheres in its avowal of its own reliance on disavowal. In other words, marking the intimate connections to phallic regulations that occur within Dempsey's spectacle may facilitate an act of insubordination to normative phallic codings that is not external to those conventions but, rather, inhabits and inhibits their normative articulation. Butler comments: "[I]t will be crucial to find a way both to occupy such sites and to subject them to a democratizing contestation in which the exclusionary conditions of their production are perpetually reworked."[19] Indeed, for Butler, it is only *within* the process of reiteration that insubordination occurs.

Rebecca Schneider notes in a recent essay on feminist performance art that whatever exceeds appropriate vision is linked to the fearful potential of base matter to implode on all symbolic structuring: "This (blinding) point of excess coagulates in matter and becomes not a site of spirit, but rather a site at which dream or symbol defecates, is literalized. Looking back at the viewer, the blind spot made literal disallows perspectival remove and 'castrates the eye.'"[20] Dempsey's extreme literalization of female lack radically disenfranchises normative conditions of viewing precisely through a form of "blinding excess" in which the hyperbolic image shifts the lines by which the explicit female body is displayed in art. Clearly the oversized vulva and its circulation within the video is meant not only to substitute as a female phallic symbol but also to expose the artificiality of such paradigms. Again I turn to Susan Bennett, who comments that the naturalized directions for women's bodies are spun in another manner by Dempsey's "self-direction" in which "the creation of skins . . . visually perform such dilemmas."[21] The series of narrative and visual juxtapositions throughout the video ensure that viewers remain within the realm of the hyperbolic. The talking vulva is the abject figure whose presence throws into question the seemingly stable foundations of normative signifiers (even the supermarket produce is shifted in its function from food to sex toys; "Be nice to your vagina, show her some kindness / Try vegetables"), and whose own identifications are similarly haunted by the lingering (and necessary) presence of these conventions.

Similarly, Dempsey's anatomical rap and the rock-music-video format that she employs situate the talking vulva as a critique (to borrow de Lauretis's phrasing) of the representation of representation. The stage is set from the outset for the improper performance of female lack. The talking vulva, in its spectacular appearance, plays on the object-producing gaze of her audience and, through a hyperbolic miming of female disappearance within a phallic representational system, deconstructs the power of that gaze even as it relies on the same visual logic for its effects. Dempsey must risk re-inscribing woman as the object of the gaze in order to manipulate the trajectory of that very gaze. In direct contrast to Freud's seminal essay on "Femininity," in which his mode of address infamously absents women by constructing us as "the problem" to be solved, Dempsey's talking vulva specifically hails her female audience as she beckons us with "Hi Girls." Again, more than simply an absence made presence, this solicitation of a female gaze shifts the burden of problematics to representation itself. That is, the entire system of seeing is the problem, if not to be solved, then at least to be re-marked upon and potentially queered by the terrorism of an excessive lack. This oxymoron radically alters the proper function of lack as the stabilizer of male identity and potency by overstepping the boundaries of what lack is and does in the realm of representation.

Despite its wonderfully parodic and insubordinate aspects, Dempsey's figuration of an aesthetics of lack in *We're Talking Vulva* produces its own exclusionary matrix that threatens to re-cover lesbian desire and identity under the sign of woman's essential lack. Although Dempsey invokes lesbian sexuality in her narration ("Since most men are jerks we find the exceptions / Or turn to our fingers for love and affection / Some of us gals like other women / touch and suck and do tribadism / That's lesbianism"), the dominance of the visual sphere and the necessarily prominent discourse of female sexuality potentially elides lesbian specificity in favor of a woman-centered performance. I am reminded here of the dangers that accompany an apparently seamless flow between gender and sexuality and of the re-closeting potential of such maneuvers. Establishing a continuum of woman-based experience as a marker of lesbian sexuality, as Adrienne Rich does in her construction of the lesbian continuum, goes, as Blakey Vermeule suggests, "to the heart of what makes lesbian representation problematic."[22] I do not think that Dempsey's project in this video is necessarily about signifying a uniquely "lesbian" body or desire or identification. However, the talking vulva's initial invocation of lesbian sex does anticipate an articulation of lesbian desire but, instead, propels this desire along a trajectory of female representation that consistently works to ensure lesbian disappearance. I wonder, then, to what extent lesbians are included in name only in this film and if this naming, rather than foregrounding lesbian specificity, actually initiates a renewed invisibility under the sign of lack? The potential usefulness of this evasive signification of lesbian—the talking vulva's expansion of the lesbian sign perhaps resonates with Judith Butler's mandate that it be "permanently unclear what precisely that sign signifies"[23]—is undercut by the inattention to how that initial lesbian figuration is reabsorbed into the existing representational system. The initial presence of absent lesbian bodies in *We're Talking Vulva* is symptomatic of the milieu in which homosexual representation occurs. In her introduction to *Inside/Out*, Diana Fuss explains this process: "Homosexual production emerges . . . as a kind of ghost writing, a writing which is at once a recognition and a refusal of the cultural representations of 'the homosexual' as phantom Other."[24] An aesthetics of lack functions as a lesbian representational strategy, then, to the extent that it foregrounds this interlining of absence and presence and makes explicit the cultural unintelligibility of lesbians. The talking vulva remains suspended between a refusal of and a replication of a phallocentric visual economy, and lesbian entry into the realm of the symbolic must contend not only with this double movement but with a further suspension within the frame of lack itself.

STRUCTURAL INTERFERENCE

Perhaps the hyperbolic figurations of lack that these performances rely on are usefully conceptualized as destabilizing specters within a phallic economy that relies on the regulation of lack for its identity coherence. Deconstruction has taught us that no counterhegemonic strategy can be radically outside the system it seeks to oppose and, indeed, an aesthetics of lack must perpetuate what Lacan has called the "misrecognition" of the power of the phallus if the most radical effects of this aesthetics are to emerge.[25] On the other hand, according to Carole-Anne Tyler via Žižek, no ideology is totalizing because "there is always something (real) which exceeds it, which slips through the signifying net as its 'outside,'"[26] that exists as the possible politicization of *dis*identification. As the exaggeration of a pre-scripted narrative, "lack" exists in the interstices of identification and disidentification, and it is this rich paradox that potentially unravels the dichotomies of presence/absence and visibility/invisibility and further takes up the Butlerian task of "making the signifier into a site for a set of rearticulations that cannot be predicted or controlled."[27] Representing lack, like the inherently unrepresentable status of passing, opens to examination the possibility of discerning the power of the unmarked and speaks to the impossible horizon of queer identities. To invoke Peggy Phelan,

> The task . . . is to make counterfeit the currency of our representational economy—not by refusing to participate in it at all, but rather by making work in which the costs of women's perpetual aversion are clearly measured. Such forms of accounting might begin to interfere with the structure of homo-sexual desire which informs most forms of representation.[28]

The proliferation of unsettling representational gestures within *We're Talking Vulva* and the subsequent tension they generate within a phallocentric representational economy are precisely the location of humor and play and perhaps a certain transgression in this vulvic rap. Layer upon layer upon layer of parodic interventions resonate with and through each other to sustain the comedic excess that the very appearance of a hyperbolically oversized vulva (a lesbian size queen?) initiates in the opening frames.

I would hope that an aesthetics of lack, with its attentiveness to spectacular modes of performance, occasions a displacement of conventional paradigms and with renewed vigor interferes in existing representational forms. And yet as I close this piece, I realize that I have failed to define exactly what this aesthetics of lack entails or what specific possibilities it sets in motion. Perhaps this is due to the paradoxical nature of the phrase itself. Perhaps the ambiguity on which it rests ensures that the words themselves remain suspended between intelligibility and unintelligibility. Perhaps I am hedging. I am still wondering to what extent this aesthetics of lack may be used as a description of lesbian strategies of representation. What, other than the real body behind the performance, will ensure a lesbian reading of these texts? And will even that guarantee a lesbian presence given all of the aforementioned limitations on lesbian visibility within conventional representational economies as well as specifically lesbian paradigms? Can an aesthetics of lack push beyond or through or between the given-to-be-seen? Is it possible that a lesbian subjectivity may emerge out of discursive strategies themselves and thereby sidestep the seemingly inevitable reliance on a stable referent? What are the specific forms that lack may take? Does lack play out differently in different gender, racial, and sexual contexts? These are the questions with which I began this discussion and although I have suggested throughout this paper that the potential of an aesthetics of lack lies in its ability to negotiate, straddle, and queerly suspend such concerns, I must admit that I am continually frustrated by the inadequacy of such stances. I can only conclude by taking solace in Lynda Hart's dictum that "[t]he struggle is not to avoid repetition, but to repeat with differences that are transformative."[29]

NOTES

1. Krafft-Ebing, quoted in Lillian Faderman, *Odd Girls and Twilight Lovers* (New York: Columbia University Press, 1991), p. 45.

2. Donald Morton, "The Politics of Queer Theory in the (Post)Modern Moment," *Genders* 17 (Fall 1993): 124.

3. Anna Munster, quoted in Lynda Hart, "Blood, Piss, Tears: The Queer Real," *Textual Practice* 9, no. 1 (1995): 57.

4. Ibid., p. 58.

5. Shawna Dempsey and Lorri Millan, *We're Talking Vulva* (Winnipeg, Canada: String of Girls Production, 1990).

6. In her review of *We're Talking Vulva*, Janine Tschuncky neatly summarizes the reigning ideology that Dempsey and Millan's film desires to challenge: "Not only must we not touch ourselves 'down there,' we had better not risk looking either, saving ourselves for the trained eye of a doctor, male lover, or the camera. We thereby become aliens to our own anatomy, replacing pride with disgust. Often the celebration that should occur at the onset of menstruation has been replaced by a guilty silence."

7. *We're Talking Vulva* continues to provoke censorship. In October 1997, the Hallwalls Art Center in Buffalo, New York, was denied National Endowment for the Arts funding for an artists' residency program on the basis of their inclusion of *We're Talking Vulva* in their application to the funding agency. That the film was singled out by NEA committee members for censure, even though it contains no nudity, no violence, and no explicit sexual activity, points toward the power that such hyperbolic spectacles of female anatomy tend to wield within conventional representational economies. Dempsey and Millan now join the likes of Karen Finley, Holly Hughes, Robert Mapplethorpe, Tim Miller, and Andres Serrano in provoking the wrath of the NEA.

8. I borrow the concept of "knowingness" from Eve Kosofsky Sedgwick's elaboration of the homosexual/heterosexual dichotomy in *Epistemology of the Closet* (Berkeley: University of California Press, 1990). In her introduction to that text, Sedgwick unpacks the ways in which a certain Western cultural "knowingness" that circulates around homosexuality works to naturalize homosexual identity and, thereby, discount not only historical personages but also innumerable present-day variations of sexuality.

9. There are innumerable pieces that deal with the ways in which rap music functions as an identity-shoring device for its (predominantly) black American performers. Three articles that I have found particularly engaging are Mtume ya Salaam's "The Aesthetics of Rap"; Judith McDonnell's "Rap Music: Its Role as an Agent of Change"; and "Signifying Rappers" by David Foster Wallace and Mark Costello.

10. Dempsey and Millan have been collaborating on feminist performance art since 1989. They are well known in Canada for pieces such as *Mermaid in Love* (1990); *Mary Medusa* (1993); the 1994 videotape *What Does a Lesbian Look Like?* which played in rotation on Much Music; and their most recent film *Good Citizen: Betty Baker* (1996). Between 1989 and 1994 they completed a series of performances using the dress as metaphor and built sculptural costumes that accompanied corresponding performance texts: the paper ball gown of *Object/Subject of Desire* (1993); a nail-studded Saran Wrap evening dress for *The Thin Skin of Normal* (1993); a Formica house dress for *Arborite Housewife* (1994); and a stained-glass robe and halo for *Glass Madonna* (1994). The duo is, however, most infamous for the film version of *We're Talking Vulva*.

11. Elizabeth Grosz, "Re-figuring Lesbian Desire," in *Space, Time and Perversion* (New York: Routledge, 1994), p. 174.

12. Rosalind Minsky, *Psychoanalysis and Gender* (New York: Routledge, 1996), p. 225.

13. Teresa de Lauretis, "Film and the Visible," in *How Do I Look: Queer Film and Video,* ed. Bad Object Choices (Seattle: Bay Press, 1991), p. 224.

14. Ibid.

15. Susan Bennett, "Radical (Self-)Direction and the Body: Shawna Dempsey and Lorri Millan's Performance Art," *Canadian Theatre Review* 76 (Fall 1993): 41.

16. Judith Butler, *Bodies That Matter* (New York: Routledge, 1993), p. 122.

17. Bennett, "Radical (Self-)Direction," p. 38.

18. Minsky, *Psychoanalysis and Gender,* p. 154.

19. Butler, *Bodies That Matter,* p. 115.

20. Rebecca Schneider, "After Us the Savage Goddess: Feminist Performance Art of the Explicit Body Staged, Uneasily, across Modernist Dreamscapes," in *Performance and Cultural Politics,* ed. Elin Diamond (New York: Routledge, 1996), p. 169.

21. Bennett, "Radical (Self-)Direction," p. 38.

22. Blakey Vermeule, "Is There a Sedgwick School for Girls?" *Qui Parle* 5, no. 1 (Winter 1991): 57.

23. Judith Butler, "Imitation and Gender Insubordination," in *Inside/Out: Lesbian Theories, Gay Theories,* ed. Diana Fuss (New York: Routledge, 1991), p. 14.

24. Diana Fuss, "Introduction," *Inside/Out: Lesbian Theories, Gay Theories* (New York: Routledge, 1991), p. 4.

25. This deployment of Lacan does not begin to unravel the complex relations between the symbolic and imaginary registers in constituting this "misrecognition." But it does point us toward the direction of thinking about the political function of the symbolizable in Lacanian terms that are also productively taken up by Ernesto Laclau in his exchange with Judith Butler. See "The Uses of Equality," *Diacritics* 27, no. 1 (Spring 1997): 3–12.

26. Carole-Anne Tyler, "Passing, Narcissism, Identity, and Difference," *Differences* 6, no. 2/3 (Summer–Fall 1994): 232.

27. Butler, *Bodies That Matter,* p. 219.

28. Peggy Phelan, *Unmarked: The Politics of Performance* (New York: Routledge, 1993), p. 164.

29. Hart, "Blood, Piss, Tears: The Queer Real," p. 63.

PART 5.
     DE-COMPOSING THE UNNATURAL

13. Decomposition

Elizabeth Wood

In "More Gender Trouble: Feminism Meets Queer Theory," an issue of *differences*, Trevor Hope and Rosi Braidotti discuss the climate of cultural grief, decay, and crisis which marks the end of the millennium.[1] Melancholia is the recurrent symptom of modernity, they find, for the decline of patriarchal law and the paternal metaphor as bearer of law; the deterioration of social bonds and crumbling of symbolic structures; the wounded, diseased subject of modern knowledge which seems unable to cure and take care of itself; the profound discontent that lies at the heart of the phallologocentric culture.[2]

While Hope arrives at the notion of a *fraternal* regime in mourning and melancholic enjoyment for the death of the father, the paternal corpse, Braidotti fantasizes the funerary ceremonies we might arrange for patriarchy's burial. We need to devise ways to bury the dead, destroy its monuments, and organize its documents, she says. The only kinds of intellectuals she knows who are "taking time off for the burial ceremony . . . lingering on the process of death and dissolution of identities and [. . .] putting it back on the agenda, without nostalgia or false sentiments" are science fiction writers and cyberpunk artists. She wishes academics could do the same, and "think the death and the burial of classical understanding of subjectivity, dissolving the received ideas about the sexed body, as a matter of ceremonial fact."

A pivotal point of their conversation about patriarchal death throes turns on a footnote: the last endnote to Hope's essay, which draws an analogy between lesbianism and male homosexuality and simultaneously apologizes for not having dealt more extensively with the lesbian issue. Braidotti immediately spots this and invites Hope to revisit his "illusion of symmetry in the position the two sexes occupy vis-à-vis the phallic symbolic." Hope regrets having made a "dismissive, homologizing reference to lesbianism within work which takes male paradigms of homosexuality as its organizing principle," and orders hereafter a "universal moratorium on any footnoted reference to lesbianism in such texts." Agreement is forged over Braidotti's point about the "plight of lesbianism ['one of the dark continents of patriarchy'] in any theory of sexuality that fails to take seriously the profound asymmetry of sexual difference."

I preface my discussion of decomposition with a sibling drama that decomposes and then reconstitutes the lesbian as central to further discussion of sexual difference because I think the way Braidotti recovers and re-installs the footnote in the text, and invites Hope to reconsider it, suggests how lesbian subjects can revisit sites and positions in order to disengage ourselves from the hold they may still have on us, and work in remembrance together through what we have lost or are in danger of losing. I take my cue from Braidotti's departing riff: "It's time for the female death force to express itself. . . . Not all feminists are 'dutiful' daughters, mourning the death of the father, lost in melancholia," and wearing black. "We want to revisit male Thanatica—the discourse of death and the death trappings that lie at the empty heart of the phallic empire. . . . We are the guerrilla girls . . . the riot girls. We want to resist, and we want to have fun."

My itinerary is different. It may promise "resistance," but I'm not too sure about "fun." For the sites and positions I want to revisit belong to female Thanatica and its funerary ceremonies for the death of the mother. The loss I experienced recently in my own mother's death prompted in me the "need to find, rediscover, invent the words, the sentences that speak of the most ancient and most current relationship we know—the relationship to the mother's body, to our body—sentences that translate the bond between our body, her body, the body of our daughter." My quote is from Irigaray's *Sexes and Genealogies*, which continues: "We need to discover a language that is not a substitute for the experience of *corps-à-corps* as the paternal language seeks to be, but which accompanies that bodily experience, clothing it in words that do not erase the body but speak the body."[3]

Irigaray proposes we stop thinking of the mother-daughter relationship as one of pathological fusion, a threatening or devouring unity, but rather as a relational situation. We need to revisit the maternal body, she suggests, not to murder the mother or experience maternity as a symbolic death, but to renarrativize the biological ground of the mother's body in such a way as to render it as material (as opposed to essentializing it), and therefore holding the possibility for a variety of psychic structures and social and political relations. I think of the work of thinking back through the maternal body, revisiting and lamenting it in remembrance and loss, as an act of decomposition: one that breaks up or disintegrates things already composite—things that have adhered or become coherent through the activity and experience of mother-daughter composition under patriarchy. Decomposition can thereby effect and perform further acts and ceremonies of composition and allow other possibilities or expansions of understanding and reciprocation to take place within the unstable, asymmetrical categories of sexuality.[4]

My funerary ceremonies for the death of the mother are musical acts of listening to the maternal body, the daughter's body, our body, and the sounds which accompany that bodily experience—clothing it in sounds that "sing" the body and its resonances.[5]

> [*A vocal Lament performed and heard as a soundtext in speech and song is in written form already decomposed. I invite the reader to reciprocate as a listener and breathe sound in this silent body.*]

CEREMONY #1: *LESBIAN THRENODY ON MY MOTHER'S VIOLIN*

Corporeal decomposition was on my mind while my mother was dying in Australia last year. She was eighty-seven, blind, crippled with rheumatoid arthritis, her body disinvested of its accouterments and possessions and utterly dependent on others for its care and control. Skin and tissue had so decayed that her entire body was wrapped in gauze bandages—death's winding sheet, birth's swaddling clothes, the mummy's shroud—to enable nurses to touch and turn it. I was thirteen thousand miles away when I made my last telephone call to her. I asked if she had music with her. She said she was listening to an ABC broadcast of the final round in a Sydney piano competition, but the technical, mechanical perfection of the players left her cold. I don't think I fully understood at the time how Mum had relinquished the struggle with corporeal decay. I was talking about music, our listening to music together, my playing for her, the only thing we had ever shared without tension, without struggle. I do remember in that conversation wondering to myself if death would end that connection, if everything between us and left unsaid would be forever unresolved. After I hung up I felt I was losing not only my mother but the possibility of breaking silence between us which music alone could mediate and promised to fill.

"That strain again! It had a dying fall: / It came o'er my ear like the sweet sound / That breathes upon a bank of violets, / Stealing and giving odour."[6] In the aftermath of mother's death, I found myself looking and listening for consolation to instrumental and song forms of lamentation: Ravel's *"Pavane pour une enfant défunte"*; Dido's lament and Purcell's elegy on the death of Queen Mary (which begins, I heard with sudden surprise, "Incassum, Lesbia, rogas"); Schubert's string quartet "Death and the Maiden"; Pergolesi's "Stabat Mater." I began to retrieve and grieve ceremonial sound-memories of my mother and our relationship, to listen for the "dying fall" of what together we had composed, arranged, settled, adjusted, and made up: of what bound and combined us, separated and divided us, or fell silent between us. I had a reiterating impulse for weeks afterward to pick up the phone and call her—an umbilical mother-daughter metaphor for my need to connect in sound and have my voice heard; to hear her voice reciprocating mine.

Mother's was a musical family, who sang, harmonized, and improvised around the piano and in church choirs. Her father designed and built pipe organs. A sister was a church organist, music teacher, and choir director married to a professional baritone whose brother was the composer Frank Hutchens. Mum studied violin at the New South Wales conservatorium, but after she developed arthritis at the age of fourteen, playing was painful. By the time I was born, she had stopped playing altogether. The violin was laid out (composed) in a locked case and put away on the bottom of her closet.

I remember the secret, mysterious thrill I had as a child when my mother opened the velvet-lined casket to show me her instrument: the soft, varnished glow and rich grain of the belly; the flaming wood of the back; the delicate rounding and purfled inlay accentuating the body's contours; the slim arched neck, with its four rounded pegs. I ran my finger inside the scroll of the ear, slid it down the four gut strings and metal wiring to the bridge, and traced the elegant *f*-shape of the sound holes. When I massaged the bow with resin, fine horsehair strands vibrated to my touch. Tension grew like a spring in my hand when I turned the ebony pegs. The beautiful instrument I held and stroked was alive for me and respondent.

For mother, however, the velvet case in the closet encrypted a silenced instrumentality, a lost voice to music. The sound once produced in and through her body would be returned to her—only to be cut short and lost again like Eurydice in a second burial, more painful in its finality than the first—in Mum's enthralled identification with a young French violinist, Ginette Neveu. After Neveu's London debut in 1942 at Wigmore Hall in Dame Myra Hess's wartime concert series, her subsequent performances were broadcast and transmitted to Australia by the BBC along undersea telegraph cables: a watery down-under sonic umbilicus linking mother-country culture with listening colonial sons and daughters. Neveu was thirty years old, ten years younger than my mother, and unmarried, when she died in 1949 in an air crash en route to the United States, in fog, off the Azores, together with her accompanist-brother and her Stradivarius violin. After that, I don't remember seeing Mum's violin again or knowing what she did with it.

After Neveu, mother's musical desires and identifications shifted to a different ego-ideal, the Lancashire contralto Kathleen Ferrier, again via broadcast transmissions and Decca recordings which reached Australia in the 1950s. Ferrier was three years younger than Mum. Her first London recital at the National Gallery in 1942, also in Hess's wartime concert series, was of songs by Brahms, Schubert, and Wolf. But within eleven years of her debut, Ferrier's professional career was cut short by breast cancer, from which she died at the age of forty-one, just four years after Neveu. *Déplorations* eulogize the early deaths of both musicians as a tragic void in annals of performance.

Mother's Kathleen (our family used the familiar name) was the storybook heroine "Klever Kaff," whose brief ascent and flight from provincial obscurity to world fame, as told by Ferrier's sister Win, resonated with my mother's own stories of origin and youth.[7] Both had tyrannical, mean, bullying mothers. Kaff's told her she was ugly and her voice "bad," and stopped her from singing around the house. My mother's mother strapped her in a high-chair facing the wall and forbade her speak from one uneaten mealy porridge to the next. Both daughters were forced by mothers to leave school at fourteen and earn their keep. Kaff became a telephone operator, Mum a typist. But there the parallel stories divide. Ferrier's unconsummated marriage was annulled when she was twenty-five and on the threshold of her singing career. Mum's endured, and produced two daughters, but Mum stopped playing the violin.

Tombeaux by musicians who knew and loved Kathleen Ferrier (her voice teacher Roy Henderson, conductors John Barbirolli and Bruno Walter, accompanist Gerald Moore, and critic Neville Cardus), which Win appended to her sister's biography, represent an angelic virgin with "a kind of disembodied warmth about her singing." Her "consoling, comforting vocal embrace . . . soothed the nerve of music" and radiated "happiness." "There was no surface glamour in her art and little exhibition of sex." I was virtually suckled on that disembodied resonating breast, figuratively the seat of affections and private thoughts and feelings, the repository of consciousness, the place of heart, lungs, breath, the singing voice, its fluid stream. For myself when young, Ferrier's voice was a first site of connection and intimacy, erotomania's nauseous enjoyment.

The heroic fallen angel, prematurely crashed and decomposed, forever beyond the sexed body, was my parents' Kathleen. I remember my father lying flat on his back on the living-room floor listening to the Decca recording of the doomed Ferrier's embracing English folksongs, and whistling them on his way to work: "I will walk with my love," and "I know where I'm going, and I know who's going with me." Mum would stop knitting and shut her eyes for Ferrier's Gretchen at her endlessly spinning wheel, her ecstatic young nun, her sorrowing, sacrificial "sleep of death" as the forsaken wife blinded by love in *Frauenliebe und -leben*. The living room was reverently hushed for *Vier Ernste Gesänge* and *Alto Rhapsody*. The grooves of "Der Abschied," Ferrier's farewell on our old mono recording of *Das Lied von der Erde*, which I still possess, are almost erased from overuse.

It was Ferrier's Orphic opera role and mode assumed in death which held my mother's morbid, melancholy fascination. Unknown to Ferrier or her doctors, after her mastectomy the cancer metastasized. Radiation had almost destroyed her femur, and the pain was so great when she left her Hampstead flat to sing Orfeo at Covent Garden, it was "as if she were going to her own execution." In the second act, Orfeo stumbled, and fell against the scenery. Euridice handed her off the stage with a classical in-character gesture. The audience claimed not to have noticed anything amiss. "There was no hint of any catastrophe," said the dramatic soprano Dame Eva Turner. "We were just mesmerized by her beautiful singing."[8] In a short time, Ferrier was dead.

"The past is a dangerous place. One look backward can turn you into salt, or cause the loss of the woman you love."[9] My mother found it compelling but impossible to regard Ferrier's body as malignant, diseased, and rotting invisibly from within. To do so risked losing a consoling voice for all the deprivations Mum experienced in dutiful, conventional "Frauenleben." Furthermore, Ferrier's death coincided painfully with a daughter's messy adolescent rebellions.

I was not my mother's wanted son. My prepubescent pederastic fantasies of having the boy chorister's unbroken, disembodied treble—will it be male or female? will it grow breasts or a beard? what sonic sex act, what "hymeny," does this voice perform in a young girl's body?—disintegrated when I understood that boy choristers become tenors or basses. My mother had expected the *Vox androgyna* that emerged from the maternal body to develop as *Vox virgina, Vox vagina,* as hers had done, and accept its feminine fate. But I was not the voice (son/sound) my mother wanted. I was *Vox lesbiana,* undiagnosed, unspeakably rotten, alien disease. Our mother-daughter bond began inexorably to decompose around our experience in time, image, and sound of Orfeo's collapse and disintegration in the dying body of Kathleen Ferrier.

Years later, I would learn of Ferrier's lesbianism; that her last years in the Hampstead flat were shared with "the blessed Bernie," the New Zealander Bernadette Hammond, and their cat Rosie; that Ferrier was the first major modern singer to have "a visibly lesbian following."[10] The Sapphonic cult status of Ferrier, and indeed of Myra Hess and Ginette Neveu, is yet to be written. But I think I always knew my Kaff was not my mother's Kathleen. I hoarded and identified with stories of male roles Ferrier took in school plays; her athletic prowess in golf and tennis; the male adjudicator who said her singing "makes me imagine I am being stroked"; the audiences who shouted, stampeded, and "capitulated" to her, flocks of female fans who followed her concerts, the radiant diva swamped by Dutch dykes. "I've had women following me from one concert to the next, 200 miles apart," she bragged of an American tour.

I also remember my not understanding quite what her accompanist Gerald Moore meant in saying, "[T]hough we men loved her, our wives loved her themselves," and reading Moore's hysterical description of Ferrier's swarming idolatrous fans as a "disgusting pest," a "little clique" with minds "obsessed," intent on retaliatory revenge when Ferrier "would not allow [them] to progress from fanship to friendship. Anonymous phone calls were made in the middle of the night; spiteful jokes were carefully planned," claimed Moore. Once, "when Kaff emerged from her flat to sing at Royal Albert Hall, she found six cars from six different hire services waiting, all demanding payment. Or returning home after a recital at Highgate . . . Kaff found a barrage of 12 [full and heavy] dustbins moved from adjoining flats had been laid one on top of another before her door. Fortunately we knew the identity, although we could not definitely prove it, of the leader of this gang of squalid nuisances. Kathleen's solicitor interviewed her, and was given a promise that these disgusting practical jokes would not be continued."

Since I myself, in unrequited love for our school music prefect at the time, was heavily into practical jokes and anonymous calls and poems, I cherished narratives of lesbian excess and lesbian trash as exemplary, not cautionary tales, and identified both with Klever Kaff and her besotted fans. "Yes, the part suits me," she said of singing Orfeo. "Searching through hell for love is something I do all the time."[11] Didn't I know it.

No-one else at home shared or heard in quite the same way songs Ferrier sang that I loved best: "Botschaft" and "Sapphische Ode" by Brahms; Schubert's "Ganymed"; my turbulent identification (short-lived) with Purcell's "Mad Bess of Bedlam." I waited until my parents went out to strut and flaunt and sing along with Kaff up and down the living room in "Botschaft's" message of desire carried on a butchy little breeze, the singing lover's intermediary with her absent beloved, the "Holde" that shaped my lips in a kiss. Many years later, I was thrilled to discover Brahms gave the autograph score of "Botschaft" to the lesbian composer Ethel Smyth. The song derived from the Persian *ghazal* and its fourteenth-century homoerotic tradition became Smyth's signature song in seducing married women with her singing voice.

"Botschaft," op. 47, no. 1 (Message), G. F. Daumer, after Hafis

Breeze, blow softly and sweetly
around my darling's cheek;
play gently in her hair;
do not hurry away!

If by chance she should ask you
how it is with me in my misery,
say: "His pain was unceasing,
his plight very grave.

But now he can hope
to spring to life once more,
for you, beloved,
are thinking of him!" [2:07]

Nor did I tell Mum my fantasies in listening to the "Sapphic Ode," in which the sound of Ferrier's contralto voice seems inseparable from the melody. For me, the song was a lush, dank rhapsody on lesbian sex in its intoxicating images of "the scent of kisses on the shrub of your lips" and the pubic hedge drenched and dripping with moisture, and in the music's ponderously heavy limbs and slow downward movement to pirouette around the clitoral cadence; the wide-arching piano melody that spreads the voice; the metrical deviancy of the short fourth line (a peculiarity of Schmidt's text which Brahms spins on a 3/2 change) and, in the last line, the chromatic "Tauten" and rapturous turn on "Tränen."

"Sapphische Ode," op. 94, no.4 (Sapphic Ode), Hans Schmidt

I picked roses by night in the dark hedge;
they breathed sweeter scent than ever by day;
and as I moved the branches they dripped
plentiful dew, which soaked me.

Also the scent of kisses, which I gathered
by night from the shrub of thy lips,
intoxicated me as never before;
and thou, too, moved in spirit like them,
were bedewed with tears. [2:47]

For Brigid Brophy, the diva's voice evokes the sound memory of one's mother having sex and reawakens the infantile fantasy of having sex with the mother: witness the mildly incestuous, diffused familial erotics of listening that Ferrier's contralto sanctioned in our living room; the necrophiliac dimension in my making out with my mother's violin.[12] Klever Kaff's was the voice I did not have, the voice I wanted. A lesbian lover, greedy for love, I devoured with eyes and ears the corporeal mechanism which produced it: the muscular strength and suppleness of her diaphragm; the open throat, full mouth, long jawbone; the huge cavity at the back of her throat where the voice breaks through erogenous zones. "Try my break," Kaff gaily told her voice teacher. I died to.

In our family quartet, listening to music and singing were our means of meeting and exchange. To the extent that music performs our love, modulates our tensions, synchronizes our losses and longings, and fills our gaps and silences, a musical composition—whose notation has no meaning independent of the performer and reader who realizes it in the terms she brings to bear on it—can be understood as a function of players and their listeners. Ferrier's singing voice continued to composit the work of connection and continuation between my mother and me when we struggled and grew apart. In my mother's death, in Ferrier's voice, I hear the transfiguring power of voice to give life to the decayed and decomposed. Death, it turns out, is neither silent nor an end to silence, to the possibility of breaking silence, but something very different.

CEREMONY #2: *LESBIAN THANATICA*

At the risk of nostalgia, essentialism, infantilism, embarrassing self-revelation, and of collapsing femininity into femaleness and conflating psychic structures with biological material ones, my threnody on my mother's violin represents, in part, an attempt to revisit the maternal body, the biological ground of the mother's body, as a material sound system. Where Irigaray probes the maternal body as "a terrain of multiple significations" to discover a "placental economy . . . an organized economy, one not in a state of fusion, which repeats the one and the other," I revisit its resonating tissues, cells, circulatory system, orifices, cavities, heartbeat, breathing, to listen for a sonic narration in the maternal body, an *audible* pre-language pre-notation that *sings* the body.[13]

To the feminist psychoanalytical literature on mothers and daughters and theories of female reproduction and the maternal voice as acoustic envelope, I would tentatively offer an experience I once had that enabled me to listen to an amplification of the sound-filled pregnant womb. What I heard was the incredible cacophony of two bodies in one: a noise machine pulsating simultaneously with synchronicity and regularity, asymmetry and irregularity, metrical displacement and parallelism, rhythmic and cross-rhythmic mimicry—a circulatory contrapuntal narration of sonic transmission and reception in and between two autonomous, distinct, differently-sized instrumental bodies, that of the mother, that of the fetus/embryo in utero, with separate yet tethered resonating systems constructed on similar elements and parallel identities.

That sonic experience suggests for me a different set of configurations on the contested theme of mother and daughter as self and other in pathologically interdependent fusion. It suggests that sound and noise—which are not a "representation" of the body but belong to its materiality—can provide a point of entry or access to the body *and* an important and powerful coding system, one that allows women to stake a claim in the highly politicized struggle to define the body, especially the reproductive and maternal body.

Lost chords and cut cords that give rise to tears suggest as well different metaphors for the bonds and struggles between mothers and lesbian daughters over autonomy and separation. I now think the impulse I had after Mum died to dial a defunct maternal sound system was an attempt to bridge the dead interval—in music a liminal space, not subject to so-called normal principles of melodic construction and voice leading—formed between my mother's last pitch and the first pitch of a conversation her death denied me. My unspoken, perhaps unspeakable desire was to cross the Acheron as Mum's motorcycle guide, wearing black, to lesbian Thanatica in order, at last, to be heard and understood.[14]

In listening again to old Ferrier recordings I had a different understanding of the ways thought and feeling are carried in the body, how they resonate with song and the singing voice. Only then could I begin composing an unnatural act of somatic and sonic decomposition of the maternal body's soundscape: to retrieve from my mother's death a woman-to-woman, body-to-body relationship of reciprocity; to liberate myself, along with my mother's memory, for us to emerge from the subordinating myth of maternal omnipotence (last refuge of patriarchal order and compulsory heterosexuality, a crypt-aesthetics littered with corpses, the corpus of women's lamentation) and disengage its stranglehold on mothers and daughters.

CEREMONY #3: *COMPLAINTE*

A lover's lament with a homoerotic history which continues to entice musicological controversy is Schubert's well-known setting of the poem by August Graf von Platen, "Du liebst mich nicht." Karen Muxfeldt has argued persuasively that the effect of syntactic, metrical, and harmonic instabilities in Schubert's setting—instabilities that are integral to the poem and its interior stresses and shifts—replicates in the listener the poet's obsessive agony, anxiety, and bitter reproach of unrequited love.[15] To counter critics who persist in refusing homoerotic meanings in Platen's poem and in its radical and excessive musical setting, Muxfeldt raises questions about differences in perception among listeners. How can we account for Schubert's "cataclysmic stresses on the figure of Narcissus?" she asks, the "terrible fantasy of loss in this song," its "psychic disturbance" which places "the very coherence of the song in jeopardy," unless we interrogate "how our reading of the poem affects the way we account for musical events?" She concludes that the song's "expressive reach" is "limited solely by the receptive capacity of the audience."

Her argument suggests other questions as well. What constitutes musical reciprocities? What transactions and exchanges take place among players and listeners, texts and voices? How can text and melody implicate a listener in reciprocal acts? How can we account for differences of perception and capacity among listeners, and extend our receptive capacity? What difference does it make to the way "Du liebst mich nicht" is read and heard that this lament on unrequited love is derived, like Brahms's "Botschaft," from fourteenth-century Persian-style homoerotic *ghazal* by a nineteenth-century homosexual poet and a composer whose psychosexual identity is queer, to say the least? What differences and extensions in reciprocity are possible in this song's "expressive reach" when performed by a lesbian singer (Kathleen Ferrier), accompanied by a gay male composer (Benjamin Britten), and when the listener is lesbian or gay?

"Du liebst mich nicht," D756, August von Platen

My heart is torn apart, you love me not!
You have let me know it, you love me not!
Though I have pleaded with you, wooed you,
Appeared in ardent pursuit, you love me not!
You have spoken it, cast it in words,
In all too certain ones, you love me not!
What to me are the blossoming rose, the jasmine,
The Narcissi in bloom? you love me not. [2:50]

That performance, on February 4, 1952, was Ferrier's last live broadcast by the BBC. It was not released on a commercial recording until recently, in a special edition of Ferrier's complete recorded work. As the CD booklet notes,

"The recording fades out before the end, but is included here because of the historical importance of the performance." The flawed ending, the acoustic fade-out itself, is what I find especially striking about this performance.

It seems poignantly queer to me that by a happy accident of mechanical reproduction the emotional pitch of "Du liebst mich nicht," which rises with each formulaic iteration, is so literally decomposed in the very act of performance and listening. It was in *not*-hearing the ending while experiencing sonic dissolution—the plight of the lesbian footnote—my mother's dead violin—the sexual silences between us—that the idea of decomposition first arrested me as a performative act that can reconstitute, reciprocate, and give back "life" to the inanimate, "life" that is lost or decayed in historical as well as mechanical reproduction, "life" we can revisit as a matter of ceremonial fact.

CEREMONY #4: *KADDISH*

Allen Ginsberg died on Saturday, April 5, 1997. I'm finding it hard to imagine Ginsberg was seventy years old; harder still to imagine his loss to gay and lesbian lives and histories. Our sibling rivalries and lovers' complaints stop here, in common grief. A lesbian daughter, I take my final ceremonial act from a gay son: Ginsberg's elegy written three years after the death of his mother:

"Kaddish for Naomi Ginsberg (1894–1956)"[16]

and I've been up all night, talking,
talking, reading the Kaddish aloud,
listening to Ray Charles blues shout
blind on the phonograph
the rhythm, the rhythm—and your
memory in my head three years after
O mother
What have I left out
O mother
What have I forgotten
O mother
Farewell.

NOTES

For my mother, Gladys Florence Cranwell, born Leggo (1909–1996). With thanks to Carol Burbank, Monica Dorenkamp, Jan Earle, and Annea Lockwood for listening, and to Philip Brett, Sue-Ellen Case, Susan Foster, and George Haggerty for Unnatural Acts, University of California, Riverside, April 11–12, 1997. This piece, together with "The Lesbian in the Opera: Desire Unmasked in Smyth's *Fantasio* and

Fête Galante" (in *En Travesti: Women, Gender Subversion, Opera,* ed. Corinne Blackmer and Patricia Smith [New York: Columbia University Press, 1995]), received the first Philip Brett Award of the American Musicological Society, October 31, 1997.

Recorded excerpts and translations from *Kathleen Ferrier Edition,* vol. 4: Schumann, Brahms, Schubert. London: Decca CD, 1992: 433 471-2.

1. Trevor Hope, "Melancholic Modernity: The Hom(m)osexual Symptom and the Homosocial Corpse" (pp. 174–98); Rosi Braidotti's response, "Revisiting Male Thanatica" (pp. 199–207); Hope's rebuttal, "The 'Returns' of Cartography: Mapping Identity-In(-)Difference" (pp. 208–11), in *differences* (issue entitled *More Gender Trouble: Feminism Meets Queer Theory*), vol. 6, no. 2, vol. 6, no. 3 (1994).

2. Hope grounds the discussion upon Rosi Braidotti, *Powers of Dissonance* (Cambridge: Polity, 1991).

3. Luce Irigaray, *Sexes and Genealogies,* trans. Gillian C. Gill (New York: Columbia University Press, 1993), p. 19, as quoted and discussed in Alys Eve Weinbaum, "Marx, Irigaray, and the Politics of Reproduction," *differences* 6, no. 1 (1994): 98–128.

4. Rosalind C. Morris: "All Made Up: Performance Theory and the New Anthropology of Sex and Gender," *Annual Review of Anthropology* 24 (1995): 567–92.

5. "Memoirs that write a parent's death share many generic and thematic features of the elegy—a performance act of taking up and revising the precursor's task in one's own voice. This is part of the mourning process and requires a break with the past, a separation, and a replacement," Nancy K. Miller, *Bequest and Betrayal: Memoirs of a Parent's Death* (New York: Oxford University Press), 1996, p. 7. Instrumental and song forms of mourning include the lament, ode, funeral march, *planctus* (Latin), *lamento* (Italian), and *tombeau, déploration, complainte,* or *plainte* (French), in which a slow pace and beat, minor mode, and reiterating descending bass or ostinato supporting the melody are characteristic.

6. William Shakespeare, *Twelfth Night,* opening lines to act 1, scene 1.

7. Winifred Ferrier, *Kathleen Ferrier: Her Life* (1955), with *A Memoir,* ed. Neville Cardus (1954), published together in one volume (Harmondsworth, Middlesex, England: Penguin, 1959).

8. Maurice Leonard, *Kathleen: The Life of Kathleen Ferrier,* with a foreword by Elisabeth Schwarzkopf (London: Hutchinson, 1981), pp. 231–32.

9. Susan Cheever's review of *The Kiss,* Kathryn Harrison's controversial memoir of father-daughter incest, in *The New York Times Book Review,* March 30, 1997, p. 11.

10. Terry Castle, *The Apparitional Lesbian: Female Homosexuality and Modern Culture* (New York: Columbia University Press, 1993), pp. 218, 219, 229.

11. On Ferrier's first *Orfeo* at Glyndebourne in 1947, and second (and last) at Covent Garden in 1953, see *C. W. von Gluck: Orfeo,* ed. Patricia Howard (Cambridge: Cambridge University Press, 1981).

12. Brigid Brophy, *Mozart the Dramatist* (New York: Da Capo, 1988), pp. 38, 43.

13. Luce Irigaray, "On the Maternal Order," in *je, tu, nous: Toward a Culture of Difference,* trans. Alison Martin (New York: Routledge, 1993), as quoted in Weinbaum, "Marx, Irigaray," pp. 113–14.

14. The leather-jacketed "Paisan"-guide to divine lesbian comedy in Monique Wittig's *Virgile, non* (Paris: Edition de minuit, 1985), trans. David Le Vay and Margaret Crosland as *Across the Acheron* (London: Peter Owen, 1987).

15. Karen Muxfeldt, "Schubert, Platen, and the Myth of Narcissus," *Journal of the American Musicological Society* 49, no. 3 (Fall 1996): 480–527.

16. Allen Ginsberg, "Kaddish," in *Eight American Poets,* ed. Joel Conarroe (New York: Vintage Books, 1997), pp. 236-61.

Contributors

Philip Brett is Distinguished Professor of Music at the University of California, Riverside. He is general editor of *The Byrd Edition* and co-editor of *Queering the Pitch: The New Gay and Lesbian Musicology,* and has written extensively on the music of Benjamin Britten.

Sue-Ellen Case is Chair, Department of Theatre and Dance at the University of California, Davis. She is author of *Feminism & Theatre* and *The Domain Matrix: Performing Lesbian at the End of Print Culture,* and has written extensively in the field of gender studies.

Susan Leigh Foster, choreographer, dancer, writer, is Professor of Dance at the University of California campuses of Riverside and Davis. She is author of *Reading Dancing* and *Choreography and Narrative* and editor of *Choreographing History* and *Corporealities.*

Amelia Jones is Professor in the Art History Department at the University of California, Riverside. She is author of *Postmodernism and the En-Gendering of Marcel Duchamp* and *Body Art/Performing the Subject,* editor of *Sexual Politics: Judy Chicago's Dinner Party in Feminist Art History,* and co-editor (with Andrew Stephenson) of *Performing the Body/Performing the Text.*

Kristine C. Kuramitsu is pursuing a Ph.D. in art history at UCLA. Her master's thesis explored the 1960s work of Yayoi Kusama.

George Lipsitz is Professor of Ethnic Studies at the University of California, San Diego. He is author of *The Possessive Investment in Whiteness; Time Passages; A Life in the Struggle; Dangerous Crossroads;* and *Rainbow at Midnight.*

Catherine Lord, Professor of Studio Art and Core Faculty, Program in Women's Studies at the University of California, Irvine, is a writer, artist, and curator whose work addresses issues of feminism, queer identity, cultural politics, and colonialism. She is author of numerous critical essays and pieces of fiction.

Ronald Radano is Associate Professor of Afro-American Studies and Music at the University of Wisconsin–Madison. He is author of *New Musical Figurations: Anthony Braxton's Cultural Critique* and co-editor (with Philip V. Bohlman) of *Music and the Racial Imagination* (forthcoming). He is currently completing a history of racial ideologies of "black music."

Timothy D. Taylor teaches in the Music Department of Columbia University. He is author of *Global Pop: World Music, World Markets*.

Jeffrey Tobin is Assistant Professor of Anthropology and of Women's Studies and Gender Studies at Occidental College in Los Angeles. He has published essays on masculinity and popular culture in Buenos Aires and on the politics of culture in Hawai'i.

Deborah Wong, Associate Professor of Music, teaches ethnomusicology at the University of California, Riverside, where she also serves as director of the Center for Asian Pacific America. She is author of *Sounding the Sacred: History, Aesthetics, and Epistemology in Thai Performers' Rituals*.

Elizabeth Wood, a writer and musicologist, is author of a novel and essays on music, gender, sexuality, and Ethel Smyth, and co-editor of *Queering the Pitch: The New Gay and Lesbian Musicology*. She is arts reporter and obituaries editor for Times/Review Newspapers on Eastern Long Island.

B. J. Wray is a doctoral candidate at the University of Calgary, Canada, where she is completing her dissertation on nationalism and sexuality in Canadian lesbian cultural productions. She has published essays in *Performing the Body/Performing the Text* and *Gay and Lesbian Literature, Vol. 2*.

Index

Italicized numbers denote illustrations.